Mevlevi Adab and Customs

Mevlevi Adab and Customs

Abdülbâki Gölpınarlı

Translated by Refik Algan
and Camille and Kabir Helminski

First English edition published 2025
by Threshold Books

Paperback ISBN: 978-0-939660-61-2

Library of Congress Control Number: 2025937985

Illustrations included on pp. xvi, 98, 176, and 202 are courtesy of Ingrid Scharr.

Typeset by Daniel Thomas Dyer.

Threshold Books
Escondido, London, Istanbul

sufism.org

Contents

Acknowledgements vii

On Transliteration ix

Introduction xi

I. Mevlevî Glossary 1

II. Semâ' & Mukabele 49

Semâ' in Humanity and Islam 49

Mevlânâ's Attitude toward Semâ' 57

The Nature of Mevlânâ's Semâ' 73

After Mevlânâ 88

III. Mevlevî Mukabele 99

Semâ'hâne 99

Mukabele 100

Reading the Mesnevî 105

Post Duasi ("Sheepskin Prayer") 107

Devr-i Veledî ("Sultân Veled Cycle") 109

Semâ' and Selâms 112

Dua-gû Duası 120

Garipler Semâ'ı ("Semâ' of the Poor Ones") 122
Niyâz Âyini ("Ritual of Entreaty") 123
Some Information Relating to Semâ' 127
Days of Mukabele, Nights of Grace 129
Shaikhs from Other Ṭarīqahs within the Mukabele 131
A Mevlevî in a Sufi Tekke 131
Ayn-ı Jem ("Unity Ritual") 131
Sheb-i Arûs ("Wedding Night") 134
Bayram Celebrations 137
Semâ' Meshki ("Practice") 137
Beginner's Mukabele 139
Symbolic Significance of the Mukabele for Mevlevîs 140

IV. Mevlevî Evrâdi 145

V. Ādāb & Erkan 157
İsm-i Jelâl 157
Meydân-ı Sherîf ("Sacred Space") 164
Somat/Sımât ("Table") 165
Muharrem and Ashûre 170
To Offer the Fātiḥah 171
Sefer ("Journey") 171
Burial Ceremony 173
Mevlevî Headstones 175

Acknowledgements

We wish to thank Daniel Thomas Dyer for his fastidious editing and proofreading, as well as the final typesetting of this very complex text; Nuray Akalın and Aykut Akalın for extensive consultations and explanations of various Turkish vocabulary and cultural matters; Mahmoud Mostafa for assistance with translation and insights into Arabic passages; Leila Bahreinian and the late Saeid Rahmanpanah and Amer Latif for help with intricate Farsi along the way; Amira Abd El-Khalek and Iman Mortagy for faithfully assisting with questions of Arabic meaning and rendering of Arabic text. We are grateful to be able, with God's assistance, after over twenty-five years of cooking, to bring forth this volume. We pray that it will be of nourishment for souls on the journey, and we ask God's forgiveness for our mistakes.

* * *

I dedicate my translation work on this volume to my dear father,
Cenahattin Algan, who was a man of real *edeb* and *erkan*.
~ Refik Algan

On Transliteration

The editing and transliteration of this book have presented some unusual challenges because of the number of different languages that are woven into Mevlevî tradition. Because the language of Mevlânâ's time was actually a mixture of Farsi, Arabic, and Turkish, and because all of the vocabulary underwent a major change at the founding of the Turkish Republic, the original vocabulary was transformed into a new Turkish language, based more or less on Roman letters, with some special Turkish adaptations.

Gölpınarlı commonly used Turkish spellings for many Arabic words, which obscured the origins of some of these terms. For example, *qadi* (Arabic) becomes *kadı* in Turkish. Many words used in the tradition are Arabic in origin and have fairly standard academic transliterations in English. In those cases, we have dropped the Turkish spelling in favor of the more common academic translation. *Hak* ("Truth") becomes *Ḥaqq*. (Sometimes, however, when these words and names refer to published texts in Turkish, we keep the Turkish spelling.)

At other times it has been a hard choice between, for instance, *Mathnawī* (the academic Arabic translation) and *Mesnevî* (the way the word is commonly pronounced in the tradition within Turkiye or Turkish circles). In other cases, words that are actively used today in the tradition, also of Arabic or Farsi origin, have their own particular Turkish transliteration. When such words are also commonly used today within the Turkish Sufi tradition, we will sometimes keep the Turkish spelling. And so, we keep Mevlânâ and not Mowlānā or Mawlānā, Mevlevî and not Molavī or Mawlawī.

So, dear reader, please be patient with us and the choices we have had to make. No single method of transliteration would have worked for this book. Since this is a living tradition, some Turkish and Farsi spellings have been maintained in words that are commonly used inside and outside of Türkiye, while some other words that are commonly transliterated in academic English will appear in that form for English-speaking readers, rather than the less familiar Turkish form.

We offer here a table of special characters for your assistance:

Turkish	**Pronunciation in English**
Ç, ç	Pronounced as "ch" (like in "chair" or "chocolate")
C, c	Pronounced as "j" (like in "joy" or "jungle")
Ğ, ğ	Silent, lengthens the preceding vowel
I, ı	Pronounced as "ih" (like in "lip," but from the back of the throat)
İ, i	Pronounced as "ee" (like in "see")
Ö, ö	Pronounced as "u" (like in "fur," lips rounded)
Ş, ş	Pronounced as "sh" (like in "shy")
Ü, ü	Pronounced as "oo" (like in French "tu," with rounded lips)
Â, â	Long "aa" sound
Î, î	Long "ee" sound
Û, û	Long "oo" sound

Arabic	**Pronunciation in English**
Ā ā	Long "aa" sound
Ḍ, ḍ	Strong, emphatic "d"
Ḥ, ḥ	Breathy, emphatic "h"
Ī, ī	Long "ee" sound
Ṣ, ṣ	Strong, emphatic "s"
Ṭ, ṭ	Strong, emphatic "t"
Ū, ū	Long "oo" sound
Ẓ, ẓ	Strong, emphatic "dh"
ʿ	"a" pronounced as in "at" (but half-caught in back of throat)
ʾ	Glottal stop

Introduction

For more than seven centuries, the Mevlevî order has exemplified Islamic civilization on this vast and bountiful earth, especially throughout the three continents once ruled by the Ottomans. Its aesthetic and technical achievements have been of enduring importance–it has produced magnificent works of music, poetry, and art. Wherever Mevlevîs have established themselves, they have made profound contributions to society, nurturing a deeper humanity. They have courageously spoken their minds, often taking a determined stance against those who oppose progress; and, as much as they have cultivated an appreciation of the mystical life, they have also added to the pleasures of a fully human one.

Mevlevîhood is like a crucible: the raw material thrown into it is transformed according to its potential. If a particle of dust enters the Mevlevî atmosphere, it gains a state that radiates light to the suns. This state is described in the following couplet, often sung in the Mevlevî whirling ceremony:

> Whoever, today, is faithful to Veled and prostrates,
> if he is poor, he becomes a prince;
> if he is a prince, he becomes a sultan.

Such a one commands sovereigns, and, without crown or throne, becomes a king of hearts. He joins with nothingness, leaving behind name and reputation to become an elixir for humanity, one who has penetrated into the lungs of those who inhale, giving an added vitality to life itself. Such a human being is evidence of the couplet:

> O Neshati! In becoming clearly manifest, we have been raised such that
> on the polished and fully radiant mirror, we have turned into a secret.

The speaker of such words has vanished from being and appeared as existent in the realm of Nonbeing. We are listening to a drop that has evaporated into the air from the ocean, raining down again to flow forth once more. In these words we might hear an awesome roar or perhaps a melody that pounds upon the heart. Pearls are scattered to the shore by such a one.

Through the glance of Mevlânâ, the most beautiful perspective has been found; in the conservatory of Mevlânâ, the sweetest voices have been harmonized in song; in the institute of Mevlânâ, the most profound knowledge has been systematized, resulting in masterful accomplishment; and in the intimate chamber of Mevlânâ, the most noble sentiments have matured into intense states of being.

Research the history of religion and of literature, plunge into the history of art, listen to the history of music: the image that most enchants your eyes will be the *Fahr-i Mevlânâ* adorned with the *destâr-ı giysûdâr-ı Mevlevî* (the conical hat of a Mevlevî shaikh adorned with a winding cloth). The sound that most charms your ear will be "*Yâ Hazret-i Mevlânâ!*" ("O our Master!") in all the different ways it is sung. Throughout the centuries, Mevlânâ has continually blazed a trail for our thinking, accelerating our creativity, fortifying our strength and deepening our values. As time has gone by, he has also embraced the western world. This sun that has risen in the east is everlasting; it also rises in the west. The one who becomes illuminated by Mevlânâ says, "*Lāa ʾuḥibbul ʾāfilīn*" ("I love not that which sets").[1] The one who praises him, praises himself: *Mâdih-i horşîd meddâh-ı hodest.*

The attained ones (*erenler*) who have experienced this feeling, who have embodied this joy and led others to it, have placed great importance on *ādāb* (courtesy), and, as the saying goes, "*Kelâm-i samt-ı deryalar gibî hâmûş söylerler*" ("They have said little, but expressed a lot"). While training beginners on the Path, the attained ones have spoken words that have become proverbs, such as: "*Kan et, kanûn etme; kan eden gelsin, kanûn eden gelmesin*" ("Spill blood, but don't violate the law").

Ceremonies based upon *ādāb* have always been held in high regard by Mevlevîs. Discourteous, lax, or idle behavior has never

---

[1] See Qurʾān, *Surah al-Anʿām,* 6:75–79.

been acceptable in their assemblies of knowledge (*irfan*)–and even if it has entered, it has been transformed. Mevlevîs have regarded the violation of the attained ones' established standards (or the violation of the order's traditions) as worse than murder. They may give a place to someone with bloody hands, but not to someone who violates these standards. All the rules (*töres*) and traditions (*gelenek*) that make up the *ādāb ve erkan* (courtesy and customs) are collectively called "the Path" (*Yol*), and the attained ones have established this incontrovertible maxim: "*Hatır kalsın, yol kalmasın*" ("Let the heart stay back, but don't let the Path stay back").

In our book *Mevlânâ Jelaluddin,* Mevlânâ talks about his life in his own words; while in *Mevlevîhood after Mevlânâ* we examine the Mevlevî order from humanistic, social, political, and cultural perspectives and trace its path through history. This book, *Mevlevî Ādāb and Customs,* will examine the beliefs and practices of the institution from its earliest sources through to its current form.

We hope this work will fill an important gap in the history and philosophy of religion, and also in psychology, sociology, literature, and music. We are not examining *ādāb ve erkan* with a outsider's eye—within its crucible we were formed and experienced great emotion (*duygulanmak*). We have lived it and have helped others experience it. The feeling, thought, and pleasure which we describe here are actually within us. We are documenting this *ādāb ve erkan* in writing because it is the responsibility of those who walk the Path to archive and preserve it for posterity.

Discover the treasure in *Truly, we have laid open.*
Tell the secrets of the being of Muḥammad Muṣṭafā.[2]

Abdülbâki Gölpınarlı

[2] Taken from a ghazal by Mevlânâ Rumi. *Truly, we have laid open* is a quotation from the Qur'ān (48:1).
Mahzen-i inna fetahna bergusha
Sirr-i can-i Mustafara baz gu

I

Mevlevî Glossary

Turkish and Arabic words are used throughout this book. Some of these words arose from within the Mevlevî tradition, but some are also found in other Sufi orders, especially in the Bektâshî tradition. These words have rich cultural and spiritual connotations that give them meanings beyond their literal English translations. For this reason we have found it appropriate to define them at the beginning of the book and to use the original words in the text that follows.

Agâh ol: "Be aware." This phrase means "bring your mind to your head," "come to yourself," or "awaken your consciousness." It is used when one is awakening someone who is asleep. In order not to startle the person, one approaches his or her bed slowly, taps lightly on the pillow with the edge of one's hand, and softly says, "*Agâh ol, erenler.*"

Allah derdini arttırsın: "May God increase your trouble." For Mevlevîs, trouble (*derd* in Turkish, *dard* in Persian) is the trouble of love: it comes with the effort to reach the Truth. For this reason, if any *nev-niyâz* ("new adherent"; see **nev-niyâz)** shows a manifestation of love or ecstasy (*cezbe,* pronounced *jezbe,* "the pull of the Divine"), if he or she weeps or burns within, their *dede* or shaikh, or a great one who sees their state (*hal),* prays for the traveler (*sâlik)* with these words.

Allah feyzini arttırsın: "May God increase your radiating grace." These words are a prayer for bountifulness and enlightenment; for spiritual power that emanates from a person and inspires others.

Allah eyvallah: "Whatever comes from God is good." That is just the way it is. This phrase is used by the Bektâshîs as well as the Mevlevîs. "*Allah eyvallah,*" reassures the person being addressed.

Ana Bacı: "Mother-Sister" (pronounced and sometimes written *Ana Baji*). Common to all paths of *taṣawwuf,* this title is reserved for the wife of the shaikh. *Bacı Anne* ("Sister-Mother") or only *Ana* or *Anne* are also used.

Âstân: A big *dergâh*. Please see **dergâh.**

Arâkîyye: "Soft felt cap." This word, which can mean "cap" or "that which soaks sweat," is the commonly used term for the short *serpuş* which is worn on the head. Made of white or brown woolen felt, usually its upper part is flat and wider than the lower part, and there is a line across it formed by the meeting of the sides. It might be worn under a winding cloth or at the time of prayer.

Although early on in the path, there were female *khalifs* (representatives and successors of shaikhs) of Mevlânâ, and his followers,[1] during the later epochs women could not formally receive dervishhood, shaikhhood, or khalifhood. In earlier times, *sikkes* were not used to honor (*tekbîr etmek*) women; *arâkîyyes* were used instead. Therefore, when a woman was receiving a title, an *arâkîyye* was given to her during the ceremony.[2]

The kitchen souls (*matbâh canları*), who had been accepted into the status of *çile çıkarmak,* but who had not yet progressed to *semâ' çıkarmak,* also used to wear *arâkîyye.*

If an *arâkîyye* is flat and wide, especially towards the top, and if two sides come together at the top forming a complete line, then it is called *elifî arâkîyye. Arâkîyyes* are also used by the other Sufi orders, and it is a custom of shaikhs to wear an *arâkîyye* and to wrap a cloth

---

[1] See *Mevlevîhood after Mevlânâ,* Abdülbâki Gölpınarlı, pp. 278–81.

[2] However, Destine Hatun and Gunesh Hatun of the Karahisar Mevlevîhâne in Afyon did wear a shaikh's *sikke,* the *destar,* and presided over the *semâ'* ceremony. See *Women of Sufism, A Hidden Treasure,* Camille Adams Helminski, Shambhala Publications, 2003, p. 124.

around it when it is not in use.

Aşk olsun; aşk vermek; aşk almak: "May it be love"; "to give love"; "to receive love." Mevlevîs have the view that everything is reached through ecstasy (*cezbe*–pronounced and sometimes spelled *jezbe*) and love (*aşk*–pronounced and sometimes spelled *ashk*). The proverb, "*Aşk olmayınca, meşk olmaz*" ("Without love, there is no practice"), is a guide for the Mevlevî in everything he or she does. For this reason, the words *aşk olsun* are used in many situations, for example:

1. When a Mevlevî sits down as a guest in the *dergâh* or in someone's home, the host says, "*Aşk olsun*" to the Mevlevî. In reply, the Mevlevî makes a prostration (*sajdah*) of *niyâz* ("longing"): wherever he is seated he puts his hands on the floor and kisses the floor.
2. To a person who is drinking something, such as water, tea, or sherbet, one says, "*Aşk olsun,*" in response to which the drinker bows his head (*baş kesmek*) and replies, "*Eyvallah.*"
3. The same word is used to address someone who is eating.

In the Bektâshî Order, when one is greeted with "*Aşk olsun,*" it is the custom to reply, "*Aşkın cemâl olsun*" ("May your love turn into beauty"), to which the proper response is: "*Cemâlin nûr olsun*" ("May your beauty turn into divine light"), and the reply then returned is, "*Nûrun âlâ nûran olsun*" ("May it be light upon light"). Some Mevlevîs who have a Bektâshî temperament (*meşreb*) also practice this customary exchange.

Aşk u niyâz: "Love and longings." Mevlevîs use this greeting in a variety of situations. For example, in a letter one may write, "We express love and longings." When asked, "How are you?" one may reply, "We express our love and longings." This expression is used by other Sufi orders, but not as commonly as among the Mevlevîs. Note that a Mevlevî avoids using the first person singular, because it is an expression of the ego. The first person plural is used instead.

The act of saying "*Aşk olsun*" ("May it be love") is an act of *aşk vermek* ("to give love"), and to receive these words is *aşk almak* ("to receive love"). For example, when telling someone about the greetings exchanged during a visit, a Mevlevî may say, "We visited a certain person; they gave love and we received love."

Âteşbâz: "One who plays with fire" (pronounced and sometimes written *Âteshbâz*). This Mevlevî term refers to the cook and the kitchen. İzzeddinoğlu Shemseddin Yûsuf, whose *türbe* ("tomb") is on the right side of the old way to Meram in Konya, and who died on the 15th of the month of *Rajab* in the year 684 H. (1285 C.E.), was known as *Âteşbâz*. Evidence of this is in the epitaph (*kitabe)* above the "window of need" (*niyâz penceresi*) where one offers prayers by his stone sarcophagus in the *zîr-i zemin* ("graveyard"). According to Mevlevî history, İzzeddinoğlu Shemseddin Yûsuf was the cook at Mevlânâ's *madrasah.*[3] This is why the cook and kitchen are called by this name.

The term *Âteşbâz* may also be related to the term *aşpez,* which means "the one who cooks the food." (It could also be understood as "the noble one who is lost in God's fiery love.")

Avâm: "Common people." When used by Sufis, this term does not refer to those who are illiterate or of low social status (as it can when used by others). According to Sufis, people are divided into three groups: The *avâm* are those who have not reached the Truth, who are preoccupied with eating, drinking, and satisfying their animal selves (*nafs)*—the majority fall into this category. Those who know the Truth are called the *hawass* (*khawass,* meaning "the noble"). Those who actualize the Truth are called *hawass-ul hawass* ("the noble of the noble"), *ahass-ul hass* or *hass-ul hawass.*

Yunus Emre (died 720 H.; 1320 C.E.) refers to this last group in the following lines:

> The two worlds seem as prisons to my eye;
> the one who knows Your love, becomes one of the *hass-ul hass.*[4]

---

[3] See *Mevlevîhood after Mevlânâ,* Abdülbâki Gölpınarlı, pp. 330–34.
[4] *Divan,* Yunus Emre, p. 46, couplet 14.

> Fasting, prayer, ablution, and pilgrimage are a shame for lovers;
> a lover is free of these among the *hass-ul hawass.*[5]

Yunus Emre also used the word *avâm* in the form of *âmî-nâdân:*

> How long will I be *âmi* ["ordinary, without knowledge"], will I be *nâmi* ["developing"], will I be *câmî* ["gathering"]?
> How long will I be *kâmî* ["wishing"], will I be *nâkâm* ["raw"], will I be *nâdân* ["ignorant"]?[6]

Mevlevîs use the word *avâm* for those who are not Mevlevîs, or, generally speaking, for those who do not perceive the Divine Unity (*Vahdet*).

Ayak mühürlemek: "To seal the feet." This term means to place the big toe of the right foot upon the big toe of the left foot and remain in that position. This pose is also called *mührpây durmak* ("to remain sealed"). The one in this position also puts the right hand on the chest with the fingers open over the heart, and puts the left hand on the left hip in the same way. Alternatively, one puts the left hand on the right shoulder and the right hand on the left shoulder, with the right arm on top and the hands and fingers straight, holding the shoulders. This position is called the *niyâz vaziyeti* ("the pleading position").

There are many stories about the origins of the custom of sealing the feet. Alevîs and Bektâshîs say that when Hazrati ʿAlī was passing away he said, "When my corpse is ready for burial, an Arab with a veiled face will come and ask for it; give it to him and he will tie my coffin to his camel and take it away." When this happened as Hazrati ʿAlī had said, Imām Ḥasan and Imām Ḥusayn began wondering who this veiled man was. They went and found him, and when he removed his veil they saw that it was Hazrati ʿAlī himself. Ḥasan ran and hit his left foot on a stone, and it began to bleed–he was ashamed and covered his left toe with his right.

According to another story, Salman-i Farsi had no left toe, so

[5] Ibid., p. 78, couplet 281.
[6] Ibid., p. 186, couplet 1305.

when he was doing service, whenever he stood still, he put his right toe over his left foot to cover it.

There is a Mevlevî oral tradition that one day Âteshbâz-ı Velî said to Mevlânâ, "We have run out of wood," and Mevlânâ told him, "Put your feet under the cauldron." So Âteshbâz-ı Velî said, "*Eyvallah,*" sat down and stretched his feet under the cauldron. Flames sprang from his toes and began to heat it. Only when he doubted, thinking to himself, "I wonder if my toes are getting burned," did his left toe get burned. When Mevlânâ found out what had happened, he called out "Âteshbâz!" In order to hide his burned toe from Mevlânâ, Âteshbâz-ı Velî put his right toe over his left.

The *Burhân-ı Kaatı',* in the section *Pây-mâçan,* relates that this is also a term used by Sufis to mean "shoe shelf," and that when one commits an error, one goes near the threshold and stands on one foot, holding one's left ear with one's right hand and one's right ear with his left hand.[7] "To stand on one foot" means "to seal the foot." This pleading position came from the Qalandars (wandering dervishes); however, as we have said, the Mevlevîs do not hold their ears, but rather their shoulders. This position means: "I have neither hands nor feet; I have surrendered; I accept everything."

Sealing the foot is practiced by other Sufi orders besides the Mevlevîs, and *ayak mühürlemek* is a general Sufi term.

Âyin; âyinhân: "Ritual; ritual reciter." Mevlevî *ilâhîs* ("songs") with lyrics which have been specially chosen from the *ghazals* and the *rubais* of Mevlânâ, and which are intended to be sung during the *semâ',* are called *âyins.* One who has been trained (*meşk etmek*) to sing them is called an *âyinhân.*

Ayn-ı Cem (Ayn-ül Cem'): "Unity Ritual." The word *cem'* (pronounced and sometimes spelled *jem'*), which means "unity," and the word *tefrika,* which means "separation" or "being contrary," are Sufi terms. *Tefrika* means seeing and understanding people as separate from the Truth (*Ḥaqq*). This is also called *fark* ("difference, diversity"). *Cem'* means seeing and understanding that all beings are

[7] *Burhan-ı Kaatı'* (Istanbul: Matbaa-i Amire, 1268, p. 145).

a manifestation of God, and realizing that there is no being other than God. There is servanthood (*kulluk*) in *tefrika* and in *fark,* but no servanthood remains within *cem'*.

For this reason, Sufis have said, "The one who does not know *fark* has no servanthood, while the one who does not know *cem'* has no gnosis (*ma'rifah*); *fark* without *cem'* is atheism, *cem'* without *fark* is blasphemy, but *tawḥīd* ("oneness") is the simultaneous existence of *fark* and *cem'*."

If a Sufi reaches the *makam* ("station") of *cem'* and then returns to the *makam* of *fark,* recognizing people as manifestations of the Truth, and knowing the Truth as Absolute Being manifesting through each person according to their receptivity (*mazhariyet*) and potential (*isti'dat*)–and if he or she sees that everything is perfect, according to its receptivity, while also understanding individual responsibility correctly–then he or she has matured. This second *fark* is also called *Fark-ı Muhammedi* ("Muḥammadan Diversity").[8]

Among Mevlevîs, *Ayn-ül Cem'* is used to describe the coming together of the companions (*ikhvan*) as one ecstatic whole, and describes penetrating into the moment (*dem sürmek*) with *semâ'* and *sefa* ("joy"). The term used by the people is *Ayn-ı Cem.* Please see **semâ'** for further information about the *Ayn-ül Cem'*.

Baş kesmek: "To bow the head" (pronounced and sometimes spelled *bash kesmek*). The foot is "sealed," and as described in the definition of *ayak mühürlemek,* the hands are placed on the chest with the right hand on top. Alternatively, the right hand is placed on the heart with the left hand placed on the right side and bent forward a little, the head meanwhile bending straight down towards the body. This position is also called *niyâz etmek* ("to plead") or *niyâz durumu* ("the pleading position").

Berk-i sebz: "Green leaf." The literal rendering of "green leaf" refers to a gift that a Mevlevî offers to his or her *dede* or to the *dergâh.* The present does not serve the purpose of satisfying a need, nor is it charity. It is a way of making the heart happy; it is a *cemile* ("a

[8] See *Risale-i Qushayriya,* pp. 46–47.

beauty"), and is presented in absolute secrecy. Other terms for *berk-i sebz* are *niyâz* and *nezr* ("a vow"). Please also see **niyâz** and **nezir.**

Can: "Soul" (pronounced and sometimes spelled *jan, jahn,* or *jaan*). Those who have been initiated (*intisab etmek*) into Mevlevîhood address each other either as *Can,* or add *Can* to the end of each other's name. For example: Ali Can or Veli Can. A kitchen soul is called *Can* and it also has the meaning of "dear." Please also see **çile** and **matbâh canı.**

Celâl: "Majesty" (pronounced and sometimes spelled *jelâl*). This term refers to all the wrathful or stringent Attributes of God.

Cemâathâne: "Communal house" or "house of the congregation" (pronounced and sometimes spelled *jemâathâne*). This word, which is used in the *Manâkıb-al Ârifîn* (*Deeds of the Mystic Knowers*[9]), refers to the place where the devotees (*muntesipler*) would come together to read or listen to the *Mesnevî* (*Mathnawī*). The same term is used in *Minhâc-al Fuqara* by Shârh-i Ankaravî. According to the *Minhâc,* the *cemâathâne* corresponds to the *tâbhâne* of the mosque–a visitor who has traveled from afar stops here and is served food, and then with the guidance of a dervish visits the shaikh, presenting a *berk-i sebz* ("a green leaf").[10]

Cemâl: "Beauty" (pronounced and sometimes spelled *jemâl*). This term has various meanings and uses:

1. It refers to the gracious or gentle Attributes of God.
2. It refers to the face. When a person is conveying Divine

---

[9] See *Rumi and His Friends, Stories of the Lovers of God: Excerpts from the Manaqib al-'Arifin of Aflaki,* translated by Camille Adams Helminski and Susan Blaylock, Fons Vitae, 2013.

[10] See *Sefer Adabina ve Hankaha nuzule ait* (*About the Rules of Traveling and Halting at a Khanaqah),* Ist. Ashir Efendi Hani, Riza Efendi Matbaasi (the issue having been printed by Al-Hajj Hasan-al Mevlevî; 12 Rabbi-ul Awwal 1286), ch. VIII, pp. 53–60).

Attributes, one says his or her *cemâl* is beautiful.

3. It can mean favor, goodness, beauty.
4. *Dâr-ı Cemâl,* "Place of Beauty," refers to the next world.
5. *Cemâl seyri,* "touring the Beauty," refers to looking at beautiful faces.

Cümbüşlenmek: "To celebrate or revel" (pronounced *jümbüshlenmek*). A general term meaning to eat or drink something, as in "let's celebrate with tea." This term is used in all Sufi orders.

Çark: "Wheel" (pronounced and sometimes spelled *chark*). This is a variation of the Persian word *cerh.* The most well-known meaning of the word *cerh* is "sky" or "that which rotates." Among the Mevlevîs, the word refers to the left foot. *Çark atmak* ("to make *çarks*") means "to turn." See "Semâ' Meşki ('Practice')" in the chapter entitled "Mevlevî Mukabele."

Çelebi: "Man of God"; "divine" (pronounced and often spelled *chelebi*). In Mongolian, *Çalab* means "God" (*Tanri*). This word is either a Persian *isim-i Mensup,* or, like *bali* or *ari,* is a word derived from Turkish, in this instance from *çalab* ("to be filled with feelings"). It suggests a relationship (*nisbet*).

This title is applied to the descendants of Mevlânâ and is placed after their name. An exception is made for Husâmuddin Hasan, Mevlânâ's khalif. Because he did not belong to Mevlânâ's family, *Çelebi* is placed before (rather than after) his name (Çelebi Husâmuddin). Those who come from the maternal side of Mevlânâ's family are of the *İnas Çelebis.*

At the same time, *çelebi* also means "polite," "noble," "tall," "elegant," "gentlemanly," or "courteous." Men like this are called *çelebi* men. Until the end of the sixteenth century, *çelebi* was used to describe learned and noble people.

Çerağ; Çırağ: "Light"; "lamp" (pronounced *cherağ*). This is a general term.

Çille (çile): "Ordeal"; "trial"; "suffering" (pronounced and sometimes spelled *chille*). In Persian, *cheleh* is short for *chehel which* means "forty." It refers to the act of purifying the body and mind (the ego or *nafs*) by eating, drinking, and sleeping very little, and spending most of one's time in worship. Mevlevîs complete the *çile* by serving for 1001 days. See the chapter "Ranks in Mevlevîhood."

Çilekeş: "One who suffers greatly" (pronounced *chilekesh*). This term is used for someone who passes through a severe ordeal. It may refer to a kitchen soul (please see **matbâh canı)** who has accepted (*ikrâr*) dervishhood and who has begun the period of service (*çile*).

Çivi: "Nail" (pronounced *chivi*). This refers to the nail on the *meşk area* or wooden floor where *semâ'is* practiced (*semâ' meşk etmek*). When the big toe and the adjacent toe are placed around it, it serves to fix the left foot to the floor.

Çivi tutmak: "To hold the nail." This means to keep one's left foot fixed to the turning place during *semâ',* without wandering from it. Someone who has the ability to do *semâ'* in this way is described as *çivisi sağlam* (their "nail is strong").

Dâire: "Circle"; "tambourine without cymbals." This is a general term.

Dal sikke: "Naked" *sikke.* A *sikke* without a *destâr* wrapped around it.

Dal tennûre: "Naked" *tennûre.* A *tennûre* worn without a *destegül.* Please see **destegül.**

Dede: "Grandfather." This is a term for someone who has completed his service of 1001 days, has attained the title of dervishhood, and has a cell in the *dergâh.*

Dem: "Moment." In Arabic it literally means "blood," and in Persian it means "time" or "breath." As a Mevlevî term it has various meanings and uses:

1. "Time" (*vakit*). According to Sufis, time is an abstract, mental concept (*zihnî*) that arises from the successive ordering of phenomena in the mind. The past is only in the mind; the future flows on all the while and one cannot reach it–like the horizon, as one moves forward, it too keeps moving forward. However, the present state (*hâl*) is continuous. Therefore, the truth of time is the moment (*ân; o'n*) in which we are, which is an indivisible part of time. But the universe is being created each moment anew; a moment ago the universe passed away and was gone. In the moment we find ourselves now, we and the universe have been manifested (*zuhur etmek*) from Absolute Being again. Therefore, one has to submit to the manifestation (*tecelli; tajallī*) of the moment that one is in. Since each moment is a manifestation of the Truth, the only everlasting (*bâkı*) thing that remains when all else passes away is the Truth. From this point of view, the meaning that should be derived from the words "*Dem-i Hazreti Mevlânâ, Hû diyelim!*" ("By the moment of Hazreti Mevlânâ, let us say *Hū!*"), is as follows: Mevlânâ, who was the receptive one, the graced one (*mazhâr olmak*) of *Hakıykat-i Muhammediyye* ("Truth of Muḥammadhood")–which is the mature (*kemâl*) manifestation (*mazhâr*) of the grace of Absolute Being and Truth–is in the universe of eternity (*ebedîyet*). For those who have annihilated themselves within him, each moment is a moment of maturity (*kemâl*) and beauty (*cemâl*). That time (*dem*) or moment (*ân*) is called *Hū;* that appearance (*zuhur*) is the appearance of the Truth. *Hū* exists; nothing else exists or has ever existed.
2. "Breath." With each breath the universe is recreated; it goes to the knowledge (*ilm*) of the Truth and from His knowledge it comes into the universe of *ayn*–that is: "the universe of relative being."
3. *Dem tutmak* ("accompanying the moment"). Towards the end of an improvization (*taksîm*), while one *ney* player is playing,

another accompanies him in a lower octave.

4. *Rakı.* According to this last meaning, *demlenmek* or *dem görmek* ("becoming the moment" or "to see the moment") is a term that means to drink *rakı.* Although it is a term that belongs to Bektâshîs, some unconventional Mevlevîs also use it. (It can also refer to the act of breathing upon food or water which is to be eaten by the sick to help them heal.)

Dergâh: "The place of the door." This Persian word refers to all of the buildings that house the dervishes and the shaikh. It is a general term. The honor and greatness of a *dergâh* depends on the honor and greatness of the saint buried (*yatir*) there. If the *pir* who founded the path of the *dergâh* is buried there, or if on the way there is a *türbe* of someone whose station is close to the *pir*, then the *dergâh* is called the *âstân(e)* ("threshold of the door"), which means the "great" or "main" *dergâh.* If, according to the people of that path, the *pir's* station is not of the highest level, then it is referred to simply as a *dergâh.*

In addition to the word *dergâh*, the word *tekke* (pronounced *tekye* by the people and meaning "a support one leans on") refers to a place where the Sufis come together and perform their ceremonies. It follows that both *âstânes* and places of lower status are called *dergâh* and *tekke.* Places that are regarded as having lower status than *dergâhs* are called *zaviye,* which means "corner"; "nook"; "subdistrict."

Mevlevîs have generally built *dergâhs* outside of cities. The *dergâhs* that exist within cities have gradually seen these cities spread up around them.

A Mevlevî *dergâh* has a *harem*, *selâmlik*, *semâ'hâne*, *türbe*, *masjid*, *meydan*, *matbâh*, and cells for the dervishes. One enters the *dergâh* through the main door, which is called the *Cümle Kapısı.* The *harem* is the building where the shaikh lives with his family; this building is always away from the *semâ'hâne, masjid*, *matbâh* and the cells, in a relatively secluded location. It also has a separate door leading outside. The *selâmlık* is the place where guests visit the shaikh. It is a separate building which consists of a few rooms. There is always a coffee room and a cell for the *meydancı* ("caretaker of the meeting room"). Sometimes the *masjid* is right next to the *semâ'hâne*, as in Konya, while in other *dergâhs* it is located nearby. A large room called *meydan-ı şerîf* is usually located close to the cells. People gather here after the morning *ṣalāh*. The *matbâh* ("kitchen") is also close to the cells, and besides the area with stoves (*ocak*) where the food is cooked the *matbâh* souls also have cells or several places to lie down and rest. The *semâ'hâne* is a separate building, and most of the time it is under the same roof as the *türbe*. Generally, there is also a *türbedâr* ("caretaker of the *türbe*") room next to the *türbe* and a door opens from this room to the *türbe*.

The cells are close to the kitchen, and they are usually along a corridor. They are small rooms designed for one person (see **hücre)**. We are not familiar with the place referred to as the *cemâathâne* ("the place for the gathering"), although such a place is mentioned in the *Manâkıb* and in the *Minhâc*. However, we understand that the *dergâhs* used to have a room to shelter their guests, and perhaps it would be appropriate to say that in such a room people must have read the *Mesnevî* and met for discussion.

Small *dergâhs* are known as *zaviye*. Dervishes are not trained in a Mevlevî *zaviye*. *Zaviye* are stopping places for dervishes who are traveling. They have dervish cells, a *semâ'hâne*, *türbe*, *meydan*, *harem* and *selâmlık* chambers. A dervish who is traveling stops here for a few days and gathers provisions for his journey. A traveler who is not a dervish is welcomed as a guest. He can rest, wash and be purified, and attend to his needs before continuing on his way.

There were five *Mevlevîhânes* in Istanbul: Kulekapısı, Yenikapı, Kasımpaşa, Bahariye, and Üsküdar. Üsküdar Mevlevîhânesi was a *zaviye* and the others were *dergâhs*.

The doors of the Mevlevî *tekkes* were closed during the call for the evening *ṣalāh*; after the call for the *ṣalāh* no one could enter (except during the month of Ramaḍān). The doors were opened while the call for the morning *ṣalāh* was being recited. The task of closing and opening the door belonged to the *bevvap dede* ("gatekeeper").[11]

The *dedes* who were in charge of the administration and discipline of the *dergâh* were called the *dergâh zabitânı* (*dergâh* "officers"). See **zabitân.**

[11] For further information about Mevlevî *tekkes* see *Mevlevîhood after Mevlânâ*, pp. 329–63.

Derviş: "Poor" ("dervish" in English). This word refers to those who are connected (*müntesip*) with the *ṭarīqah*, and it is a general term. Among Mevlevîs the word is used for the *çilekeş matbâh canları* (the "kitchen souls" who have been accepted as dervishes and who have begun to serve) and the dervishes who have completed the *çile* and been awarded a cell (*hücre*).

Destâr: "Winding cloth." Among Mevlevîs, the right to wrap a winding cloth around one's head belongs to the shaikhs and khalifs. If the shaikh is a *seyyid* (a descendant of the family of Hz. Muḥammad), he wears a green *destâr*; otherwise he wears a white *destâr*. Khalifs and *chelebis* wear smokey, dark (*dühânî*) violet *destârs* that look almost black. *Chelebis* wrap the *destâr* in such a way that their *sikke* is not visible underneath it, while those who are not *chelebis* wrap the *destâr* so that their *sikke* is visible.

The Mevlevîs have six types of *destâr*: *Örfî*, *Cüneydî*, *Şeker-âvîz*, *Hüseynî*, *Şeker-âvîz kafesî*, and *Dolama*.

The *Örfî destâr* is stuffed with cotton; it has a rounded shape and is at least three fingers thick. It is made of muslin and is wrapped halfway from the bottom up and halfway from the top down, with slight spaces in between. Shaped like a a sweet melon, the lower and upper parts are narrower than the rounded middle. The *destârs* of Sultânel-Ulemâ, Mevlânâ, and Sultân Veled's sarcophaguses are *Örfî*. During the Ottoman period, before the Tanzimat, the Şeyhülislâms and the Nâkibüleşrafs used to wear *Örfî destârs*. One comes across very beautiful examples of these on gravestones.

The *Cüneydî destâr* is half as long as the *Örfî destâr* and is in the same style. The great ones of the Mevlevîs, being sensitive to etiquette (*ādāb*), have never worn the type of *destâr* worn by Mevlânâ, but have worn instead the *Cüneydî* (*Junaydi*) *destâr*. In the *huzur* ("presence"—the area near the sarcophagus where Mevlânâ is laid to rest) the sarcophaguses of Ulu Arif Chelebi and of most of the departed Mevlevîs have *Cüneydî destâr*.

The *Şeker-âvîz* is a *destâr* where the lower part is rounded and the upper part tapers in until it is the same thickness as the *sikke*. This *destâr* is wrapped by folding a narrow muslin four times at two fingers width, then wrapping from right to left and then in the opposite direction from left to right. The *Şeker-âvîz kafesî* is a *destâr* with the cloth–the "sugar" – hanging from it. The cloth is wrapped in a trellis pattern downward.

The *Dolama destâr* is wrapped in a plain fashion.

Hüseynî is the manner in which a *destâr* is wrapped from left to right and the other way, from right to left.

Destegül: Mevlevî "jacket" (from the Persian, meaning "a bouquet of roses"). This type of jacket is collarless, with plain, tight arms and it ends at the waist. Attached to the right edge is a band one finger wide which can be tucked into the *gaytan* ("tie band") of the *elifî nemed* ("belt") to keep the jacket from opening and flapping while one is turning in the *Semâ'*. Please see **elifî nemed** below.

Destûr: "Permission." Mevlevîs use this word to ask for permission, for example, "If you give me *destûr*" ("If you allow me to speak"). Also, when one arrives at a Mevlevî's cell, one says, "*Destûr*," with a soft, harmonious voice, lengthening the last syllable. When the person inside replies, "*Hū*," one may open the door and go in. If there is no answer, one says, "*Destûr*," two more times, and if there is still no answer one departs.

Dışarı vermek: "To give it to the outside" (pronounced *dıshan vermek*). This term refers to showing one's ecstasy (*vecd; wajd)*, or revealing something that should be kept secret (which was considered very poor *ādāb* and inappropriate). Among the Bektâshîs, to vomit after drinking (*demlenmek*) is "to give it to the outside."

Dinlendirmek: "To put to rest." Mevlevîs do not say "put out" or "extinguish" because of the harshness of these expressions. Instead they use the expression *dinlendirmek*, as in "to put the stove, candle, or light to rest."

Direk: "Column"; "pillar"; "post." The *direk* is the left leg of someone turning during *semâ'*. The leg must stay straight and turn on its axis. Performing *semâ'* on the same spot without wandering from it is called *direk tutmak.*

Düşkün: "Fallen"; "immoral"; "unchaste" (pronounced *düshkün).* Someone on the Path who does something contrary to good manners or *ādāb*, or who does something insolent, is called "fallen". Please see **küstah.**

Eksikli: "The one who is lacking or guilty." This term, which is seen in the old texts, means "someone who has erred," and it is a general term.

Elifî nemed: "Belt." This is a woolen felt *(nemed)* belt which is four or five fingers wide. Its end is pointed, and it resembles the Arabic letter *alif.* It is wrapped around the *tennûre* at the waist, one-and-a half times. At its end it has a long *gaytan* (a braided cotton or silk cord which wraps around the waist twice). To secure it, the end of the *gaytan* is then attached to the main part of the belt that is wrapped around the waist. The band of the *destegül* is also tucked inside the *gaytan.* In everyday speech the word has become *eliflâmet.*

Er: "Man"; "manly man"; "soldier." This word refers to someone who has control over his or her *nafs.* Among the Sufis, "erhood" is a station (*makam; maghaam*). The Qur'ān mentions people whom business and trade cannot distract from remembering God, performing *ṣalāh* (prayer) and giving *zakāt* (alms). These are people who have reached the *makam* of *er.* From this point of view, a woman who has reached this station is also regarded as an *er*, while a man who has not been able to reach this station is not.

Erenler: "The attained ones." This word refers to people who have reached the Truth or Oneness (*Vahdet*). This is also a general expression used to address the great ones of the Path.

Eşik: "Threshold" (pronounced *eshik*). Sufis regard the threshold as the foundation of the structure and of the station of dervishhood. This belief, which is shared by all paths of *taṣawwuf,* is also an old

Turkish tradition. The threshold, and the furnace or stove (*ocak*), are sacred. One must never step or sit on the threshold.

Eyvallah: "Good by God"; an adaptation of *iyi vallâh* and *iy vallahi.* This expression can be found in Mevlânâ's letters. When someone replies with this expression, he is confirming what was said to him, or implying, "Yes, I'll do it." When called, instead of saying, "Yes, sir!" one replies instead, "*Eyvallah!*" If one does not understand what was said, one asks, "*Eyvallah?*" When guests arrive, this word also welcomes them. When someone is eating or drinking, this word is said in place of *"Afiyet olsun!"* ("May it turn into health!"), and it is also said in reply to "*Aşk olsun.*" People swear by *Allâh eyvallah.* It is a general term.

Fâhir: "Sumptuous"; "splendid"; "honorable"; "one who glories in his deeds." The Mevlevî *sikke* and the Bektâshî *tac* ("crown") are called *fahir* and *fahr-i şerif.* They are common words on the respective paths.

Fakıyr: "Poor"; "nonexistent." Mevlevîs use this word in place of "I," and it signifies nonexistence. If a Mevlevî accidentally says "I," he immediately says, "Curses upon my *benlik* (I-ness)." He confesses his mistake and says, "*fakıyr.*"

Ganî (Ghani): "Rich." This word–meaning "the one who does not need anything," "the one who does not ask for anything," or "the one who is rich"–is common among Mevlevîs and Bektâshîs. When something is offered, instead of saying, "I don't want it," one says, "*Ganîsiyim*" ("I am rich with it"). The abundance of something is expressed with the word *ganî.*

Göçmek; göçünmek: "To immigrate" (pronounced *göchmek*). This word is used with the meaning "to die." It is a general term used by all paths of *taṣawwuf.*

Görmek: "To see." This word means "to pay attention," or show meticulous care towards something. For example: "He saw such and such person; see us a little, too." This is also a general term.

Görüşmek: "To see with each other (a mutual seeing and being seen)" (pronounced and sometimes spelled *görüshmek*). According to Mevlevîs, everything has a soul and human beings are obliged to show respect to everything that serves them. For example, in a mosque, a Mevlevî will first prostrate and kiss the place of prostration; then, when he stands up to do the *ṣalāh,* he and the place of prostration perform "a seeing with each other." After he completes the *ṣalāh,* he again "sees with" the place of prostration, before standing up.

When going to bed, first a Mevlevî "sees with" the pillow, and then lies down. Then, when he is pulling the quilt over himself, he "sees with" that too, kissing its edge. Before he drinks water, tea or coffee, he kisses the glass: he "sees with" it.

A Mevlevî is forbidden to display something shameful or dirty. For this reason, after drinking tea or coffee, he makes a *niyâz*, "sees with" the dirty cup, kisses it, and hides it somewhere nearby. When the one who is serving comes and bows his head (*baş kesmek*) to the seated dervish who has finished his drink, the seated dervish covers the top of the cup with his left hand, "sees with" it, and presents it to the soul who is serving. The one serving covers the top of the cup with his left hand, "sees with" it, and takes it away.

When a Mevlevî takes a book to read, he or she "sees with" the book. After she finishes reading it, again she "sees with" the book and puts it lightly back in its place, never throwing or hurting it. She picks up the *tasbīḥ* (prayer beads) and "sees with" them, and when she has finished chanting, she "sees with" the *tasbīḥ* and puts them gently back in their place.

This practice applies to everything. Even with something that should not be kissed, such as a dirty handkerchief or a mouthpiece, the Mevlevî moves it towards his mouth as if to kiss it, and kisses his own index finger instead. If he is passing an object to someone, the receiver takes it and kisses it in the same way.

In addition, when Mevlevîs simultaneously kiss each other's hands it is called *görüşmek.* According to Mevlevîs, every human being is equal; there is no notion of inferiority or superiority. When a Mevlevî meets a friend on the Path, he takes his friend's right hand in both of his hands, while his own right hand is taken in his friend's hand. The thumbs are either left resting on the hands, or they are held upright so that their insides touch each other. The two bow slightly towards each other and simultaneously kiss each other's hands. In this way, regardless of temporary things such as age, status, and knowledge, two souls have celebrated each other.

Among the Mevlevîs, one also "sees with" the shaikh and the khalif in this way. A shaikh does not let his palm be kissed or smelled, and such things as letting another kiss one's feet have no place in Mevlevîhood. However, if moved by sincere love and rapture during a *sohbet*, one may kiss the knee of a great one. Then, immediately, the one whose knee has been kissed responds by kissing the person's *sikke* or the back of their neck.

Gönül etmek: "To make heart." This is a general term on the path of *taṣawwuf.* It refers to unseen help (*himmet*) from God, or from a saint a long distance away, or some other form of unseen, spiritual help. For example, one might say to someone, "Please make a heart, so that I may complete this book."

Gönül koymak: "To put heart." This idiom means "to be hurt by someone because of something." For example, "So-and-so put heart in this business."

Gülbâng: "Rose voice." This Persian compound word describes the singing of the nightingale. It is used in all Sufi orders, and it may also be pronounced *gülbenk.* It refers to composed prayers. In Mevlevîhood there is a different *gülbâng* for every occasion.

Habbe: A faceted carnelian or agate. This is a common term among the Mevlevîs and Bektâshîs. A *habbe* is a round, facted carnelian or agate no bigger than a nut. It is strung on a thin silver chain with a loop of silver wire at the end. There is a pin at the end of the wire to attach it to a shirt. A *habbe* signifies love of the Truth.

The influence of the Bektâshîs may have introduced the *habbe* to Mevlevîs. Among the Bektâshîs, those who have visited the fourteen innocent ones–the Blessed Prophet, Hz. Fatima and the Twelve Imāms–attach seven *habbes* on a chain on one side of their chests, and another seven *habbes* on the other side. Although Mevlevîs do not traditionally wear such things, on the photograph of Fahreddîn Chelebi (1305 H.; 1887 C.E.) one can see two *habbes*, one on either side of his chest.

Hakta; Hak vere: "In the Truth"; "the Truth has it"; "may the Truth give it." Mevlevîs say these words instead of "there is none." For example, by saying, "The sugar is in the Truth," one means that the sugar has run out. If someone asks for something, one can reply with "Let the Truth give it," to say that there is none left.

There is a story about this practice. During a time when there had been many fires, a Mevlevî shaikh heard a noise outside and said to a newly initiated soul, "Dervish brother, go out and see! Is there a fire?" Because the dervish had been previously warned not to say, "There is not," but rather to say, "Let the Truth give it," when he saw that there was no fire outside he said, "My *erenler!* Let the Truth give the fire!" Hearing this, the shaikh said, "No, dervish brother! Let the Truth give us everything, but not the fire!"

Hak erenler: "True attained ones." This expression describes the absolute *erens*. It means "the true *erens*."

Halife (khalif): A Mevlevî who has gained the authority to bestow khalifhood on someone else (please see the chapter "Ranks in Mevlevîhood").

Halile: "Cymbal." This is a large cymbal, bigger than the palm of the hand, the inside of which is slightly concave. One puts one's hand into the leather band on the convex side. The musician holds one in each hand and makes a rhythm by gently hitting them together while pulling one of them downwards. The musician who plays the *halile* is called the *halilezen*.

Hânkaah (khanaqah): A big dergâh. This word is a synonymn for *âstân* and *âstâne* (please see **dergâh)**.

Hâmûşân: "Silent ones" (pronounced *hâmûshân*). This literally means "those who are silent", but it is used to refer to those who have died. It also means "cemetery."

Hâmûşhâne: "Silent home" (pronounced *hâmûshhâne*). This is a synonym of *hâmûşân* and is used instead of the word "cemetery." (*Hâmûş*, "Silent One," was one of the names of Mevlânâ.)

Havâlet: "Permission." This term is used by all paths of *taṣawwuf*. For example, "If you give *havâlet*; let me go!" or "I will go with your *havâlet!*"

Hayderî; hayderîye: "Waistcoat." This is a plain waistcoat without arms or a collar. It is worn over a shirt. The front is open, and it is waist-length. Over the shoulders it has a crescent-shaped part made of the main fabric (not an addition) that comes down two or three fingers from the top of the shoulder.

Hırka (khirka): A long robe, sometimes padded and quilted. This is a long cotton jacket worn by dervishes. Mevlevîs have two kinds of *khirka*. One is worn when going out on the street and is an over-garment without a collar. Its arms are a little wider than a jacket's, but from the top to the bottom its body is about as wide as a jacket's body. It comes down to the heels, and the waist is not tight. The other kind is called the *resim hırkası* (ceremonial *khirka*) and Mevlevîs wear it during their rituals. This *khirka* does not have a collar either, but its arms, upper part, and lower part are one, and they are very wide. Its body is plain. If one does not put one's arms in the sleeves, it seems like a cloak, and its length comes to the heels. When one's arms are in the sleeves and the hands are brought together at the front, the width of the sleeves falls below the knees. A *khirka* is worn by a dervish who has expressed acceptance, whose time of service is complete and who is staying in a cell. It is also worn by a khalif when he is receiving khalifhood.

Hora geçmek; hora geçirmek: "To eat" (pronounced *hora gechmek*). This comes from the Persian *horden* (*khordan*), meaning "to eat." It is a general term that can mean both "to eat" and "the thing that is eaten."

Hora geçmek means that the meal is appreciated. *Hora geçirmek* is "to eat." It is a general term.

Hû (Hū): "He." This Arabic word is the pronoun of Divine Presence. In reality, it is beyond gender. It expresses the meaning of Allāh. *Hū* is recited at the end of every *gülbâng*.

Hücre: "Cell" (pronounced and sometimes spelled *hujre*). This word means a "small room", "corner," or "nook." The dervish who completes his service of 1001 days becomes a *dede*, and he is permitted to have a cell at the *dergâh*. The cell's door opens from a corridor, and when one enters, there is a little *methal* (entry place) where shoes are left. The place for the shoes can be on the wall. The cell floor is one foot higher than the ground, and has a window that looks outside onto the courtyard of the *dergâh*. Just inside the door, to the right or left, there is a furnace (*ocak)* for the *dede* to make coffee, and next to it is his *kerevet* (cot-like, wooden bed) on which is placed his sheepskin (*post*). The *dede* sits there and his visitors sit on the *kerevet*. Some cells also have an additonal furnace or fireplace.

İcâzet: "Permission" (pronounced and sometimes written *ijâzet*). This word has two meanings. It can mean the permission required to leave the presence of a respected person. There is a Mevlevî proverb that says, "To come depends upon will, and to go depends upon permission" (*Gelmek irâdet, gitmek icâzet*). The second meaning refers to the permission given to someone to educate dervishes and lovers of the Path. This permission is confirmed in writing, and the written document is called an *icâzetnâme*.

İhvân: "Siblings." "The faithful are siblings" (Qur'ān, 49:10). In Mevlevîhood, siblinghood is emphasized through being born from the soul, because those who have accepted Mevlevîhood have in reality become the children of the Path of Mevlânâ. However, in Mevlevîhood one does not call the shaikh *Baba* ("Father"), because the shaikh is only a representative; he represents the Path within the limits of his capacity. For this reason, unlike other Sufi orders, one does not say that someone is the "disciple" or "son" of a shaikh, but rather that he is the "brother" (*ihvân*) of the shaikh. In his letters, Mevlânâ refers to one who is bound to him as "my son" and himself as "father,"[12] but this is an authority that belongs to him alone.

İkrâr: "Admittance"; "declaration"; "acceptance." This word literally means "to declare." In Mevlevîhood it is the promise to become a dervish and to begin serving.

İsm-i Celâl: "The *Celâl* Name"; "the Name of Majesty." The name Allāh, which signifies the *Dhāt* ("Essence") of God, is called *İsm-i Celâl* (*Ism-e Jalal*). It means "the Name of Majesty," "the Majestic," or "the Greatest Name." It is common to all paths of *taṣawwuf.* Instead of *İsm-i Celâl,* some say *Lâfza-i Celâle.*

İstivâ (istiwa): "Equableness"; "straightness"; "uniformity." *Sivâ* is used for the equality of two things in volume or weight. It is also used in regard to quality. *İstivâ* means that two things are equal and at the same level. If it is used as a verb with the word *ala* it means "to grab" or "to cover."

The *er,* who knows and sees, and turns this seeing into being, so that all actions, all attributes and all being are perceived as the Truth, becomes existent through the Truth's being and knows that all attributes are manifestations of one single Self within objects (*mazhar*) according to their capacity (*istidat*). The *er* sees that actions are the appearances (*zuhur*) of the attributes; therefore, he regards everything in the correct way according to the thing's capacity. He does not fall into despondency (*meskenet*) because he has understood that this universe of opposites is a universe of endeavors (*şüûn*) and he treats everything and everybody appropriately. From then on,

[12] See *Letters of Mevlânâ,* Abdülbâki Gölpınarlı.

according to him, the people (*halk*) are an appearance (*zuhur)* of the Truth and have no independent being; and the Truth is the Absolute Being made manifest through the veils of actions and attributes, being the whole of the people. To the *er,* this manifest (*zahiri*) duality is all one. Someone who has reached this degree of maturity (*kemâl*), even if the Truth may not have given him an authority, has reached the spiritual (*manevî)* khalifhood; he has the station (*makam*) of *istivâ* (equableness).

As a proof and sign of this, he places a band of black or green wool, two fingers wide, on his *sikke.* This band is called the *istivâ.* Emerging from the *destâr* at the midpoint between the eyebrows, it goes over the top and returns to the bottom of the *destâr* at the back. Some couplets of Esrar Dede (d. 1211 H.; 1796–1797 A.D.) mention the *istivâ*, and lead us to understand that its color was green:

Ol nûr-ı sebze bî ser ü bî pâ olan erer,
Bîhûde alma başına sevdâ-yı istivâ.

One without head or foot reaches that green light;
don't take the love-sickness of *istivâ* upon your head lightly.

Bir Mevlevî ki râsti âl-i Rasûl ola,
Mevrûsudur alâmet-i hadrâ-yı istivâ.

Such a Mevlevî as he, true descendant of the Prophet,
the green *istivâ* is the sign of his heritage.[13]

However, on the sarcophagi in the "presence," and on some sarcophagi at Yenikapı and Istanbul, the *sikkes* have black *istivâs.* In the second couplet of the same *qaside* Esrar Dede writes:

Ser tâ-be pay mazhâr-ı nûr-ı siyah olan
Gerdûn-ı devr-i zâta olur cây-ı istivâ

One who has been honored by the black light from head to foot,
who has ascended from the world, the *makam* of *istivâ* is his.

As he alludes here to its color being black, it is likely that *istivâs*

[13] Ist. *Takvim-i Vekai Matbaasi,* 1257; pp. 10–11.

were either black or green. Perhaps, as in the case of the *destâr* (please see **destâr)**, those who were descendants of the Prophet wore a green *istivâ*. This seems most probable to us. Şâhidî (d. 951 H.; 1544 A.D.), who wrote *Gülşen-i Esrâr* (*The Secret Rose Garden*)**,** meets someone named Fenâyî in a mosque in Kozluk; this person has a green *istivâ* on his *sikke*.[14] In the Kulekapisi *dergâh*, Mevlevî Ali Dede, who rests at the foot of the *Mesnevî* commentator Ismail Rusûhî, and who is one of the dignitaries of the same century, wears an *istivâ* on his *seyfî sikke* although he does not have a *destâr*. Mevlevîs, therefore, had the *istivâ* in the sixteenth century, and the tradition must come from the fifteenth century.

We have heard that the *istivâ* was not given by a khalif or *chelebi* with khalifhood, but that the *er* who came to the realization that he had reached such a level (*mertebe*) of maturity (*kemâl*) attached an *istivâ* to his *sikke* himself. Such is what we understand. But in *Sefine,* it is written that khalifhood *sikkes* with *istivâ* were given to the Shaikh of Gelibolu, Ağazâde Mehmed Dede (d. 1063 H.;1652-1653 A.D.) and the Shaikh of Yenikapı, Sabûhî Ahmet Dede (d. 1057 H.;1647 A.D.), by the station of chelebihood.[15]

However, we do not find any gravestones or sarcophagi with *istivâ* after the eighteenth century. In recent times, *istivâ* have not featured at all. In the "presence", the *sikkes* of the sarcophagi of Mevlânâ, Sultân Veled, Mevlânâ's father, and Chelebi Husâmuddin do not have *istivâs* either. Ulu Arif Chelebi, those who rest near him, and some of the later Mevlevî *chelebis* do have *istivâs* on their sikkes. However, we wonder if they were there initially, or if they were added after the *destârs* were washed or renewed–while they were being wrapped perhaps. We surmise that they were added later, because we suspect that the use of the *istivâ* came into Mevlevîhood through the influence of the *Hurûfis* (another *ṭarīqah*).[16]

In the *semâ'hâne*, the imaginary line from the edge of the sheepskin (*post*) of the shaikh to the middle of the *semâ'hâne* door just across from it is called the *hatt-ı istivâ* (the *istivâ* line), and one never

[14] Ist. Halet Efendi, Mulhak 74, 71a-97b. For Fenayi please see *Mevlevîhood after Mevlânâ*, pp. 104, 119, 121, and 135.
[15] Part II, pp. 26 and 76.
[16] See *Mevlevîhood after Mevlânâ,* pp. 310–17.

steps upon it. This line divides the *semâ'hâne* into two halves.

On ceremonial *khirkas,* there is a green border, a cord which begins from the collar and goes all the way around the edge of the whole *khirka.* This cord is entwined behind the collar in a circular form as per figure 1:

This is also called an *istivâ.* Due to the way it is entwined, this cord takes the following form as per figure 2:

The dervish who wears this is in the rank of an *alif* inside of it, the form becoming as per figure 3:

This symbol shows the *kalimāt at-tawḥīd* ("declaration of oneness") and indicates that real being is the existence of the Truth (*Ḥaqq*), and that the one who has worn the *khirka* is liberated from his imaginary and relative existence and has come into real being through the Being of the Truth. On the gravestones of Melami-Hamzavis, figure 2 above shows that the one who has passed away is in the station of nothingness, and figure 3 above shows that the person has reached the Being of the Truth, the degree of maturity.

The border and collar of the *destegül* and the *tennûre* have *istivâ,* too. In his *İstivâ Kasidesi,*[17] Esrar Dede notes this fact with the following couplets:

Yazmish kenar-i hirkaya adab-i fakri hep
Hatt-i sebizle matla-i garra-yi istivâ
Tennûrelerde suret-i La'da iyandir
Sine-i gayri nefyide ta La'yi istivâ

He has written the *ādāb* of poverty fully on his *khirka's* collar.
With the green line, the brightness of *istivâ* arises.[18]

[17] *Divan,* p. 10.

[18] *Matla:* the place where the sun begins to rise. It also means a point where inner and outer meanings unite, and the epiphany of Allah received by a

In *tennûres*, the form of "la" is apparent–
drive out everything in your breast but the "la" of *istivâ*.[19]

Kaaf-i fenada Mevlevî pervaz eylesun
Var hirkasinda sheh-per-i ankaa-yi istivâ

May Mevlânâ soar upon the *fana* of Kaf–
the longest feather of the anqa's *istivâ* is upon his *khirka*.[20]

Besides the ceremonial *khirka*, the non-ceremonial *khirka* had eighteen tight stitches the same color as the *khirka* itself. Beginning at the *khirka's* collar and coming down to the level of the heart, these stitches formed a *lām-aleph* at the collar again, in this way making an *istivâ*.

Kadem: "Foot." Although it means "foot," this word also means "good luck." When guests arrive, they are welcomed with the words, "You have brought *dems* and *kadems!*"

Kafesçi bacı: "Lattice sister" (pronounced *kafeschi bajı*). When a *mukabele* was held at the *dergâh*, one of the sisters who was in need used to collect whatever the women in the lattice chamber were inspired to give, and she would take it to the shaikh. The shaikh would give part–or, usually, all of it–to that sister, who was called "the lattice sister." Sisters in need would take turns as the lattice sister. The practice is from the later period of Mevlevîhood.

Kanını içine akıt: "Shed your blood within yourself" (pronounced *kanını ichine akıt*). With these words the *dedes* caution the devotees

---

mature one who is reading the Qur'ān. The *istivâ* may be embroidered in green. This also suggests the green line that appears upon the horizon just before dawn.

[19] This indicates the *lā* of *lā ilāha illā Allah*. Dispell everything but the unity of the One Reality.

[20] The legendary mountain of Kaf supposedly surrounds the entire world. Beyond Kaf mountain is the home of the *anqa* (phoenix). *Fana* is annihilation. What remains is the Truth.

never to reveal their rapture (*cezbe).* In Mevlevîhood, it is strictly forbidden to reveal one's rapture during a *semâ'*, or when listening to a *naat* or *taksîm*, or during a recitation of the Qur'ān, because such displays are also deployed the hypocrite. It is forbidden to shake, to harmonize with the melody, to sigh aloud, or even to let others know that one is weeping.

Kapıdan geçmek: "To pass through the door" (pronounced *kapıdan gechmek*). When a dervish has completed the service of 1001 days, he or she is given a cell. This expression refers to the moment he or she enters the cell (see the chapter "Ranks in Mevlevîhood").

Kemer: "Belt." Mevlevî dervishes and shaikhs did not usually wear a specific belt, but some Mevlevîs who were influenced by Bektâshîs used to wear a woven belt with a whitish carnelian or agate attached. Such a belt can be seen in the photographs of Fahreddîn Chelebi.

Kıdem: "Seniority." This refers to one's time on the Path. In Mevlevîhood, it is not one's age but the length of one's time on the Path that is considered. Except for the superior ranks, Mevlevîs are seated according to seniority.

Kılıflı maşa: "Tongs with a sheath" (pronounced *Kılıflı masha*). This is a symbolic object. The kitchen soul assigned to serve outside and buy meat and vegetables places long tongs within a sheath into his *elifî nemed.* In this way, he informs others that he has a service to perform, and the souls who cross paths with him do not talk with him for too long or keep him from his service.

Köçek: "Little one"; "male dancer" (pronounced *köchek*). The *nev-niyâz*–the soul that has recently set out on the Path (and especially the young man who has recently made a commitment to learn the *semâ'*)–is called a *köçek* or *Mevlânâ köçeği* (the *köçek* of Mevlânâ). Besides this, the kitchen soul or *dede* assigned to serve the shaikh is also called *köçek.* For example, in Instanbul's Hâlet Efendi Library, in manuscript no.74 among the indexed books, we read the following:

Min kutubil fakiyr Dervish Ibrahim
Al Mavlaviyy al Kunavi sakin der hankaah-i
Bab-i cedid hala der hidmet-i
Kuchekiyy-al Shayh-al Mavlavi
Aliyy-al Nutkiy

From the records of the poor one, dervish Abraham,
a Konya Mevlevî at peace in the *khaneqah*,
the new door still acknowledges his service.
Köçek of the Mevlevî Shaikh Ali-al Nutkiy

Kudüm: "Percussion instrument." People call the *kudüm* "the double shouts." It is made of two metallic bowls that taper toward the bottom, and each has a skin stretched over the top. In addition, they each have a rounded piece of felt at the bottom on which they sit. One kneels down or crosses one's legs in front of this instrument and, according to the rhythm (*usûl*), beats the skins using slender drumsticks with rounded ends. The one who plays the *kudüm* is called the *kudümzen*, and the one who conducts the *kudümzens* is called the *kudümzenbaşı* (the head *kudümzen*).

Kurban tığlamak: "To lance a sacrifice"; "to sacrifice an animal." This means to sacrifice an animal in accordance with Islamic law (*sharīʿah*). The word "lancing" is also used for cutting a sweet melon. Words such as "cut" or "slaughter" are almost never used. This term is common to all paths of *taṣawwuf*.

Küstah; küstahlık: "Insolence"; "impertinence"; "shamelessness." To do or say something that is not in harmony the Path is called *küstah* (please see **serpâ**).

Mangır: "Money." This term is common to all paths of *taṣawwuf*.

Matbâh; matbâh canı: "Kitchen"; "kitchen soul" (pronounced *matbâh jahni*). These words refer to the kitchen of the *dergâh* and those who serve there. The kitchen is also called the *Âteşbâz* (please see the chapter entitled "Ranks in Mevlevîhood").

Mazhâr: A *halîle* is also called as *mazhâr.* A tambourine without cymbals is called as *mazhâr* too. *Mazhâr* is a general term.

Meydan: "Open field"; "chamber." This is a wide, rectangular room in Mevlevî *dergâhs* where the *dedes* come together in contemplation after the morning *ṣalāh.*

Meydancı: "*Meydan* man" (pronounced and sometimes spelled *meydanji).* This word refers to the dervish responsible for taking care of the meeting chamber in the *dergâh.* He lays out the *post* (sheepskin) of the shaikh in the *semâ'hâne* before the *mukabele*, accompanies the shaikh when he enters the *semâ'hâne*, and rolls up the *post* after the *mukabele* has finished, putting it back in its proper place. According to the rules of courtesy, the *meydancı* informs people about mealtimes and when there will be a *mukabele*, and performs other services in a similar vein.

Mihmân: "Guest." This term is common to all paths of *taṣawwuf.*

Muhib: "Sympathizer"; "lover" in the sense of "to like." *Muhib* means "the one who loves" (or "has affection for") and refers to a person whose *sikke* has been "*tekbired*" (blessed with an initiation ritual which includes the *tekbir: Allāhu Akbar*) and who has entered on the Path. With Bektâshîs, too, the one who has joined Bektâshîhood, but who has not yet accepted full dervishhood, is referred to with the same term. It is clear that this word has been used since the thirteenth and fourteenth centuries, as Yunus Emre uses it in one of his poems:

> Forty people bring down a tree from a mountain with difficulty.
> How will so many disciples (*murīds*) and sympathizers (*muhibs*) pass over the *sirat?*[21]

[21] *Divan,* p. 135, couplet 1001.

Mutrib; mutribân; mutribhâne: The place for the Mevlevî musicians is known as the *mutrib* or *mutribhâne*. The orchestra of musicians and singers is called the *mutribân* or the *mutrib heyeti* (*mutrib* board). The *ney*, *kudüm*, and *halîle* are essential instruments in the Mevlevî *mutrib*. If they are available, the *rebap*, *kanun*, *oud*, and even the violin are included. On several occasions during the later period, cello was also included. The first piano brought to Türkiye was played at the Kulekapısı Mevlevîhânesi in Istanbul, but the musicians soon realized that it was impossible to perform with it (because of the tempered scale), so it was only included in the *mutrib* once. The piano is now in the Museum of the Istanbul Municipality. Because the last shaikh of the Bahariye tekkye, Baha Efendi (died 1937), had difficulties with the other Mevlevî shaikhs, there have also been times when the *mukabele* had to be performed with just *kudüms* at the Bahariye tekkye.

Naat (Na't): "To praise someone." This word is used in particular reference to poems that praise the blessed Prophet, his four companions, the Twelve Imāms, and the great ones of the religion.

Among the Mevlevîs, the terms used are *naat*, *Naat-ı Şerif*, and *Naat-ı Mevlânâ*. During the *mukabele*, one of the *mutrib* (called the *naathân*) recites the *naat* after the *ṣalāh*. The music that accompanies the recitation is by the famous composer Itrî (d. 1124 H.; 1712 A.D.).

The two most famous *naats* are recited in all *Mevlevîhânes*. One of them is known as *Senâyî* and is the seven-couplet *ghazal* of Mevlânâ that begins with the *matla* (first verse):

İy cerâğ-i âsmân u rahmet-i Hak bir zemin
Nâle-i men gûş dar u derd-i hâl-i men bibîn[22]

The other one is known as *Şems,* and is the six-couplet *ghazal* of Ulu Arif Chelebi that begins with the verse:

Yâ Habîballâh Rasûl-i Hâlık-ı yekta tüyı
Bergüzîn-i zül-celâl-i pâk-i bî hemtâ tüyî.

[22] *Divan-i Kebir*, volume 4, p. 52.

Besides these two famous examples, Mevlevîs might recite any of Mevlânâ's *ghazals* as the *naat*, because they believe that each word, each poem of Mevlânâ, interprets and explains the *āyāts* of the Qur'ān and the *ḥadīth* and praises the blessed Prophet. However, while this is true, as time has passed, several sects (due to personal inclinations, fear of progress, and propaganda) have attributed additional words and poems to Mevlânâ which do not belong to him—it is quite impossible for them to belong to him. Unfortunately, these imitations have been accepted as authentic in the *tekkes*. Shaikhs who were too preoccupied with collecting money for the *tekke* and protecting their status did not critically examine or discard them. When such poems were recited, Mevlânâ's temperament and aesthetics were not properly considered. It is with sadness that we are obliged to admit that inauthentic poems are sometimes recited as *naats*.[23]

We have examined the *naats* in two manuscripts that have transcribed compilations of rituals. Of these, the one recorded as no. 1606 certainly belongs to the nineteenth century, because although the names of the scribes were not recorded, it contains the rituals of Musahip Ahmet Ağa (d. 1209 H.; 1794 A.D.) and Hamamî İsmail Dede (d. 1247 H.; 1832 A.D.). Within it, nineteen poems are recorded as *naats*, but only three of these can be ascribed to Mevlânâ. Thirty-six *naats* are recorded in the other manuscript, which belongs to the same century. Again, twenty-four of these *naats* cannot be ascribed to Mevlânâ; only twelve.

One cannot understand how these "*naats*" entered the manuscripts, how shaikhs closed their eyes to what was in front of them without proper diligence. Actually, it would be better to say that we understand how it happened, but we do not wish to dwell on it.

Nâz: "Playful, pretended opposition" to someone with whom one is very close; "coyness"; "capriciousness". It refers to being loved by God in such a way that one is not found guilty even though it appears as if one speaks or does what is forbidden. This term, which

[23] In the original text, six pages of counterfeit *naats* follow, which are not included in this edition.

is common on all Sufi paths, is associated with a group of *erenler* ("attained ones") called the *nâz ehli* ("people of caprice").

Nazar: "Glance." Sufis, and especially the *melâmet ehli* (the people of *melâmet*, the Bayrâmi Melâmîs-Hamzevîs), who insist that love and the Divine pull (*cezbe*) are essential for the spiritual journey (*sülûk*)–and also the Mevlevîs who rely on *melâmî* essentials–attribute great importance to the glance. According to them, the godly (*hakkaanî*) glance of the people of states (*hâl ehli*) and the guide (*murshid*) annihilates the imaginary being of the spiritual traveler (*sâlik*); it takes the traveler into the Divine pull (*cezbe*) and allows him or her to reach high ranks (*mertebe, martabeh*). For this reason, during the *Devr-i Veledî* ("Veled's Cycle"–the three circumabulations of the *semâ'hâne* at the beginning of the *semâ'* ceremony–please see the chapter on *mukabele*), those who meet face-to-face look in each other's eyes and the place between the eyebrows, and bow their heads (*baş kesmek*). The spiritual traveler is always in need of the glance of the guide: he or she reaches the Truth by means of this glance.

Nazarım; nazarlarım: "My glance"; "my glances." These words are used instead of "thou" and "you," based on the concept of the glance (from *nazar man* which means "my attention," *nazarım* also has the meaning "my aim"). These are common terms among all paths of *taṣawwuf.*

Ney (nay): "Wind instrument." During the time of Mevlânâ, the *rebap* was played at his gatherings. He himself, his son, and his grandson all played the *rebap.*[24] After Mevlânâ's time, the *ney* and the *kudüm* became the prime instruments of Mevlevî music.

The *ney* is a musical instrument made from a reed; it has a mouthpiece made of tortoise shell or bone and it has seven holes. It is played with the breath; the mouthpiece is called the *başpâre* ("headpiece"). To play the *ney* is referred to as "blowing the *ney*," and the

[24] *Mevlânâ Celâleddîn*, third edition, pp. 212–17; *Mevlevîhood after Mevlânâ*, pp. 455–56.

one who plays it is called the *neyzen*. The one who conducts the *neyzens* is called the *neyzenbaşı* (the head *neyzen*).

Nezir: "Vow"; "promise"; "votive offering." This is the term for something given as a present after a goal has been reached or a wish fulfilled. However, because Mevlevîs do not take alms, the money given to the *murshid* or *dede* has the effect of a blessing, and belongs in the category of favors.

In Mevlevîhood, the numbers associated with the *nezir* are nine and eighteen. After eighteen come the other multiples of nine: 27, 36, 45, 54, 63, 72 and 81. The one who wants to donate a favor (a quantity of the money amounting to one of the numbers mentioned above) to the *dergâh*, or who wants to help his *dede*, secretly places this amount of money into his hand while he is speaking with him, or, while he is doing the *niyâz*, he leaves it under the sheepskin (*post*) without anybody seeing.

The holiness of nine and eighteen is based on the following belief: The Absolute Being has an active manifestation which is His Self-Requirement–this active manifestation is called the Complete Intellect (*Aql-ı Küll*) or the Truth of Muḥammadhood (*Hakıykat-i Muhammediyye*). This active capacity created a passive capacity, the Complete Self (the Created). The nine layers of the heavens formed from these two. The movement of the nine heavens manifested the four elements, and together they formed the three categories: mineral, plant, and animal. Added together this makes eighteen. In Arabic, the highest numbers were expressed in thousands, and one was equated with a thousand, so the expression "eighteen thousand worlds" was formed as a result of this. At the same time, according to *abjad* (Arabic numerology), the name *Ḥayy,* which is one of the Attributes of God meaning "Ever Living", has a numerical value of eighteen. That which exists, and everybody and everything within the universe of Being, is an object of manifestation receptive to this Attribute. Mevlânâ wrote the first eighteen couplets of the *Mesnevî* in his own hand. All of these reflections explain why the number eighteen is regarded as sacred.

Mevlevîs have *nezr-i Şems*, too, which is associated with the number six; the reason being because even the least particle has six directions–below, above, right, left, before, and behind. Multiplying the number six with the minerals, plants, and animate beings gives the number eighteen. The Mevlevî shaikh of Bahariye, Hüseyin Fahreddin Dede, wrote about *nezr-i Mevlânâ* in his manuscript as follows:

> *Nezr-i Mevlânâ* and *Nezr-i Mevlevî* have entered into literature through Mevlevîs, and while indicating a specific date, riddles have been arranged using the number eighteen or subtracting with it.[25]

Where a text says "together with *Nezr-i Mevlânâ*," it is understood that one should add eighteen to the date, and where the text says "subtracting *Nezr-i Mevlânâ"* one understands that eighteen should be subtracted from the date of the line.

Niyâz: "Yearning"; "entreating." This word is a common term among the paths of *taṣawwuf* and has the following useages:

1. To entreat, humbling oneself in prayer.
2. To bow one's head in front of a guide (*murshid*) or a great one.
3. To bow one's head or kiss the threshold when entering a place.
4. To send greetings with the words "I entreat…"
5. Money given or a gift to someone.

Nevniyâz: This word refers to someone who has recently entered Mevlevîhood; someone who has recently begun to do the *semâ'*.

Niyâz penceresi: "Entreating window" (pronounced niy*âz penjeresi*). In the *türbes*, this is a viewing window at the feet or the side of the sarcophagus. If the *türbe* is closed and one cannot enter, one can visit and offer prayers through the window. This is a common term among Sufis.

[25] A couplet or a literary piece is written whose letters have a numerological value of eighteen; or when the numerological values of the letters are added and eighteen is substracted, one finds a number which gives an important date, such as the date of someone's passing.

Ocak: "Furnace"; "fireplace for cooking" (pronounced *ojak*). Also, the smallest unit where a family lives. The *ocak* is sacred to all Sufis. "May your *ocak* keep on burning," is a blessing; "May your *ocak* extinguish," is a curse. The expression, "He planted a fig tree in his *ocak,*" means that someone has exterminated someone else's whole family lineage. The expression, "Smoke does not rise from his or her *ocak*," means that the people of a house are poor.

Among the Mevlevîs, *ocak* is the station (*makam*) of Âteşbâz-ı Velî. One does not begin working without entreating (*niyâz etmek*) the *ocak.* This entreating is done by kissing it if it is clean, or, if it is in such a condition that one cannot kiss it, by bowing one's head, touching it with one's hand, and kissing one's index finger. When a dervish takes a dish of food from the *ocak* he or she recites the *gülbang.* The most holy places within a Mevlevî *dergâh* or home are the threshold and the *ocak.*

Örtmek: "To cover." Mevlevîs do not use the word "close" because it has a negative connotation. Instead, one says, for example, "I covered the door," or "I turned the door into a secret (*sırlamak*)."

Paşmak: "Shoe" (pronounced *pashmak*). The origin of this word is *başmak.* It is a common term among Sufis.

Paşmak çevirmek: To turn the *paşmak* (pronounced *pashmak chevirmek*). In Mevlevîhood, the shoes of the guests that come to a house, a cell, or a *dergâh* are never pointed towards the outside, because this means, "Go and never come back." The shoes of the guests point towards the inside and are arranged in a tidy and even manner. Just as the one who enters comes in facing the house, the one who leaves does likewise: he puts on his shoes and "sees with" (*görüşmek*) the host, and while still facing inside, steps outside with his right foot, then turns around and departs.

According to the tradition of the people, to turn the *paşmak* means to turn the shoes of someone towards the door, because of a mistake that person has made.

Peymançe: "Agreement"; "acceptance" (pronounced *peymanche*). Please see **ayak mühürlemek.**

Post: "Sheepskin." The *post* indicates a spiritual station (*mânevî makam*). Dedes and the shaikh possess *posts*. The *post* in the kitchen is regarded as indicating the station of having surrendered one's will to the guide (*murshid*); this *post* is called the *saka postu* ("sheepskin of the waterman"). Life exists because of water–as is indicated in *sūrah* 21:30. Everything has come to life through water and is alive because of it. From this point of view, the lover is also in need of water; he or she is thirsty. The waterman is filled with water and contented; then he quenches the thirst of the lovers (*muhib*). This is the reason why this *post* is called the *saka postu.*

The *post* of the shaikh is dyed a dark red, because this color is associated with coming into appearance or manifestation. The color black indicates colorlessness and the Self (*Dhāt*). Although the *Dhāt* contains all the Divine Attributes, Names, actions, judgments, and works in potential, they are like butter in milk, or like the speaking, listening, walking, and acting of a person who is still and silent. For this reason, night is associated with the *Dhāt* and day is associated with the Attributes. (It is for this reason, too, that in Sufi literature the hair that covers the face is associated with the Attributes, and the face itself associated with the *Dhāt.*)

The night encompasses and covers everything, and the day reveals everything that the night covered. The night begins with the red dusk that appears with the setting of the sun; the day begins with the red dawn that appears while the sun is rising. It is due to this that dark red is regarded as the color of appearance (*zuhur*) and manifestation (*tecelli*), and is a symbol for return after reaching the *Dhāt*. It is therefore a symbol for maturity (*kemâl*) and khalifhood (*khilafet;* the human being as representative of God upon Earth).

Mevlânâ begins a *ghazal* in the *Divân-ı Kebîr* with a couplet that demonstrates this symbolism:

Nurist miyan-i shar-i ahmer
Ez dide vu vehm u nur berter

There is a light within the passionate poem
better than eyes and illusion and light.

On the paths of *taṣawwuf* that traverse the spiritual journey (*sülûk etmek*) with the Attributes (*Aṣmā*), the *nafs* or soul of the human being has seven modes or attitudes (*tavir*): *ammārah* ("commanding" *nafs*); *lawwāmah* ("repentant" *nafs*); *mulhamah* ("inspired" *nafs*); *muṭma'innah* ("satisfied," "contented" *nafs*); *rādiyyah* (the *nafs* that accepts and is "pleased" with all manifestations of God); *mardiyyah* (the *nafs* accepted by and "pleasing" to God); *kāmilah/sāfiyyah/zakiyyah* ("purified" or "completed" *nafs*).

Ammarāh is taken from *sūrah* 12:53; *lawwāmah* from 75:2; *mulhamah* from 91:8; *muṭma'innah, rādiyyah,* and *mardiyyah* from 89:27–28; and *zakiyyah* from 87:14. The *dhikr* of the spiritual traveler (*sâlik*) in *ammārah* is *lā ilāha illā Allāh;* in *lawwāmah* it is *Allāh;* in *mulhamah* it is *Hū;* in *muṭma'innah* it is *Ḥaqq;* in *rādiyyah* it is *Ḥayy;* in *mardiyyah* it is *Qayyūm;* and in *zakiyyah* (or *kāmilah*) it is *Qahhār.*

In each of these seven modes, the spiritual traveler will see Divine Lights (*Nūr*) of manifestation during meditation and in dreams. These lights are respectively: blue, yellow, scarlet, black, green, white, and colorless.[26]

Here too, scarlet is the color of reaching the Self, because in *mulhamah* the traveling (*sayr*) of the traveler is *billah* (together with God).

Post-nişîn: "The shaikh who sits on the *post*" (pronounced *post-nishîn*). It is also a general Sufi term referring to the shaikh of a *dergâh* with a station (*makam*).

Resim hırkası: "Ceremonial *khirka.*" *Resmî hırka* refers to the *khirka* worn during ceremonies (please see **hırka**).

Rızâ: "Acceptance"; "surrender." This word means to accept and be pleased with all that God bestows and to endure difficulties and

[26] Abu Ridvan M. Sadik Vijdani: *Silsilename of Halvetiyye* from Tumar-i Turuk-i Aliyye.

troubles for the sake of the Path. There is a proverb that says, "This Path is a bazaar of *rızâ* ('acceptances')."

According to *abjad* calculation, the numerical value of the word *rızâ* is 1,001. Mevlevîs have 1,001 days of *çile,* so *rızâ* also has that association in Mevlevî literature.

Safânazar: "Clear glance"; "clean, purified, serene look." These words describe the *murshid's* glance at the *sâlik*, and how the *sâlik* should strive to look at everything and everyone with an eye that knows unity. The *sâlik* should not look at anything with a darkened glance (*kem nazar*) or see things in a negative light as "bad" or "worthless"; he should see everything as appropriate according to its receptivity (*mazhar*) and aptitude (*isti'dad*). In this way, the *sâlik* will continually be in the presence of God—he will be contemplating the manifestations of God—and the eventual result will be the realization of unity (*vahdet*).

Sâlik: "Wayfarer." This is a common Sufi term referring to someone who has begun the spiritual journey.

Seccâdenişîn: Another term for the *postnişîn* (pronounced *sejjâdenishîn*). This is a more pious and humble term meaning "one who sits in prostration." It is a general term.

Secde-i şukur; secde-i niyâz: "Prostration of thankfulness"; "entreating prostration" (pronounced and sometimes written *sajdah-i shukur* and *sajdah-i niyâz*).

When a Mevlevî enters a gathering of brothers (*ikhvan meclisi*), after he "sees with" (*görüşmek*) the elder, and sits down in a suitable place (the place appropriate to him according to his length of time on the Path), the elder of the gathering says to him, "*Aşk olsun!*" Together they prostrate themselves on the floor and entreat (*niyâz etmek*) and kiss the floor. This is a *secde-i niyâz* ("entreating prostration")—it is not a prostration of worship.

In a mosque (*masjid*), a Mevlevî prostrates on the floor and kisses the floor as he stands up to do *ṣalāh*; this is called a *secde-i şukur* ("prostration of thankfulness"), and it is done in thanks for the blessing of the Truth (*Ḥaqq*).

*E*very action of *niyâz* contains either entreating (*niyâz*) or thankfulness (*şukur*).

Semâ' (samā): The basic movements of the *semâ'* involve turning counter-clockwise accompanied by music. If wearing a *khirka*, one holds the neckline with the right hand and opens it a little at chest level, while with the left hand one holds the right side of the *khirka* at the level of the waist, keeping it closed. One may also open one's arms if one is wearing a *tennûre*.

To learn and to teach *semâ'* is called *semâ' meşki* (the practice of *semâ'*), and the one who performs the *semâ'* is called a *semâ'zen*.

Ser-pâ etmek: "To dismiss from the order." If a dervish makes a serious mistake, his elders take away his *sikke,* turn his *paşmaks* so that they face outside, and order him to leave the *dergâh* and the Path and wander for a time.

Seyahat (siyâhat); ah vermek: "Travel"; "to command to travel." In Mevlevîhood there is a belief that after initiation (*intisap*) a journey will inevitably appear before the *sâlik*–a journey to visit Konya and the *Huzûr-ı Pîr* ("Presence of the Pir").

To command a period of travel (*ah vermek*) can be a form of *ser-pâ*, which entails sending a Mevlevî away from the *dergâh* and the Path due to a mistake he or she has made. If a person is ordered to travel but his *sikke* is not taken away from him, this means that he has not been made *ser-pâ* but has only been sent away from his *dergâh.* His *paşmaks* are turned and his *khirka* is placed on his shoulder, he prostrates on the floor (*niyâz etmek*), stands up, turns his shoes back to face the inside, puts them on, kisses the threshold, and exits without turning his back. He leaves the *dergâh* for another *dergâh.*

If he has been made *serpâ*, in the same way he turns his shoes (which were turned to the outside) back towards the inside, puts them on, kisses the threshold, and exits without turning his back. After a period of time, the dervish has a mediator apply to the *aşçıbaşı* (the head cook of the *dergâh*) on his behalf, and if it is found to be appropriate, he pays a penalty for his mistake and makes an *Ayn-ı Cem* (please refer to this term in the glossary and also see the chapter about *semâ'*). The dervish has a sheep sacrificed, and a ceremony is held to *tekbîr* his *sikke* and *khirka* again. In this way, he is freed from pathlessness, and no further objections are raised. Or, if the dervish believes he is in the right, he goes to Konya and applies to the *tarîkatçı* ("order man," the officer of the order) and a decision about him is reached there.

Ser-tabbâh; ahçıbaşı: "Chief cook" (pronounced *ahchibashi*). The head officer of the *dergâh* is the *aşçıbaşı*. Their service is not in cooking food, as one might conclude from the name; the title is a metaphor. The *aşçıbaşı* is the person who spiritually cooks and matures the souls of the dervishes. The spiritual order of the *dergâh* belongs to him; it is his responsibility. The shaikh is a representative, and the educator (*murebbî*) is the *aşçı dede* ("cook dede").

Sır olmak: "To turn into a secret." These words are used when something gets lost, or runs out, or has disappeared. If this happens to something, it is said that "it became secret" or "it turned into a secret" or "it is in the secret."

Sırlamak: "To turn something into a secret." Because the words "put out the candle," "turn off the light or electricity," or "extinguish the fire" have negative connotations, Mevlevîs use instead the words "turn it into a secret" or "it became a secret."

At the same time, "to hide something" is also expressed as "to turn something into a secret," and to bury someone is "to turn someone into a secret." For example, one could say, "Today we turned so-and-so into a secret in such-and-such a place."

Sikke: "Stamp"; "brand"; "sign." This is the name for the Mevlevî *külah* (conical hat). It is called this because the Mevlevî *külâh* is a sign that someone is on the Path of Mevlânâ.

A *sikke* is a two-layered conical hat made of beaten felt. It is a little thinner at the top than at the base and its height is one span and three inches. It is the color of camel's wool, usually dark brown, but sometimes lighter. In earlier times, the top naturally ended in a slight point. In later times, it became the custom to mold or reblock it, and even to iron and shine it.

We know that Ulu Arif Chelebi was the first one to wear a white *sikke*.[27] We have heard some people say that the white *sikke is* a sign for *khalifhood*, but we do not have documented evidence of this. However, it is possible that in some places this tradition was followed.

If the *sikke* is flattened at both sides towards the top so that its top becomes pointed, it is called a *külâh-i seyfî* ("*külâh* like a sword"). We learn from Sefine that Dîvâne Mehmet Chelebi and his dervishes used to wear *seyfî külâh*, and we also see the *seyfî külâh* on the gravestones that belong to him.[28]

Sefine also says that Dîvâne Mehmet Chelebi wore a twelve-segmented *tac* (crown), and Jalaluddin Ergun Chelebi a seven-segmented *tac*, which Sefine calls the *Şemsî Tac*.[29]

In recent times, one never encounters the *seyfî külâh* nor the *tac* with either seven or twelve segments.

Somat: "Table." The correct form of the word is *sımât*. This is the word for a Mevlevî table, and the place in the kitchen where meals are served is called the *Sımâthâne* ("table home").

Soyunmak: "To undress." This refers to the decision to become a dervish: taking off one's old garments and putting on the *tennûre* and *arâkîyye* for the period of service, and then the *sikke* after one completes the *semâ'* training.

During the time of Galip Dede (d. 1213 H.; 1799 A.D.), the shaikh of Kulekapısı, someone who had decided to become a dervish applied to him saying, "My Master! If you permit me, I will undress." The applicant's clothes were meager and shabby, so after Galip Dede learned that the applicant had nobody to look after him and was all

---

27 *Manâkıb-al Ârifîn* II, p.862

28 See the photographs at the end of *Mevlevîhood after Mevlânâ*, pp. 14–16.

29 Ibid, pp.109, 123.

alone, he called the *aşçı dede* and said, "*Erenler!* Take this soul away and let him get dressed up!"

Sülûk: "Journey." This is a common term on all the paths of *taṣawwuf*; it refers to the spiritual journey.

Şeb-i Arûs: "Wedding night" (pronounced *Sheb-i Arus*). *Şeb-i urs* can refer to the feast at a literal wedding. In the evening of the fifth day of Jumadhi al-akhirah (672 H.; 17th December 1273 A.D.), the day of Mevlânâ's birth into infinity (passing away), a ceremony would be held in all the Mevlevî *dergâhs*. That night was called *Şeb-i Arûs*, which means "nuptial night." (Please see the chapter "Mevlevî Mukabele".)

Şebkülâh: "Night hat" (pronounced *shebkülâh*). The hat which is one layer, made without a mold, and shorter than a *sikke* is referred to as the *şebkülâh*.

Şeyh (shaikh): "Old chief." In Arabic, it means "old, great one" and "leader." In Sufism, it describes the person who educates *muhips* and dervishes and can claim this authority with a written *icâzetnâme* from another shaikh. Because the status of a shaikh is not superior to that of a *khalif,* someone who is assigned somewhere as a shaikh, receives a *khalifhood* from a *khalif*, too; in this way, he completes titles (*meratip*).

In Mevlevîhood, one addresses the shaikh as *Efendi* ("Master") and *Efendi Hazretleri* ("Blessed Master"). In the *dergâh,* the shaikh is the representative and the final authority on Mevlevîhood. But, in the *dergâh*, the spiritual educator is the *aşçıbaşı.*

Taylasan: The end of the *destâr*. According to the way in which the *sikke* is worn, the end of the *destâr* comes down the rear, left hand side. When it remains hanging at the back, it comes down to the waist; when it is taken over the shoulder to the front, it comes down to the chest at heart-level. In poetry this has been called *giysû-yı Külâh-ı Mevlevî, zeyl-i Külâh Mevlevî*, etc. As it is left wide and can be taken under the chin and over the right shoulder to the back when necessary, in Arabic the *taylasan* is also called the *tahtel-hanek* which means "under the chin." According to legal tradition (*sher'an*), it is a *sunnah* (custom of the Prophet Muḥammad) to leave it free during *ṣalāh.*

Tennûre: A garment worn during service at the *tandır* (a traditional oven made by digging a hole in the earth) and *ocak* ("stove" or "furnace") without sleeves or collar. The neckline descends to the mid-chest area; its upper part is tight-fitting down to the waist, and its lower part is wide.

There are two kinds of *tennûre*: the service *tennûre a*nd the *semâ' tennûre.*

The *matbâh* souls wear the service *tennûre.* Its skirt is wide enough to walk comfortably in, but it is tight compared to the *semâ' tennûre.* Its color is black or dark brown (i.e. a color that will not show dirt). The kitchen soul wears this while perfoming service and does not wear the *destegül* over it. He wears it only when he is going outside, and he places tongs within a sheath under his belt to show that he is going out in service.

The skirt of the *semâ' tennûre* is very wide. A cloth three fingers in width is sewn into its bottom edge. When the *tennûre* is opened, this stops the *tennûre* from gathering, even if the *semâ'zen* slows down. It is said that sometimes in the past they sewed lead pieces into the skirt.

When the *tennûre* opens, the *semâ'zen* seems to follow in its wake. If the *tennûre* hits someone, it could even knock that person down. When the turning is fast, the *tennûre* opens into a shape like the lid of a copper food dish (*sahan*); when the turning is slow, it opens in a triangular form. If the skirt of the *tennûre* is wavy, or if one side is higher or lower, it is not considered a good thing, because from one side of the *tennûre* the undergarments of the *semâ'zen* might be seen up to the waist. For this reason, after they tie the *elif-i nemed* of the *semâ'zen's tennûre*, *dedes* adjust the folds that are formed in the *tennûre*, making sure the length is the same on all sides.

Terceman: "Interpreter" (pronounced *terjeman*). This name is given to the prayers composed to be recited while certain activities are performed. The term is common among the Bektâshîs and Mevlevîs.

Tıyg-bend: "Sword belt." It is a long rope made of wool. During the *Devr-i Veledî*, to stop the skirt of his *tennûre* from touching the floor, the *semâ'zen* ties this string to the lower part of his waist and pulls the tennûre up with it. During the third *devir* (circuit) of the *Devr-i Veledî,* he unties the *tıyg-bend* (without letting anybody see) and lightly leaves it where he stops.

Uyandırmak; uyarmak; uyanmak: "To awaken"; "to warn"; "to wake up." Because the expression "to burn" has a negative connatation, it is avoided. The expression "to awaken" the furnace, lamp, candle, light or electricity is used instead.

"To awaken" and "to warn" are also used to mean "to guide" a traveler (*sâlik*) in any subject relating to *taṣawwuf.* "To awaken" means to be aware, to understand and to know.

Vahdet: "Aloneness"; "to be alone." It is used to refer to sleeping. "He is in *vahdet*" or "He has arrived at *vahdet*" means "He is asleep" or "He has gone to sleep." It is a general term.

Yolsuz: yolsuzluk: "Pathless"; "being without a path." It is means "guilty" or "having committed a crime." To be pathless means to have fallen away from the *ṭarīqah.*

Zâbitân: "Officers." The soul of the Mevlevî *dergâh* is the kitchen (*matbâh*). The primary educators (*murebbis*) of the *dergâh's* kitchen are: the head cook *dede* (*aşçı dede; ser-tabbâh*), the cauldron *dede* (*kazancı dede*), the inner court dervish in charge of housework (*içeri meydancısı*), and the dishwasher *dede* (*bulaşıkçı dede*). The head cook's task is to manage the expenses of the *dergâh*; he is also responsible for courtesy (*edep/ādāb*) and training (*terbiye*) of the souls. The cauldron *dede* is regarded as the assistant to the head cook *dede*. The khalif *dede* trains the new initiates (*nev-niyâz*) in the kitchen; he teaches them about manners and behaviour. The inner court *dede* (*meydancı dede*) is under the order of the shaikh and communicates his commands.

In Konya, there used to be two small centres called the Shams Zaviye and the Âteşbâz Zaviye. The shaikh of the Shams Zaviye was called the Shams *dede* (Shams *dedesi*). The shaikhs at these two locations used to visit the Mevlânâ Dergâh on Fridays, sit at their appropriate places during the *semâ'* ceremony (*mukabele*) and participate in it. When a shaikh was appointed somewhere, usually the *ataşbaz dede* ("one who plays with fire") would take his certificate of appointment (*icâzetnâme*) to him.

Because the *dergâh* was also a home for music and a *madrasah for* literature, the *neyzenbaşı*, the *kudümzenbaşı* and the *mesnevîhân* had honored places among the high officers (*erkân*) of the *dergâh*. They would teach and train the *âyinhâns* about the ritual performed during the *mukabele*. They would also train *neyzens* and teach them about the rhythms (*usûl*). The *mesnevîhân* would teach the *Mesnevî* to those that had a talent for it. He would teach them about language and literature, give lessons in Sufism (*taṣawwuf*) and award diplomas (*icâzets*) to those who had matured to a point where they were qualified to give explanations and commentaries on the *Mesnevî*.

The *dedes* listed above, who held great responsibility and took care of the spiritual and material needs of the *dergâh*, were called "*dergâh* officers" (*dergâh zabitânı*).

There were eighteen kinds of service in the *dergâh*. Those who served were as follows:

1. *Kazancı dede* ("cauldron" *dede*): He was in charge of the discipline, manners, and training of the souls. Like the *aşçıbaşı* ("head cook") he also had a separate *post* and held a revered position.
2. *Halife dede* ("khalif" *dede*): he taught about the Path and trained those who were new to the kitchen in manners.
3. *Dışarı meydancısı* ("outer court" dervish): The dervish who was in charge of matters outside of the *dergâh*. In Konya, he would convey the orders of the *tarikatahçı* ("order man"), and in other locations the orders of the *aşçıbaşı,* to *dedes* in the cells.
4. *Çamaşırcı dede* ("laundry" *dede*): He would wash the laundry of the dedes and the souls, or arrange and oversee it.
5. *Âb-rîzci dede* ("ewer/pitcher" *dede*): He would look after the cleanliness of the toilets, faucets, and *şadırvan* ("reservoir of water" with faucets at the sides for ablution).

6. *Şerbetçi* ("sherbet-maker"): He would prepare the sherbet for the one who delivered it to the dervish cells and, when the *dedes* came to visit the *matbâh* ("kitchen"), he would make sherbet and serve it to them.
7. *Bulaşıkçı* ("dishwasher"): He would look after the dishes and their cleanliness; he would either wash them himself or have them washed.
8. *Dolapçı* ("cupboard keeper"): He would also look after the dishes and pots and would have the pots tinned if required.
9. *Pazarcı* ("bazaar attendant"): In the morning, he would go to the bazaar with a basket, buy what was necessary and bring the provisions back to the *tekke.*
10. *Somatçı* ("table attendant"): He would prepare the table and cover it. He would also sweep the floor or have it swept.
11. *İç meydancısı* ("inner court housekeeper"): The dervish who looked after internal matters and was in charge of housework within the *dergâh.* He would prepare coffee for the souls in the *matbâh*, and when the *dedes* visited the kitchen on Fridays, he would make coffee and serve it to them.
12. *İçeri kandilcisi* ("inner court candle-lighter"): He would clean, prepare, "awaken," "put to rest" or "turn into a secret" the oil lamps or candlesticks.
13. *Tahmisçi* ("coffee roaster and grinder"): He would break the coffee granules into powder by pounding or hammering (*dövmek*). He would grind coffee for the kitchen and the *dedes.*
14. *Yatakçı* ("bed-maker"): He would spread the beds of the souls, roll them up, and take them away.
15. *Dışarı kandilcisi* ("outer court candle-lighter"): He would take care of the oil lamps, candlesticks, and candles outside the *tekke.*
16. *Süpürgeci* ("sweeper"): He would sweep the garden and the surrounding area, or he would have it swept. He would attend to general cleanliness.
17. *Çerağcı* ("light attendant"): He would inspect the oil lamps and the candlesticks of the kitchen (*matbâh*) and he was regarded as the assistant of the *türbedar* ("the one who takes care of the *türbe*").

18. *Ayakçı* ("footman"): He would do foot service; he would bring or take away things as necessary. When someone had put aside his clothing and accepted dervishhood (*ikrar vermek*), he would begin with this service.

If there were many souls living in the *dergâh*, one or two assistants were assigned to those holding these roles. An assistant was called a *refiyk* ("friend"). If the number of the souls were few, one person might perform two or three duties.

Zahme: This is the name given to the thin drum sticks with rounded ends used to beat the *kudüm*.

Zaviye: Please see **dergâh.**

Züvvâr: "Visitors"; "guests"; "pilgrims." Those who came to observe the Mevlevî *mukabele*, to listen to Mevlevî music, to receive spiritual grace (*feyz*), or to be informed about it, were referred to as züvvâr, meaning "visitors."

Women would go to the latticed area. Men would go to the area surrounding the *semâ'hâne*, separated from it by a balustrade. Nobody was sent away as long as he or she was cleanly dressed and followed etiquette (*ādāb*), because as Shaikh Galîp says:

> Those who come to the *khaniqah* of the saints (*awliyā*)
> are all invited to joy, Galip.
> Beware! Don't focus on their outside (*ẓāhir*), you will err–
> they wouldn't come, if they didn't have permission.

II

Semâ' & Mukabele

Semâ' in Humanity and Islam

The words *semâ'* and *sima'* literally mean "to hear," or "to hear beautiful praise and remembrance." For Sufis, the word refers to the experience of listening while moving to music, entering into ecstasy, and losing oneself while dancing and turning. Of course, we know that dancing and moving rhythmically to music (whether choreographed or spontaneous), as well as singing in harmony with a melody, losing oneself and loudly crying out, are all experiences as old as humanity. Such experiences do not belong exclusively to one culture; they are part of being human. Music and dance were of a religious nature in primitive societies, but as societies evolved, two separate aspects of music developed. Sacred music developed its own aesthetics and techniques, while popular music, having no relation to religion, stimulates sensuality.

Ever since the early eras of Islam, scholars of religion have debated whether music and poetry (which is the essence of music) are *ḥalāl* ("religiously acceptable") or *ḥarām* ("forbidden"). The Holy Qur'ān says that pagans called the Blessed Muḥammad a poet, but insists that he was not taught poetry and that poetry is not appropriate for him. Rather, the words brought down to him are meant to be read as a body of wisdom, because the Qur'ān contains guidance on all matters.[1] Furthermore, the Qur'ān criticizes poets with the following *āyāts*:

[1] See the following *sūrahs* of the Qur'ān: 31:5; 37:36; 19:4; 36:69.

And as for the poets[2]–[they, too, are prone to deceive themselves: and so, only] those who are lost in grievous error would follow them. Art thou not aware that they roam confusedly through all the valleys [of words and thoughts[3]], and that they [so often] say what they do not do [or feel]?

[Most of them are of this kind–] save those who have attained to faith, and do righteous deeds, and remember God unceasingly, and defend themselves [only] after having been wronged, and [trust in God's promise that] those who are bent on wrongdoing will in time come to know how evil a turn their destinies are bound to take!

However, commentators on the Qurʾān mention faithful poets who were exempted from the judgements in the last two of these *āyāts,* such as Abdullah son of Revâha, Kâ'b son of Malik, and Hassan son of Sabit. These poets rejected the satires of the pagan poets[4] and became famous among the *sahaba* (companions of the Prophet). But it would be no exaggeration to say that almost all Arabs were poets. During the tribal wars among the Arabs, they read *recez,* women encouraged the warriors with heroic poems while playing the tambourine and cymbals. The satirical poems about the enemy tribes had a certain character; maintaining this character was an established tradition, and there was little way of avoiding it.

The Prophet also praises poetry in the *ḥadīth* ("traditions"): "Truly, some poems contain wisdom."[5] He also expressed pride in

---

[2] "An allusion to the fact that some of the pagan Arabs regarded the Qurʾān as a product of Muḥammad's supposedly poetic mind. See also Sūrah Yā Sīn 36:69." (Muhammad Asad, *The Message of the Qurʾān,* The Book Foundation, 2003.)

[3] "The idiomatic phrase *hāma fī widyān* (literally, "he wandered [or "roamed"] through valleys") is used, as most of the commentators point out, to describe a confused, aimless, and often self-contradictory playing with words and thoughts. In this context, it contrasts the vagueness often inherent in poetry with the precision of the Qurʾān, which is free from all inner contradictions. See also Sūrah an-Nisāʿ 4:82." (Ibid.)

[4] *Kur'ân Kerîm ve Meali* (*The Holy Qurʾan and Its Meaning*), Abdülbâki Gölpınarlı, II edition, Istanbul, Remzi Publishing 1958, commentary, LXXXIX.

[5] Câmî'al Sagıyr, Egypt, Hayriyya Print, 1321, I, p. 82.

his own eloquence in the *ḥadīth*, "I am the one of you who speaks the most beautifully; I am of the Quraysh; my language is the language of the Banî Sa'd Ibn-i Bakr."[6] The Blessed Prophet, who viewed some poems as "wisdom," said in another *ḥadīth* that "wisdom is the lost property of the believer and he takes it wherever he finds it,"[7] and it is impossible not to make a connection here. Among Qur'ānic commentators, there have been those who have interpreted *He multiplies in creation what he wills* (35:1) as referring to "the beautiful habits and beautiful voice."[8] It has also been reported that the Blessed Prophet said, "Allāh has sent each messenger with a beautiful voice,"[9] and that he instructed his followers to "embellish the Qur'ān with your voices."[10] This is also implied in the following *ḥadīth:* "Everything has an embellishment and the embellishment of the Qur'ān is the beautiful voice; whoever does not recite the Qur'ān with a beautiful voice, he is not one of us."[11]

The Holy Qur'ān praises the voice of the Prophet David and says that even the mountains and birds obeyed his voice.[12] Blessed Muḥammad said that a psalm of the children of David was given to Abū Mūsā because of his beautiful voice.[13] When Blessed Muḥammad emmigrated from Makkah to Madīnah, he did not stop the women of Madīnah when they welcomed him by playing tambourines and reciting poems.[14] The day he conquered Makkah, as he rode on his camel he recited *Sūrah al-Fatḥ* with a melody.[15] The Qur'ān criticizes ugly voices in *Sūrah Luqmān* 31:19.[16] One *ḥadīth* reports that the Blessed Prophet recited the words, "I am a prophet,

---

[6] Ibid, p. 90.

[7] Kunûz-al Hakaayık, Câmiî-al Sagıyr's postscript, the same printing, II, p. 51.

[8] Tabrasi: Mecma'-al Bayan, Tehran; 1267–68, 153, b.

[9] Câmî', II, p. 120.

[10] Ibid.

[11] Müslim, Ist. Amire Print. 1334, vol. 1, p.4.

[12] See the following sūrahs of the Qur'ān : 21:79, 34:10.

[13] Kunûz-al Hakaayık, II, 147; Müslim, II, 192–93.

[14] *Al Sîrat-al Halabiyya,* Egypt, Print. Muhammed Efendi Mustafâ, II, p. 60.

[15] Müslim, II, p. 193.

[16] *Hence, be modest in thy bearing, and lower thy voice: for, behold, the ugliest of all voices is the [loud] voice of asses.*

I am not a liar; I am the son of 'Abd al-Muṭṭalib," in two rhyming lines,[17] and during the Hayber War, when Âmir ibn-al Akva'a recited his poem comprising seven lines beginning with the couplet "My Allāh! If Thou had not shown us the right path, we would not accept You, nor would we do the *ṣalāh*," the Prophet answered him with a poem of three lines.[18]

During the Handak War, while they were digging ditches, the *sahaba* used poetry and song to make the labor easier, and they began to recite the poem, "We are those people who have taken an oath of allegiance to Muḥammad, to fight together, as long as we are alive." When they recited this couplet, the Blessed Prophet replied with the rhyming lines, "My Allāh! Life is life only in the next world; Place your Grace and Favor upon the *Anṣār* [inhabitants of Madīnah who invited Muḥammad and his friends there] and the *muhājir* [immigrants]."[19]

There is also a famous *ḥadīth* that relates how the Prophet praised a couplet from Lebîd (d. 4 H.; 661 A.D.), saying "The wisest words of the Arabs are these that Lebîd spoke: 'Know that whatever exists besides Allāh is nothingness.'"[20]

The Prophet listened to the *qaṣīda* ("laudatory poem") of Kâ'b ibni Zuhayr, and he himself corrected a line of it. The Blessed Prophet threw his own *khirka* ("cloak") to the poet, but said also that dirt should be thrown into the faces of those who praise a poet; in this way he taught that praising a poet is inappropriate, but at the same time showed that *caize* ("reward" given to a poet for a laudatory poem) was legitimate.[21] Because of this event, the *qaṣīda* of Kâ'b became known as *Qasida-i Burda* and the *qaṣīda* of Bûsırî (d. 694 H.; 1294 A.D.), known as *Qasida-i Bur'da,* is regarded as holy and as possessing healing powers.

For centuries, Sufis have paid attention to the effects of poetry and music on the human soul—how they cause spiritual ecstasy—and have discussed whether *semâ'* is *ḥalāl* or *ḥarām.* Sufi scholars have

[17] Câmî', I, s. 89.
[18] Müslim, VII, pp. 186–88.
[19] Müslim, V, p. 188.
[20] Câmî', I, p. 36; and in a slightly different manner, Müslim, VII, p. 49.
[21] Câmî', I, p. 9.

said that Anas, Ja'far ibn Abdullah, and Omar ibn Abdullah, who were companions of the Prophet, and many people who followed Omar Abdullah, all accepted *semâ'* as *ḥalāl.* Meanwhile, although the scholars of *ḥadīth* have said that this is uncertain, they have said that a female servant recited poems in the presence of the Blessed Prophet in the house of ʿĀʾishah and that the Blessed Prophet did not stop her. Also, they confirm that two female servants were singing in the Blessed Prophet's presence and ʿUmar (or, according to other sources, Abū Bakr) wanted to stop them, but the Blessed Prophet said, "Leave them alone! Every society has its own celebrations." Scholars have insisted on the authenticity of these accounts and furthermore have said that Imām Ash-Shāfiʿī (d. 204 H.; 819 A.D.) regarded *semâ'* as acceptable as long as it was not against the honor of masculinity, and he only regarded it as *ḥarām* if it was made with the wrong intentions or encouraged immorality.

Since the early periods of Islam, Sufis have accepted *semâ'*, *wajd* (ecstasy), moving the body while listening to poetry and music, and turning. Junayd (d. 297 H.; 909 A.D.) said that (the right) time, space, and brotherhood (*ihvan*) are essential for *semâ'*. He also said that *raḥmah* (grace) descends upon *fakirs* at three times: during *semâ'*, because they hear the eminating sound of the Truth and rise in ecstasy; during a scholarly discussion, because they discuss only knowledge of the states of reality; and while they are eating, because they eat only when it is necessary. Husrî (d. 371 H.; 981 A.D.) described *semâ'* with these words: "Thirst goes on and drinking water, too; as much as one drinks water, one's thirst increases." Bundâr ibn-al Husayn (d. 353 H.; 981 A.D.) said that *semâ'* is *mubāḥ* (permissable; neither commanded nor forbidden by the religious law) if it is done without bad intentions.

Shaikh Abû-Nasr, one of the dignitaries of the fourth century *hijrah,* concluded that *semâ'* is *ḥalāl* according to the following *āyāts: There are clear evidences on the earth and in your own essence, do you still not see?* (51: 20–21) and *We shall show them Our portents on the horizons and within themselves until it will be manifest unto them that it is the truth. Doeth not thy Lord suffice, He is Witness over all things* (41:53). He also said, "Allāh informs us about 'a thing and its opposite' through our five senses. The eye sees the beautiful and the ugly; the nose discriminates between pleasant and unpleasant smells; the tongue tastes the sweet and the bitter; the hand understands the soft and the hard; and the ear distinguishes the difference between the beautiful and the ugly voice, and this is possible only by hearing the beautiful voice."

Abū Sa'id ar-Rāzī (d. 298 H.; 910 A.D.) said,

> There are three kinds of *semâ'*: the *semâ'* of the beginners (*mubtedî*), of the disciples (*murīds*), and of the truly learned (*arifeen*). The beginners want to experience elevated states through *semâ',* but one worries about them being caught in attention-seeking and vanity. The true disciples fall into ecstasy (*wajd*) during *semâ'*, and the people of wisdom (*arifeen*) pass beyond themselves during *semâ'.*

It is reported that Abü Bakr-al Kettânî (d. 322 H.; 932–933 A.D.) said,

> The *semâ'* of the ordinary people (*âvâm*) is to follow and obey their lower nature. The *semâ'* of the disciples is an effort to reach the truth. The *semâ'* of the attained ones (*erenler*) is to see the abundance and grace of God. The *semâ'* of the people of wisdom (*arifeen*) is by seeing, and the *semâ'* of the people of the truth is by finding it through clear vision. Each group has a pleasure and a station.

Dhu'l Nūn (d. 245 H.; 956 A.D.) saw *semâ'* as a favor from God that takes hearts to the Truth; however, he also said that if it is listened to while under the influence of the *nafs* it turns one into a blasphemer (*zındık*). Abū Bakr Shiblī (d. 334 H.; 946 A.D.) taught that *semâ'* is outwardly a test and inwardly a lesson, and that it is *ḥalāl* for one who listens to it for the sake of God.

One day, some musicians were playing at a gathering and Shaikh Junayd was in a reserved mood. People asked him, "O Shaikh! What has happened to you—hasn't it been granted to you to receive anything from this *semâ'*?" In response, Junayd recited this *āyāt*: *And thou wilt see the mountains, which thou deemest so firm, pass away as clouds pass away: a work of God, who has ordered all things to perfection! Verily, He is fully aware of all that you do* (27:88).

Hâris-i Muhâsibî (d. 243 H.; 857 A.D.) used to listen to the *kavvâls* (those who recited *neşîdes* with a melody) and he would stand up and go into rapture, sobbing to such an extent that others felt pity for him. Abû Hamzat al Horasânî (d. 290 H.; 902 A.D.) was criticized by some of his brothers because he revealed his ecstasy to others. Shiblī and Abû Muhammed al Murtaish (d. 338 H.; 949 A.D.) were known to recite poetry. When Sahl ibn ʿAbdullāh at-Tustarī (d. 284 H.; 897 A.D.) heard a beautiful voice, he would go into ecstasy, stop eating and drinking, and even if it was the middle of winter would begin sweating. Once, when Ma'rûf-i Karhî (d. 20 H.; 815 A.D.) fell into ecstasy, he embraced the pillar of a building and squeezed it.

Abû-l Husayn Nuri (d. 295 H.; 907 A.D.) did *semâ'* while chanting the name of Allāh. Abdullah ibn Manâzil (d. 329 H.; 940 A.D.), Abû-l Hasan-ı Husrî, and Abū Saʿīd-i Abūʾl-Khayr (d. 440 H.; 1049 A.D.) all used to take part in *semâ'*. The *kavvâl* Shaikh ʿAlī used to join the gatherings of Abû-l Kaasım-ı Nasrâbâdî (d. 369 H.; 979 A.D.). ʿUthmān al-Maghrībī (d. 373 H.; 983 A.D.) asked for a *semâ'* to be held near him even while he was dying. Abu'l Hasan-i Harkaanî was in favor of *semâ'*, and when he was asked, "What would you say about moving during *semâ'* and falling into ecstasy?" he replied, "Dance is to the benefit of the person who sees into the depths of the earth, and who watches the empyrean as he opens his arms to the sky."

Clearly, Sufis have been fond of *semâ'* since the early days of Islam. Very few among them have not accepted *semâ'* and the open expression of ecstasy. In fact, almost all of them have agreed that *semâ'* is *ḥalāl* for "the people of states" (*hâl ehli*), those who truly experience the extraordinary on the Path. According to some, there have even been Sufis who died during *semâ'* or relinquished their souls while listening to the Qurʾān.

Sufis have developed a refined conduct for *semâ'* called the *ādāb* of *semâ'*. If a *semâ'zen* gets caught by ecstasy and his *khirka* falls down while he turns, or if he throws his *khirka* away unconsciously or tears off parts of his clothing, his *khirka* and clothing then belong to the *kavvâls* ("singers"); even if the *semâ'zen* wishes to pay for them they cannot be returned. If there are many *kavvâls,* then the *khirka* and clothing are divided into pieces and shared among them. If there are poor people at the gathering, like the *kavvâls,* they also receive a share. *Semâ'* should not be done merely as a performance or an empty show. It is never appropriate to interfere with the *kavvâl* and dictate to him what to sing. [22]

Mevlânâ's contemporaries, as well as Sufis who lived before his time, accepted *semâ'* as *ḥalāl* for those who were qualified, and they themselves participated in it. Muḥammad al-Ghazālī (d. 505 H.; 1111 A.D.) devoted a chapter of *Iḥyā' 'Ulūm ad-Dīn* to *semâ'.* His brother Aḥmad Ghazālī (d. 517 H.; 1123 A.D.), for whom the Sufis have even more respect and who was a member of Mevlânâ's lineage, was also very fond of *semâ'.*[23] Ayn-al Kuzât-ı Hemedânî (d. 533 H.; 113–1138 A.D.) used to dance together with Aḥmad Ghazālī.[24] Two great Sufi poets for whom Mevlânâ had great respect, Sanā'ī (d. 521 H.; 1127 A.D.) and 'Aṭṭār (d. 624 H.; 1226–1227 A.D.), and his *khalif* Majdeddîn-i Bağdadî (d. 616 H.; 1219 A.D.), used to do *semâ'.*[25] At the gatherings of Sa'deddîn-i Hamavî (d. 650 H.; 1253 A.D.), a powerful Sufi in his time,

---

[22] For further reference see: Abû-Nasr Abdullâh ibn-i Alîyy-al Sarrâc-al Tûsî: *Kitâb-al Luma'fit Tasawwuf*; Reynold Alleyne Nicholson publication; Leyden: E. J. Brill; London 1914, "Kitâb-al Sama'", pp. 267–300. Hucvayrî: *Kaşf-al Mahcûb*; Ist. Universty Library; Persian Writings; no: 1282–1307; "Kaşf-al hâdî aşer fis-Semâ'", beginning from p. 408. Kuşayrî: *Al Risâlât-al Kuşayrîyyâ*; Egypt-Bulak, 1284; "Bâb-al Sama'"; pp. 197–206. Abû-Bakr Muhammed ibni Ibrâhîm al Buhârî: *Kitâb-al Taarruf li Mazhabi Ah-al Tasawwuf*; Ist. Uni. K. Arab. Writings 3317; pp. 161–62. Abû-Abdurrâhman-al Sulamî: *Tabakaat-al Sûfîyya*; I. Edition; Nûreddin Şarbiya edition; 1372_1953; pp. 60, 191, 305, 328 and especially 329–500. Suhravardî: *Avârif-al Maârif*; in the addendum to "Ihyâu Ulûm-al Din"; Egypt Print. Maymaniyya; 1306, vol. I, pp. 81–141; vol. II, pp. 199–214. Nûr-al Ulûm min Kalûm-al Shaikh Abû'l Hasan-ı Harkaanî; *Al-Muntahab min Kitabi Nûr-al Ulûm*; E. Berthels edition and translation; Iran, vol. III; Leningrad 1929; pp. 155–224; p. 176. Attâr: *Tazkirat-al Avliyâ*; R.A. Nicholson publication; with Mîrza Abdul Vahhâb-ı Kazvîni's foreword and notes; London 1905–1907; vol. I, pp. 255, 271; vol. II, pp. 50, 107, 205, 288–89, 308, 311, 314–15, 333. In his *Huccat-al Samâ'*, Ismâil Rasûhî-i Ankaravî has used material from most of these sources, from books of the traditions of the Prophet, from the *Futūḥāt* of Ibn al-'Arabī, from many commentaries, and from the *Iḥyā'* of Al-Ghazālī; at the end of *Minhac-al Fukara* by the same writer; Ist. Aşır Efendi Han; Rızâ Efendi Print, Al-Hâcc Hasan-al Mavlâvî edition, 1286.

[23] Lâmiî: Nafahât Translation Ist. 1289 Hal trans., pp. 404–05.

[24] Ibid., pp. 471–73.

[25] Ibid., pp. 475–85, 666–70.

people used to do *semâ'* and he also took part in it.[26] Awhadeddin-i Kirmânî[27] (d. 635 H.; 1237 A.D), who was very much bound to Ibn al-ʿArabī and who gained the great respect of his stepson, Sadreddîn, (and who was criticized by Shams due to some of his tendencies) used to do *semâ'* at every occasion.[28] Fahreddîn-i Irâkıy (d. 688 H.; 1289 A.D.), author of *Lamaât*, was a very exuberant practitioner of *semâ'*.[29]

Mevlânâ's Attitude toward Semâ'

Now, let us read the words of Mevlânâ about *semâ'*:

> Dervishes fall into ecstasy and hold *semâ'* so that their love and longing for God, as well as their faith in the next world, may increase, and so that their hearts' attachment to this world will dissolve, making them and the world strangers to one another. They follow the great shaikhs whose miracles (*keramet*) the world has acknowledged, who have become more renowned than the sun and whose greatness is expounded from the pulpits. Believers look to the earth on which their feet have trod; they put their eyes there so that the eye of their hearts may be enlightened, perceiving secret worlds as they are plunged in God. It is they who have established the *semâ'* ceremony; they are the inheritors of the Prophet. The knowledge of inheritance belongs to them and also the knowledge of understanding and intuition. Scholars who know about the outer forms have the knowledge to teach others and help them learn—but they do not possess the knowledge of understanding and intuition. However, Mustafa has said that God also grants the knowledge of understanding and intuition to the one who acts according to what he or she knows.

---

[26] Ibid., pp. 485–87.

[27] Please see the third edition of our book named *Mevlânâ Celaledin*; Ist. Inkılâp Books, 1959, pp. 236–37.

[28] Lâmiî: Nafahât Trans., pp. 659–63.

[29] Ibid., pp. 670–74. Please also refer to *Mevlânâ Celâleddîn*, p. 232 and 240.

And to whomever He grants this knowledge, that one joins the ranks of the attained ones (saints). Everything established by the shaikhs is similar to that established by the prophets, because "a shaikh is like a prophet among his community."[30] Such people even discover the secret of "He hears through Me and he sees through Me."[31] What they do may be seen as included within the statement, *God threw it* (8:17).[32]

Some scholars have forbidden *semâ'* while some have said it is permitted–both are right. If those who follow their *nafs* and are ruled by their lust engage in *semâ'*, it is arrogance and ignorance. They have no knowledge concerning the states of the next world; their *semâ'* is a futile act and nothing but a game. They must face Divine Stringency due to their actions, because the *nafs* and lust belong to this world. *The life of this world is but a play and a passing delight* (47:36). As for the *semâ'* of the shaikhs and the sympathizers (*muhibs*), because they are pure and free of empty games their *semâ'* is even greater than the good works of the people of outer forms. This is because "deeds are evaluated according to intentions."[33] If someone speaks the truth with the intention of making two Muslim brothers fight, or with the intention of revealing something shameful about another Muslim, it is *ḥarām*; it is nothing but antagonism towards that person. The prophets have condemned this type of "truth-speaking" as worse than adultery: "To speak or act against someone while he or she is not there is worse than adultery."[34] But it is *ḥalāl* to tell a lie in order to make two Muslims come into harmony; in fact it is even considered a good deed. The Prophet said, "Those who tell this kind of lie go to Paradise." Both food and jokes are *ḥalāl* for the mature people. But since you are not mature, do not eat and be quiet.[35]

---

[30] Câmî', II, p. 36.
[31] Ibid., I, p. 59.
[32] Abdülbâki Gölpınarlı; *Fihi ma-fih,* trans. Ist. Remzi Books 1959, p. 224.
[33] Al-Tacrîd-al Sarîh, Egypt 1323, I, p. 4.
[34] *Kunûz-al Hakaayık,* II, p.121.
[35] Abdülbâki Gölpınarlı; *Fihi ma-fih,* trans. Ist. Remzi Books 1959, pp. 224–25.

> *Semâ'* is *ḥalāl* for the chosen ones (*havâss*), because they have hearts that have freed themselves from all ties. The feeling 'To love for the sake of God and to hate for the sake of God' is also within the heart that has been liberated from everything...[36]

We also present some of the *ghazals* from Mevlânâ's *Divân-ı Kebîr* that relate to *semâ'*:

O moist branch, dance–the soul's spring has arrived!
Like Joseph entering into Egypt, sweetnesses are entering this world. So start dancing![37]

O sultan, nourished with the mother's milk of love!
Step joyously, lion-like soul of your father,
and dance at once!

Her hair was like a bat so you ran at it like a ball.
Now you've neither head nor foot,
dance without them!

Some knife-wielding assassin was here, asking how I am.
"The news is good?" I asked.
"No, bad," he said.
"Start dancing."

Even a sultan melts into moisture on the breast of that Love.
What's the use of a kaftan?
O you with the beautiful belt,
keep dancing!

O drunkard immersed in being,
nonexistence awaits you.
The decree of nonexistence:
"Get ready for the road–

---

[36] Ibid., p. 230. These words have been conveyed from the manuscripts of Mevlânâ; please refer to the headline on p. 219.
[37] See our *Divân-ı Kebîr* translation; Ist. Remzi Books, Vol. I, 1957, p. 231.
Amed behar-i canha iy shai ter beraks a
Chun Yusuf eneramed Mısr u sheker beraks a

dance!"

A goblet of wine in His hand, my Beautiful One strode by.
If you're a man, dance with love for this maned Lion!

The war has ended, the sound of the harp is heard
and Joseph is out of the well.
O inept and clumsy one–go!
Dive into the dance!

How long will all the promises and prostrating last,
and separation divert the purity of my endeavor?
Join the dance!

"You who are aware of nothing–get lost!"
When will He say this?
"You who are aware of everything–
Stand up! Dance!"

When will our peacock come and the signs appear?
When will the soul-bird trill, "Dance without arms,
without wings"?

The Messiah cured the blind and deaf of this world;
Jesus, son of Mary, called, "O blind and deaf, dance!"

Shamsuddin is the direction to which we chose to turn;
even China is jealous of Tabriz.
Both branch and trunk dance in the springtime of his beauty!

* * *

Each heavenly particle–dancing for wine
and love of God–sees the Sun of eternity.[38]

---

[38] Ibid., Trans. II, Ist. Remzi Books, 1958, pp. 41–42.
Her zerre ki der bala mey nushed u pa kubed
Horshid-i ezel bined vez ishk-i Huda kubed

If He makes you smile, your arms and sleeves will dance;
if He frightens you: your lips will dance with prayer.

Even the beautiful sky is heavily drunk with wine,
and keeps thundering the call to prayer.

Love Itself got drunk and staggered to the vineyard of Alast.[39]
Its tender feet now press the grapes of existence.

If Love isn't drunk and doesn't worship wine,
why enter the vineyard to press grapes?

You, too, are striking your feet all the time,
though you don't see the grapes, your Sufi soul keeps pressing them.

You've worn Joseph's *khirka*, that's why you keep striking your foot on the floor!
Whoever hears "Strike your foot on the floor!" strikes his foot of fidelity. Join the Dance!

It was Joseph's chanting that made Jacob dance.
And sweet-lipped Joseph keeps striking his foot, dancing!

O souls in the Presence of the Beloved, strike your foot, dance!
You may brush feet with Felicity and be taken for a whirl.

My soul, this is the Love that rains
on leaf and herb, meadow and field.
And all of a sudden they may sprout up green!

The friend of God[40] entered Nimrod's dancing fire;
toward a blade of troubles danced the throat of Ishmael.[41]

God's seabird stamped its foot upon the waves

---

[39] Referring to the moment when our souls were asked by God, "Am I not your Lord?"
[40] Abraham.
[41] A name given to Ishmael, the son of Abraham, meaning "the sacrificed one."

and ascended through the air on *miʿrāj.*[42]

Be silent.
Without tongue or lips say, "May his beautiful life be long."
Know the evil eye won't dance upon this one.

* * *

The *rebab*[43]–source of love and companion of the friends–
means "cloud" to the Arabs.[44]

As a cloud waters the rose garden,
the *rebab*, cupbearer of essences, feeds the heart.

Breathe into the fire and the flames flare up.
Breathe into the ground: nothing but dust.

The *rebab* is an open call: "Come near to the Sultan!"
Crows flee at the beating of drums.

It unties the difficult knots of lovers,
and when the knots are gone,
like water, how sweet and cool it is!

The goal is grass for the troubled beast.
Its dough was kneaded with the yeast of heedlessness,
so its seed is lust.

Can a donkey discourse on the love of Jesus?
God, who opens doors, has shut this one.

To reach for Love is the garment of the soul,
shedding veils within union's sultanhood.
This is the necklace of *We have honored the children of Adam.*

---

[42] Referring to the ascension of the Blessed Prophet.
[43] Stringed instrument typically played with a bow.
[44] Ibid., Trans. Vol. III, Remzi Books, 1958, p. 91.
Rebab meshreb-i ishkest u munis-i ahbab
Ki Ebrra araban nam kerdeend rebab

When God calls, the real workers tend to their one task
and are soon freed from distraction.

Don't speak of Love to those still defined by the body;
their task: the fear, the hope, the good deed, the guilt.

* * *

Come, come! You are the soul of the soul of the soul of *semâ'*;
you are thousands of flaming candles in the dynasty of *semâ'*.[45]

The hearts of stars–hundreds of thousands of them–burn
because of you.
Come, you are the waxing moon in the sky of *semâ'!*

* * *

Come, come! You are the soul of the soul of the soul of *semâ'*.
Come, O strolling cypress of the garden of *semâ'!*[46]

Come! Nothing like you has been, nor ever will be.
Come! *Semâ'* never set eyes on anything like you,
nor shall it.

Come! Even the source of the sun is your shadow;
in the sky of *semâ'* you are a thousand Venuses!

Semâ' says thank you in a hundred lucid tongues.
This once, say a few words in this language of *semâ'*.

Entering *semâ'* is exiting both worlds:
semâ' goes beyond.

---

[45] Ibid., p. 224.
Biya biya ki tuyi can-i can-i can-i Sema
Hezar shem-i munevver be hanedan-i Sema

[46] Ibid., p. 225.
Biya biya ki tuyi can-i can-i can-i Sema
Biya ki serv-i revani be bustan-i Sema

Though the roof of the seventh heaven is high,
the ladder of *semâ'* goes even higher.

Whatever you have, if it's not Him,
put it under your foot,
then press.

Semâ' is all you own,
and you are owned by *semâ'*.

If Love puts Her arms about me, what can I do
except hold Her tight to my chest in *semâ'?*

When the laps of particles become filled with sunshine,
they dance without prompting from *semâ'*.

Come! Shams of Tabriz is love made manifest.
The mouth of *semâ'* is yearning for his lips.

* * *

What is *semâ'*? A greeting to the heart from the hidden men of God; when their letters arrive, the heart finds tranquility.[47]

The knots of the mind release with this breeze;
with the striking of the strings, the body finds peace.

From the cry of this spiritual rooster the dawn will break,
and victory will be heralded by the kettledrum of Mars.

The soul's essence shot arrows of wine at the jar of the body;
as it heard the tambourine, it began to froth.

A strange sweetness enveloped the body
as the tongue tasted the sweetness from the *neyzen's* lips.

---

[47] Ibid., pp. 261–62.
Semâ' chist zi pinhaniyan-i dil peygaam
Dil-i garib biyaded zi nameshan aram

See now a thousand scorpions of sorrow slain,
and a thousand toasts without glasses.

As the resurrection of all the people
will take place with the blowing of the trumpet,

the dead will jump out of their slumber to the joy of
hearing the whisper of love.

The one who is not moved by that blowing
is less than a nobody.

The body and the heart that drink from this clear and clean wine
are safe from the burning sorrows of separation.

Warm up the *semâ'* and ignore the donkeys.
You are the core and kernel of *semâ'*, the prosperity of the times.

I'll sell my tongue and buy a thousand ears
because the sweet-spoken orator has risen to the pulpit.

* * *

You are the *Ka'bah* of souls: I am circumambulating you.
I am not some raven flapping over a ruin.[48]

I have no other skill, no other occupation.
To keep turning like the sky is my art—what I do.

* * *

O *ney's* wail, *ney's* wail, *ney's* wail,
making the whole world of secrets stand erect![49]

---

[48] Ibid., Trans. IV, Ist. Remzi Books, p. 371.
Kabe-i canha tuyi gerd-i tu arem tevaf
Cugd neyem ber herab hich nedarem tevaf

[49] Ibid., p. 267.
Iy deraverde cihanira zipay

What is the *ney*?
That thing the elegant Beloved kisses,
and kisses
and kisses.

Yet the *ney* is only a pretext
for that which is beyond the means of the *ney*.
It's only the wing beats,
not the bird of fortune itself.

* * *

Musician! Begin again about Love
and loosen, just a little,
one or two of those silk strings.[50]

Providence has presented wine to you
so build your house on the roof of the sky's dome.

You've conquered the land of drunkenness
and of self-transcendence too.
Give up the love of the land of Sanjar.

* * *

Today, there is *semâ'* and a continual flow of wine.
Honored chalices without end do the rounds.
The request "May God bestow water" is granted,
so drink!

O body, turn completely into soul.
Don't you belong to the İhvân-ı Safâ?[51]

Bang-i nay u bang-i nay u bang-i nay

[50] Ibid., Trans. V, Ist. Remzi Books, p. 146.
Mutriba ishk-bazi ez ser gir
Yek du ebrishimek furuter gir

[51] "Brotherhood of Purity." A secret fraternity of Muslim philosophers who

O era! What an era you are!
O day! What a day you are!
O rose garden of fortune!
What leaves, what fruit you've grown![52]

* * *

Though the whole world burns with troubles, trouble's fire is never seen.
Has anyone ever seen the weaving of its spell?
No, no one has ever seen.[53]

The power of His amber pulls me in every direction.
I wonder: has anyone seen who is pulling me?
No, nobody has.

We have *semâ'* but no *cheng*;[54] we have wine but no color.
One chalice after another—hundreds of them—are being offered;
where is the one who has sipped from the chalice?
Not in the open.

Love is playing with the waterskin—I look like the bottle in Her hand.
She threw the bottle under the people's feet—it broke, but
did anyone's foot get injured? No.

For those advancing on this path there is no end to shaikhs and disciples.
But neither exists when the breath of unity is drawn.

---

wrote extensively on many subjects, including music.

[52] Ibid., Trans. VI.
Imruz semâ' est u mudamest u sakaayi
Gerdan shude ber cem' kadehha-yı atayi

[53] Ibid.
Suht yeki cihan begam atesh-i gam bedid ni
Suret-i in tilismra hich gesi bidid ni

[54] A harp-like musical instrument.

Give good news to the lovers! The Celebration of attaining is
arriving.
It is such a holiday that it is neither Ramaḍān nor 'Eid.

* * *

Today there is *semâ'* and wine in the decanter,
a drunken cupbearer and revelers who see everything
as appropriate.[55]

Those who see this way belong to that world of existence,
not with the opium and cannabis eaters.
Those inane ones see everything
as appropriate.

* * *

Whirling is the peace of the soul for the living ones;
only the one with the Soul of the soul knows it.[56]

Only the one who is asleep in the rose garden
should want to wake up.

But the one who is sleeping in a prison
would be worse off awake.

Whirl where there is a wedding,
not in mourning, nor in lamentation.

The one who has not seen his own essence,
the one from whose eyes that Moon is hidden,

for such a person what use is *semâ'* and *daf*?
Semâ' is for uniting with the Beloved who satisfies hearts.

---

[55] *Imruz semâ' est u sherabest u sūrahi*
yek saki-i bed-mest u yeki cem-i mubahi

[56] *Sema aram-i can-i zindeganest*
Kesi daned ki ura can-i canest

Those who turn in the direction of prayer,
whirl in both this world and the next.

Pay heed, when a circle of friends whirl,
circling round and round, the Ka'bah is the center.

* * *

Semâ' is for the soul with no fixed abode.
Leap up! There's no time wait.[57]

Don't sit wrapped in thought.
If you're a man of God,
go where the Beloved is.

* * *

My friend, the time for *semâ'* has come.
On your feet!
It's time to work,
time to out-do everyone.[58]

* * *

God, give honey to the musicians.
Grace them with hands of iron
to strike their instruments well.[59]

* * *

[57] *Sema ez behr-i can-i bi kararest*
Sebuk berceh ne cay-i intizarest

[58] *Semâ' amed hele iy yar berceh*
Musabik bash u vakt-i kar berceh

[59] *Hudaya muribanra engubin dih*
Beray-i zarbdest-i ahenin dih

Let's go, Sufis!
At least for today,
come to yourselves.
Yes, today: *semâ'*
is a joy and a pleasure![60]

Finally, we present two of Mevlânâ's *rubais,* or quatrains, which describe *semâ',* reveal Mevlânâ's opinions concerning it, and offer advice to *semâ'zens*. We will stop there, however, because if we were to present all of Mevlânâ's poems about *semâ'* it would occupy a book almost half the size of the *Divân* itself. Here we would also like to insist that the "wine" mentioned in these poems is not the wine fermented from grapes, even though prejudice, unreasonable narrow-mindedness, ill will, and a lack of poetic sensibility may lead some to think of it as such. Mevlânâ himself made it clear that what is meant is a "wine" that is *ḥalāl*: a spiritual enlightenment (*feyz*), a love, and a joy in oneness (*vahdet*) through which the heart is made drunk and through which it matures, allowing a person to give up the "I" of egotism and reach real being.

O *semâ'zen*, keep the stomach empty,
for emptiness makes the ney moan.
A full belly means no Beloved–
no embrace, no kisses![61]

* * *

Semâ' is the heat of power,
the mountain ash,
and the falcon on the threshold of God.

Semâ' polishes the hearts of the people of states (*hal*).

---

[60] *Hela iy sufiyan kimruz bari*
Semâ' est u neshat u aysh ari

[61] *Iy merd-i semâ' mi'dera hali dar*

Though *hāram* ("unlawful") for deniers,
for circles of lovers it is *ḥalāl.*[62]

Mevlânâ also mentions *semâ'* in his *Mesnevî* whenever the subject allows it:

A Sufi stops at a *khānqah*; he ties his donkey to the stable; gives it fodder and water; and he himself goes in and becomes a guest. They eat and drink and begin the *semâ'*. The musicians begin to play the instruments and the dervishes begin to sing "The donkey has gone! The donkey has gone!" The Sufi also joins them; sometimes he hits his foot on the floor, turns, and sometimes he prostrates, and does the *semâ'* until the morning. In the morning, the Sufi wakes up early to arrive at his destination on time. He goes to the stable and sees that his donkey has disappeared.[63]

In another *Mesnevî* story related to *semâ'*, Mevlânâ speaks of a Sufi suffering from heartache who tore off his cloak during a *semâ'* ceremony, and relates that for this reason cloaks opening at the front are called *fereci* (a garment worn by *ulema* on ceremonial occasions).[64] Also, in Volume VI of the *Mesnevî,* he refers again to the same tradition with these couplets:

He is a Sufi and has flung away his robe in ecstasy:
how could he take it back again?

To repent and hanker for a mantle given away
is as much as to say, "I have been swindled:
bring back the mantle, brothers.
Love was not worth the price of it."

---

[62] *Sheh-baz-i cenab-i zul-celalest semâ'*

[63] *Furûhten-i sûfiyan behîme-i müsâfirrâ cehet-i semâ'*; Vol. II; Reynold A. Nicholson edition; London, 1925; pp. 275–79. The dervishes had been hungry for days. During the *semâ'* they had alerted him that "the donkey is gone," which he himself joyfully chanted. They had sold the donkey and bought food.

[64] *Sebe-i nam nihaden-i fereci der ibtida-yi hal der mani*; Vol. V, chp. 18.

Far be it for a lover to harbor such a thought;
if he does: dust upon his head!

A hundred mantles like the body–
which contains life, sensation, reason–
are worthless beside Love.[65]

In Volume I, in the chapter *Mujde burden-i hergush suy-i nahciran ki shir der chah uftaden,* Mevlânâ writes:

Branch and leaf set free from the prison of the earth,
lifted their heads to become comrades of the wind.

The leaves, having burst the bough,
raced to the tree tops.

Without tongue or lips,
each tree and all its fruit sing thanks to God,
saying, "The Bounteous Giver nourished our root
until we grew big and tall."

So spirits once trapped in clay,
when they make their glad escape
begin to dance in the air of Divine Love,
flawless as a full moon's orb.

Their bodies dancing, their souls–don't ask!
Their soul's delight–no, don't ask![66]

In chapter 30 of Volume IV (*Sebeb-i hicret-i Ibrahim Edhem . . .*), Mevlânâ explains,

Therefore, *semâ'* is nourishment for the lovers;
it is the vision of one's meeting with the Beloved, with God.[67]

---

[65] *Sufiyim u kikaha endahtim*
Baz nestanim chun derbahtim

[66] *Shah u berk ez habs-i hak azad shud*
Ser beraverde herif-i bad shud

[67] *Pes gaza-yi ashikaan amed semâ'*
Ki redu bashed heyal-i ichtima

The Nature of Mevlânâ's Semâ'

We cannot be sure whether Mevlânâ practiced *semâ'* before meeting Shams. Sipehsâlâr (who describes himself as following scholars of Muslim theology for forty years, while also serving Mevlânâ for an equal length of time), says that Mevlânâ followed Shams in the *usûl-i semâ'* (method or rhythm of *semâ'*), in the practice of wearing the ceremonial cloak, and in his attitude towards the *destâr*, and that it was Shams who encouraged Mevlânâ to practice *semâ'*.[68] Eflâkî Ahmed Dede, who began writing *Manâkıb-al Ârifîn* (*Deeds of the Mystic Knowers*) in 718 H. (1318 A.D.), upon the order of Ulu Arif Chelebi (died 719 H., 1320 A.D.), also says that Mevlânâ's esteem for *semâ'* grew after he met Shams, and that his enthusiasm caused conservative Muslims (who were bound to the outer aspect of the religion) to criticize him and even question his sanity.[69]

Sultân Veled's *İntihânâme,* which is a reliable document, clearly states that Mevlânâ was a pious man of God before Shams came, and it goes on to say:

> Shams invited him to a *semâ'* he had chosen himself. Upon his order, when he [Mevlânâ] began to do *semâ'*, by the favor of God, he saw that he had advanced a hundred times beyond his previous state. Practicing *semâ'* became the right way for him. Due to *semâ'*, hundreds of vineyards, orchards, and gardens sprouted and grew in his heart...[70]

In order to understand the difference in Mevlânâ's state before and after he met Shams (according to Mevlânâ himself and Sultân

[68] Ahmed Avni trans., Ist, Arsak Garoyan print. 1331; pp. 12–34 (in particular p. 26), pp. 67–68. See the English translation of Eflâkî's *Manâkıb-al Ârifîn*: *Rumi and His Friends, Stories of the Lovers of God*, translated by Camille Helminski with Susan Blaylock, p. 299 "Love from Samarkand" section, where it is related by Sultân Veled that it was his grandmother who had originally introduced Mevlânâ to a form of *semâ'*, but that it was Shams who encouraged him to fully immerse in the practice of whirling.

[69] Tahsin Yazıcı Ed., *Türk Tarih Kurumu*/Turkish History Institution pub. Ankara T. T. K. Pub.; Vol. I, 1959, p. 89.

[70] Ist. Uni. Lib. Persian Writings, 1009, 61a.

Veled), please see our book *Mevlânâ Celâleddîn.*[71]

Shams said that during *semâ'* the Friend is seen, and that men of God will step out of their existence and reach the Truth (*Ḥaqq). Semâ'* is *ḥarām* for those who have not reached this state (*hâl*):

> Semâ' is permissable (*mubāh*) for the experts of fasting (*riyâzat*) and it is an obligation (*farḍ*) for the people of spiritual states (*hâl*). Even if the people of *semâ'* are whirling in the West, they are aware of the *semâ'* in the East.[72]

According to these valid accounts, we presume that Mevlânâ did not practice *semâ'* before he met Shams, or if he did, he did not have a high opinion of it, nor was he known for participating in it. We conclude that Mevlânâ became enamoured of *semâ'* after he met Shams.

But what was the nature of Mevlânâ's *semâ'*? The following accounts from the treatise of Sipehsâlâr and *Manâkıb-al Ârifîn* will help answer this question:

A shaikh called Buzağu (meaning "calf") came to Konya, and Rükneddin Kılıch Arslan showed him great respect. During a feast that he gave in honor of the shaikh, Arslan addressed him as "Baba" and told him that he had chosen him as a father; that is, he had accepted him as his shaikh (*intisap etmek*). Hearing this, Mevlânâ felt hurt and rose for *semâ'*, and while he was engaged in it he recited a *ghazal* with the following first verse (*matlâ*):

> By God! My heart is enticed by neither sweets nor meat.
> I fawn not upon this sack of gold nor upon that golden bowl.

Continuing *semâ'* and reciting poetry, he left and went on his way.[73]

---

[71] Third ed., Ist. Inkılâb Books, 1959, pp. 69–77.

[72] *Manâkıb-al Ârifîn,* II, p. 658.

[73] *Mevlânâ Celâleddîn,* p. 86. Please see Shaikh Bâbâ-yı Merendî pp. 243–44. *Manâkıb-al Ârifîn* also reports that Mevlânâ recited this *ghazal* while he was doing *semâ'*.

> *Be Huda meyl nedarem ne becherb u ne beshirin*
> *Ne bedan kise-i pur zer ne bedan kase-i zerrin*

* * *

At a dinner given by Sultan Rükneddin, Mevlânâ rose for *semâ'* after the meal. When Seyyid Şerefeddin spoke some words against Mevlânâ to Emîr Pervâne, Mevlânâ stopped and recited this *ghazal*:

> In my heart I have heard the nonsense spoken by my enemy.
> I've seen, too, the suspicions you harbor against me.[74]

* * *

One day, when he heard someone selling a fox, calling "*Dilgü! Dilgü!*" ("Fox! Fox!"), Mevlânâ fell into ecstasy and began *semâ'*, reciting this couplet:

> Where is the heart, where is the heart? Where is the lover, where is the heart?
> Where is the gold, where is the gold? Where is the bankrupt, where is the gold?

Then, while immersed in *semâ'*, he went to the *madrasah*.[75]

* * *

Because Mevlânâ used to live on the small amount of money he earned by giving *fatwās*, he used to say to his companions, "Even if we are engaged in *semâ'*, if somebody wants a *fatwā*, bring him to us; let's give the answer so that the money we gain may be *ḥalāl*." During *semâ'*, if somebody asked for a *fatwā* from him, his companions would bring a pen and ask the question, so that he could write the answer

[74] Sipehsâlâr, p. 87.
Hezeyan ki guft dushmen bederun-i dil shinidem
Pey-i men tasavvurira ki bikerd hem bididem

[75] Sipehsâlâr, p. 91; *Manâkıb-al Ârifîn*, p. 356.
Dil ku dil ku dil ez kuca ashik u dil
Zer ku zer ku zer ez kuca muflis u zer

or dictate it.[76]

* * *

While Mevlânâ was practicing *semâ'*, a drunkard came and joined in. He kept bumping into Mevlânâ. The *semâ'zens* wanted to stop the drunkard and take him out of the *semâ'*, but Mevlânâ said, "He has drunk wine, but you are the drunkards." In this way, he told them that they should not touch the drunkard and they left him alone. The drunkard was a Christian, and at that time Christians were called *tersâ*, "frightened ones."

"But he is a Christian," the *semâ'zens* said.

Mevlânâ, who saw the humanity in each person and embraced it, tolerated this, too, saying, "If he is a *tersâ*, aren't you, also, *tersâ*? Aren't you afraid of God?"[77]

* * *

One day while Mevlânâ was passing through the jewelers market, he heard the sound of hammering coming from the shop of Salâhaddîn-i Zerküb. He fell into ecstasy, began *semâ'*, and pulled Salâhaddîn into the *semâ'* with him. Salâhaddîn participated for a while and then said that he was not able to continue because of old age. He asked for Mevlânâ's forgiveness, but he ordered his apprentices to go on hammering without a care for the loss of gold that this would incur. To the sound of the hammers, Mevlânâ continued and recited the *ghazal* which begins with this first verse:

> A treasure has appeared in this goldsmith's shop!
> What a rendering; what essence it contains!
> Such beauty! Such beauty![78]

---

[76] Sipehsâlâr, p. 96; *Manâkıb-al Ârifîn*, pp. 209, 325.
[77] Sipehsâlâr, p. 104; *Manâkıb-al Ârifîn*, Vol. I, p. 356.
[78] Sipehsâlâr, p. 126; *Manâkıb-al Ârifîn*, Vol. I, p. 379; Vol. II, pp. 709–11.
Yeki kunci bedidamed derin dukkan-i zer-kubi
Zihi suret zihi ma'ni zihi hubi zihi hubi

* * *

One day when he was holding *semâ'*, Mevlânâ recited these couplets:

The Kingdom of our Lord holds both the rough and the pure;
for Him, all kinds are wanted.
Be a carnelian or a ruby, or even a brick or a stone–
if you are truly of the faithful, He will find you;
if you are a denier, He will refresh you:
on this road, be an Abū Bakr; on that road, be a Frank.[79]

* * *

Qadi ("Judge") Izzeddin used to denounce *semâ'*. One day, when Mevlânâ was engaged in it, he approached and embraced Qadi Izzeddin, pulling him into the *semâ'*. The judge fell into a great ecstasy and after the *semâ'* became a disciple of Mevlânâ.[80]

* * *

One day during *semâ'*, Mevlânâ recited in Arabic, "Whatever I have seen, I have seen God in it."

One of the dervishes said, "The words 'in it' refer to something that contains; it is not appropriate to say this of God, because it makes Him the content of the universe; but God cannot be contained in anything."

Mevlânâ replied, "If you are drunk, we are the sober drunkards; if these words were not completely appropriate, we would not have said them. The outward appearance and the inner substance require two separate things. However, that which appears to be two is actually

[79] *Manâkıb-al Ârifîn*, Vol. I, p. 89.
Mulkist ura zuft u hosh her gunei mibayedesh
Hahi akiyk u lal shov hahi kuluh u seng shov
Ger mu'mini micuyedet ver kaferi mishuyedet
In ku birov siddiyk shov von ku birov Efreng shov.

[80] Ibid., p.104.

one. He has covered everything; He is both the outward appearance and the inner substance..." He then continued with his *semâ'*.

* * *

When Mevlânâ was leading *semâ'*, Sheyyad Abdürrahman used to fall into ecstasy and cry out loudly.[81]

* * *

While in *semâ'*, Mevlânâ recited his *ghazal* beginning:

> Didn't I tell you not to go there, for I am your friend?
> I am the source of life in this mirage of non-existence.
>
> Didn't I tell you not to go there, for trouble awaits you?
> They have talons for hands and will tie your legs.[82]

People later discovered that Rükneddin Kılıcharslan had accepted an invitation from the Mongols and was drowned.[83]

* * *

In a *semâ'* gathering arranged by someone else, Mevlânâ fell into an ecstasy and showed many signs of pleasure and rapture.[84]

* * *

---

[81] Ibid., p. 140. For Sheyyad, please refer to our book *Mevlevîhood After Mevlânâ,* Ist. Inkilab Books, 1953, pp. 24–25, Note 11.

[82] *Negoftemet merov anca ki ashnat menem*
Derin serab-i fena chesme-i heyat menem
Negoftemet merov anca ki mubtelat kunend
Ki seht dest-dirazend beste-pat kunend

[83] Ibid., p.148.

[84] Ibid., p.149.

One day, when Mevlânâ was engaged in *semâ'*, Kemâlettin Emîr-i Mahfil said, "Mevlânâ is a very great man of God but for the most part, Mevlânâ's disciples are artisans and common people. Scholars and the distinguished don't often mix with them. Wherever there is a tailor, a cotton merchant, a grocer–he accepts them readily as students."

In the midst of the semâ', Mevlânâ gave out a loud cry and said, "O accursed one, our Mansoor was a cotton-carder and Shaikh Abū-Bakr of Bukhara, was he not a weaver? And that other perfect being, was he not a glassmaker? Did their professions in any way harm their inner knowing and insight?"[85]

* * *

Again, one day while Mevlânâ was holding a *semâ'*, Kemâleddin Muarrif (the same person) turned his back to the *semâ'zens*. Mevlânâ called out to him, "O incomplete *Kemâl!* You have turned your back to the maturity of the maturity," and he cried out, loudly.[86]

* * *

One day, while Mevlana was immersed in *semâ'*, he spoke words of wisdom and shared knowledge and whirled to the *madrasah*.[87]

* * *

One day the *semâ'* lasted from the noon prayer until midnight. Kadı Kemâleddîn-i Kâbî offered honey sherbet to the *semâ'zens*. Mevlânâ paused the singing of the *kavvâls* and recited this *rubai*:[88]

> He came full of love, warmly in haste–
> his soul caught the fragrance of the rose garden of Truth.

---

[85] Ibid., p. 151.
[86] Ibid., p. 152.
[87] Ibid., p. 161.
[88] *Germ amed u ashikaane vu cust u shitab...*

Above all other judges, he came running today—
the Kadı of Kâb in search of the water of life.

Then he called Kemâleddîn to him, and, while embracing him and kissing his face and eyes, recited the ghazal that begins[89]:

If you wish to know me, ask the nights;
ask the pale cheeks and dry lips...[90]

* * *

While Mevlânâ was in the *semâ'*, Shemseddin-i Mardînî put a *dümbelek* (a kind of a hand drum) on his head and said, "Truly, this is chanting. Whoever says that *semâ'* is *ḥarām* is a villain," and he kept repeating these words.[91]

* * *

At the *tekke* of Tâjeddin-i Vezîr, someone was appointed to sit on the *post* for *semâ'*, and *semâ'* was held during the ceremony that marked his appointment. While Mevlânâ was taking part in the *semâ'*, Seyyid Sherefeddin began to gossip. Mevlânâ shouted, "O such-and-such person!" and recited from the Qur'ān: *Would any of you like to eat the flesh of his dead brother? No, you would detest it*... (49:12)[92]

* * *

During *semâ'*, Mevlânâ came before Shihâbeddin-i Gûyende and Osmân-ı Kavvâl and asked for pardon several times.[93]

---

[89] *Mera eger tu nedani bipurs ez shebha*
Bipurs ez ruh-zerd u zi hushki-i lebha

[90] *Manâkıb-al Ârifîn,* Vol. I, pp. 179–82.

[91] Ibid., p. 210.

[92] Ibid., p. 215.

[93] Ibid., p. 222.

* * *

While engaged in *semâ'*, Mevlânâ came up to Hâce Nefîseddin, held him by the collar and asked, "What will you say if they ask you, 'Why does he (Mevlânâ) keep rolling up the sleeves of his *ferece*?'"

Nefîseddin answered, "Whatever Hudâvendigâr (i.e. Mevlânâ) says."

Mevlânâ continued, "The universe is a great *khaneqah*. In this *khaneqah*, the real shaikh is God. All the prophets, all the attained ones and prominent people of the *ummah* ("religious community") are like visiting Sufis. When a poor Sufi comes to the *khaneqah*, he sees the person whose sleeves are rolled up and knows that this is the one who serves in the *khaneqah*, and so learns about the manners and traditions of the *khaneqah* from that one. In this universe, we are the servants of God and the lovers of God, too."

He then recited the *ḥadīth*, "The master of a community is the one who serves that community."[94]

* * *

During *semâ'*, Mevlânâ went into ecstasy and cried out in rapture.[95] He granted favors to the people and the singers[96] and tossed coins in the tambourines of the musicians.[97]

* * *

In Meram, while a grain mill was turning, Mevlânâ fell into ecstasy and began *semâ'*, reciting the *ghazal* that begins with this couplet:

> The heart is like the wheat, and we are like the mill;
> how would the mill know why it is turning?[98]

---

94 *Manâkıb-al Ârifîn*, Vol. I, p. 224; *Cami-al Sagiyr*, II, p. 29.
95 *Manâkıb-al Ârifîn*, Vol. I, p. 232.
96 Ibid., p. 257.
97 Ibid., pp. 320, 454, 485–86, 487.
98 Ibid., p. 371.

* * *

In order to challenge Mevlânâ, Hajı Bektash sent a dervish of his, Baba İshak, with the following message: "If you have found, why this struggle? If you have not found, why don't you search?"

Mevlânâ was participating in *semâ'* when Baba İshak arrived. Suddenly, Mevlânâ began to recite the *ghazal* that begins with these couplets:

> If you have not reached the Friend, why don't you search?
> If you have reached the Friend, why not make music and sing?
>
> Seated in sloth, you respond, "What puzzling thing is this?"
> But the puzzle is you who have not fallen under its spell![99]

Baba İshak said, "I have received my answer." He kissed the threshold, about turned and left.[100]

* * *

During *semâ'*, Mevlânâ would take hold of the *kavvâls*, beat his foot rhythmically on the floor and send greetings of peace to the Prophet.[101]

* * *

Sadreddîn-i Konavî told the Pervâne, "Tonight I had an ascension (*mi'rāj*); I have seen Mevlânâ above the Empyrean."

When the Pervâne related this to Mevlânâ, Mevlânâ replied, "He

Dil chu dane ma misal-i asya
Asya key daned in gerdish chira

[99] *Eger tu yar nedari chira taleb nehuni*
Veger betar residi chira tarab nekuni
Be kahili binisini ki in aceb karest
Acep tuyi ki heva-yi chunan acep nekuni

[100] *Manâkıb-al Ârifîn,* Vol. I, p. 383.

[101] Ibid., p. 412.

speaks the truth, but I have never seen him there," and he stood up for *semâ'* and recited the *ghazal* beginning with this couplet:

> If you are my companion and friend, tell me: what happened last night?
> What happened between this heart and that Beloved selling wine?[102]

* * *

During *semâ'*, people offered food to Mevlânâ. He refused it and recited the following couplet:

> Once you've tasted this food of light,
> you'll throw dirt on bread from the oven.[103]

Then he continued the *semâ'*.[104]

* * *

While he was passing by a wine house (*meyhâne*), Mevlânâ heard the sound of the *rebab* and began *semâ'*.[105]

* * *

During a *semâ'* held in the Pervâne's home, the Pervâne said to Hatıroğlu Şerefeddîn, "Oversee this gathering, and let me sleep a little."

During the *semâ'*, Mevlânâ recited the *ghazal* that begins with this

---

[102] Ibid., pp. 417–18.
Eger harif-i meni pes bigu ki dush chi bud
Miyan-i in dil u on yar-i mey-furush chi bud

[103] *Ger hori yek bar ezan me' kul-i nur*
Hah rizi ber ser-i nan-i tenur

[104] *Manâkıb-al Ârifîn,* Vol. I, p.488.

[105] Ibid., p. 489.

couplet:

> If you don't sleep for a night, what will it matter?
> If you don't knock at the door of separation, what will it matter?[106]

* * *

During *semâ'* someone asked, "What is *faqr* ("spiritual poverty")?"

As he was turning, Mevlânâ recited a *rubai* in Arabic, which translates as follows:

> Poverty is the substance and anything else is the accident.
> Non-existence is health–anything else is disease.
> The entire world is trickery and pride;
> nothingness, rather than this world, is the treasure, the aim.[107]

* * *

During *semâ'*, Mevlânâ recited the *ghazal* beginning with this couplet:

> As a result of my drunkenness and dissolution,
> I can no longer distinguish water from earth.[108]

* * *

At the funeral of Selâhaddin-i Zer-Kûb, Mevlânâ began a *semâ'*, crying out loudly and reciting the *mersiye* beginning with the couplet:

---

[106] Ibid., pp. 542–43.
Ger nehosbi shebi iy can chi sheved
Ver nekubi der-i hicran chi sheved

[107] *Manâkıb-al Ârifîn,* Vol.II, pp. 586–87.
Al cavharu fakrun va siva-l fakru araz

[108] Ibid., pp. 602–03.
Cunan mestem zi mesiyy u herabi
Ki hakim nemidanem zi abi

> O the one whose loss causes earth and sky to weep!
> The heart languishes in blood; reason and soul begin to weep.[109]

* * *

Selâhaddin was sitting in the corner at a *semâ'*. While Mevlânâ was overseeing the *semâ'*, he recited the *ghazal* that begins with the following couplet:

> At the end of time, there is nobody to bring help
> except Selâhaddin, Selâhaddin,[110] and nobody else.[111]

* * *

Mevlânâ went to Ilgın and stayed for forty or fifty days. His companions arrived to bring him back. On the way, Mevlânâ and his companions held a *semâ'*, with Mevlânâ reciting *ghazals*.[112]

* * *

Another year, Mevlânâ went to Ilgın again and stayed there for a while. Chelebi Hüsâmeddin came and they traveled back together. When they arrived in Konya they went to the place where Sultan-el Ulemâ is buried and they gave a feast there.[113]

* * *

---

[109] Ibid., p. 73.
Iy zi hicranet zemin u asman bigriste
Dil miyan-i hon nisheste akl u can bigriste

[110] "Righteousness of the Way."

[111] Ibid., p. 736.
Nist der ahir zeman feryad-res
Cuz Selahaddin Selahaddin u bes

[112] Ibid., pp. 759–60.

[113] Ibib., pp. 760–61.

One day, Mevlânâ was at a gathering in Pervâne's home. Chelebi Husameddin had not been called, and Mevlânâ did not speak of anything relating to education. Chelebi was then invited to join them. Chelebi arrived and sat at the table. Mevlânâ approached him and *semâ'* began. While they were whirling, they went to the *madrasah*, where the *semâ'* continued.[114]

* * *

Near the Meram Mosque, Mevlânâ held a *semâ'* and recited a poem:

> Come, come, O Sultan of sultans!
> The soul is again calling back his hawks.
> Come! The shepherd is leading the flock to the meadow.[115]

* * *

Sultân Veled had made an error. While Mevlânâ was whirling, he approached Sultân Veled, held him by the collar, pointed at him with his index finger and warned him, "Bahâeddin! Ha, ha, ha! From now on, it is up to you!"

* * *

When Ulu Arif Chelebi, the son of Sultân Veled, was born, a *semâ'* was arranged which lasted for three days. On the third day, Mevlânâ recited the *ghazal* with the opening verse:

> If the vineyard or the orchard knew of Him,
> blood would drip from the fresh branches;
> if the mind understood Him,

---

[114] Ibib. pp. 769–72.

[115] Ibib. p. 805.
Biya ki baz-i canhara shehensheh baz mihaned
Biya ki kellera chuban besuy-i desht miraned

a river of tears would flow from the eyes.[116]

* * *

During a *semâ'* a man was reciting the Qur'ān, and when he came to an *āyāt* requiring a prostration, Mevlânâ stopped to perform it.[117]

* * *

While he was engaged in *semâ',* Mevlânâ made many prostrations.[118]

* * *

Sipehsâlâr says that in *semâ'*, the turning of the foot (*chark vurmak*) signifies reaching unity, while the opening of the arms signifies reaching the heights of the universe, overcoming one's *nafs* by placing it under one's foot, and attaining unity's joy—a sign of greatness. He says that to embrace someone during *semâ'* indicates that "with complete purity, one sees one's self, one's own truth in that person," and that to encourage someone to engage in *semâ'* is to spread grace (*raḥmah*). He adds that to prostrate during *semâ'* means that one has reached the station of servanthood, or that one has glimpsed the Attributes of God in someone, and he informs us that Mevlânâ used to recite many *ghazals* during *semâ'*.[119]

As we have seen, there were no restrictions on Mevlânâ's *semâ'*. He used to spontaneously fall into ecstastic *semâ',* in the midst of which he would cry out loudly, converse with people, dictate a *fatwā*, discuss religious education, recite poems, throw coins into the tambourines of the musicians, grant favors and apologize to them, beat his foot on the floor, prostrate, and open his arms. *Semâ'* usually took place in

---

[116] Ibib. p. 828.
[117] In the Qur'ān there are traditionally seventeen *āyāts* that require a prostration as they are read.
[118] Sipehsâlâr, pp. 97–98.
[119] Ibid., p. 69.

gatherings, after a meal, but Mevlânâ even used to engage in *semâ'* on the street as he was on his way somewhere. His *semâ'* movements were not dictated by ceremony or rules; rather, he was in a state of involuntary ecstasy brought about by the rapture he felt: it was an outer manifestation of a spiritual state. Mevlânâ would even engage in *semâ'* during a funeral, and his followers continued this tradition.

After Mevlânâ

What form did *semâ'* take after Mevlânâ's time? Did people continue to practice it in the same way as Mevlânâ–in spontaneous ecstasy–or did *it* become ceremonial? The old Mevlevîs say that the *Sultân Veled Devri*, which we will discuss later, was established by Sultân Veled, and that the *mukabele* of today was composed by him; they regard Sultân Veled as the *Pîr-i Sanî*, the "Second Master."

Ahmed Eflâkî, who grew up during the time of Sultân Veled and served his son, Ulu Arif Chelebi, from the time he sat on Mevlânâ's post until his death, accompanying him on all his journeys, and writing *Manâkıb-al Ârifîn* upon his order (completed in 754 H., 1353 A.D.), recounts the following story about Sultân Veled:

Sultân Veled was reciting a *rubai* during *semâ'*.[120] It had not rained for a year, and people had asked for the Sultan's prayers. He was praying at the *türbe* when it started to rain, and he and those with him spontaneously began *semâ'*, which they continued, in great joy, all the way back to the *madrasah*.[121]

* * *

While Ulu Arif Chelebi was engaged in *semâ'*, he recited the *rubai* which begins with these lines:

---

[120] *Manâkıb-al Ârifîn,* Vol.II, p. 613.

[121] Ibid., p. 795.

> Those gifted enlightenment move very fast through that door;
> they are lion-hearted, their hands are quite swift…

He then continued on to the *madrasah* while in the midst of *semâ'*.[122]

* * *

In Tabriz, at a gathering of Iltirmiş Hâtûn, attended also by Gazan Hân, again Ulu Arif Chelebi recited a *rubai* during *semâ'*.[123] Later, when he grabbed hold of a shaikh and pulled him into the *semâ'*, he recited a second *rubai*.[124]

* * *

On another occasion, while Ulu Arif Chelebi recited a *rubai* during *semâ'*, he took off his *destâr* and *ferecî* and gave them as gifts to the singers (*gûyendes*).[125]

* * *

While engaged in *semâ'* in the *türbe*, Ulu Arif Chelebi could not contain his ecstasy. Continuing the *semâ'*, he left the *türbe* and went to the *musalla* (the stone table on which the coffin is placed during funeral prayers), and said, "With the intention of doing so for the hidden ones, let's perform the funeral prayer." After the prayer was finished, he announced, "Gazan Hân has died."[126]

* * *

---

[122] Ibid., pp. 840–41.
Onha ki ezon cenab erhordarend…

[123] Ibid., pp. 846–48.

[124] Ibid., pp. 851–52.

[125] Ibid., pp. 856–57.

[126] Ibid., pp. 857–58.

On the evening before the Ramaḍān Eid holiday in 716 H. (1317 A.D.), when Ulu Arif Chelebi was engaged in *semâ'* in Erzurum, he said to Hâce Yakut (the governor of Erzurum), "Your sultan, Olcaytu, has died, but our Sultan does not die. He is always alive, working for His servants and the entire universe. His Sovereignity has no end." He then recited a *rubai* related to this theme.[127]

* * *

In Sinop, once again during *semâ'* he could not contain his ecstasy, and recited a *rubai.*[128]

* * *

While in Konya on a holiday, Chelebi was engaged in *semâ'* with Hayran Emirci, the khalif of Barak Baba and the shaikh of his *dergâh.* He gave his white *külah* (a special hat) to the shaikh to wear, and said, "The next holiday, let us do *semâ'* again together."[129]

* * *

In Amasya, he fell into ecstasy and recited two *rubais*, and had people recite the ghazal of Mevlânâ that begins with the first verse:

> Let's set fire to both melancholy and madness;
> with each breath, let's drink from the sea of blood.

Then, continuing the *semâ'*, he recited yet another *rubai.*[130]

* * *

---

[127] Ibid., pp. 859–60.
[128] Ibid., p. 861.
[129] Ibid., p. 862.
[130] Ibid., pp. 875–79.
Bisuzanim sovda vu cununra
Derashamim her dem movc-i hura

We read that on yet another occasion Chelebi recited a *rubai* during *semâ'*.[131]

* * *

A *semâ'* gathering occured in Tokat and Chelebi could not keep his ecstasy within himself; he became exuberant, and recited two *rubais* in the midst of semâ'.[132]

* * *

In Tabriz, Ahî Ahmed-i Kazzâz arranged a *semâ'* gathering. At the gathering Chelebi became exuberant, took off his hat (*külah*) and placed it on the head of Ahî Ahmed. He then recited this couplet:

> Souls are not held back here; is a hat, or even a head, worth mentioning?
> Look to the Head for the head; receive an enlightening glance.

In thanks, Ahî Ahmed gave some of his clothes to the singers.[133]

* * *

A gift of a white marble fountain from Kütahya had been given to the *dergâh*. While Chelebi was on a journey, someone named Jelâli Kûçek carried the fountain off to his palace in Karaman. When Chelebi returned to the *dergâh* he sent a letter to the governor of Karaman, Emîr Bedreddin Ibrahim Bey,[134] informing him about the situation. Ibrahim Bey dismissed Jelâl from his position, apologized to Chelebi, and had the fountain sent back to Konya on an ox-pulled

---

[131] Ibid., pp. 878–79.
[132] Ibid., pp. 892.
[133] Ibid., pp. 894–95.
Canha diriyg nist chi cay-i kulah u ser
Ser cuy ez seran u binih ser sitan nazar
[134] Ruled during the years 1315–32; died 1356 A.D.

cart. When Chelebi heard that the fountain had been returned, he set out with the *gûyende* (singers and reciters) of the *türbe* to welcome it back. He took off his *ferecî* (ceremonial cloak) and threw it over the fountain. Then they put it back in its place and Chelebi began *semâ'*, reciting this *rubai* of Mevlânâ:

O Self, in whose radiant beneficence
sun, moon, and stars are willing slaves,
all doors have been closed to the poor one seeking refuge,
so that only Your door is open for him.[135]

* * *

In Tokat, there was *semâ'* during a ceremony to mark someone's sitting on the post, during which Chelebi recited Mevlânâ's couplet:

They have beaten the drum of war.
See the mounted Arabian horse, how it is restless and prancing.

Still engaged in *semâ'*, he took hold of two Sufis and threw them down to the floor, reciting a *rubai*.[136]

* * *

While Chelebi was ill, on the last Friday of the month *Dhu'l-Qa'dah* in 719 H. (1320 A.D.), he went to the mosque for Friday prayers. He then went on to the *türbe* and joined the *semâ'* gathering, revealing his ecstasy and reciting a *rubai*.[137]

---

[135] *Manâkıb-al Ârifîn,* Vol.II, pp. 907–08.
Derha heme besteend illa der-i tu
Ta reh nebered garib illa ber-i tu
Iy der kerem u izzet u nur-efshani
Horshid u meh u sitaregan chake-i tu

[136] Ibid., pp. 952–53.
Tabl-i gaza kuftend in dem peyda sheved
Cunbish-i palanii ez feres-i tazii

[137] Ibid., pp. 966–68.

As we can see, during the periods of both Sultân Veled and Ulu Arif Chelebi, *semâ'* remained much the same as it had been in Mevlânâ's time. Neither in the *Divân* of Sultân Veled, nor in his *Mesnevî*, nor in Sipehsâlâr's writings, nor in the *Manâkıb-al Ârifîn* is there any mention of the *naat, taksîm*, *Devr-i Veledî*, the *post* prayer, or *selâms*; nor is there any mention of the *mukabele*. *Semâ'* still took place spontaneously. Somebody would arrange a banquet, and afterwards *kavvâls*, *gûyendes*, *handers and sazendes*–known as *şeyyâds* ("reciters, singers, and musicians")–would begin to sing and play the *rebab*, tambourine, and *ney*. Those who fell into ecstasy would stand for *semâ'*. Sometimes just a single word or action could make a representative of Mevlânâ fall into ecstasy, and he would begin the *semâ'*. *Semâ'* had neither a *chark* nor a *direk* (the turning foot and the fixed foot), and was not something that needed to be learned through a methodology or practice. The writing of *Manâkıb-al Ârifîn* was completed during the time of Ulu Arif Chelebi's son, Shemseddin Emîr Âbid Chelebi. Therefore, at least until the year 754 H. (1353 A.D.), when the writing of this significant resource was completed, there was no *semâ'* ritual in the form of a *mukabele* with ceremonial rules.

The books we have cited were written in the same period as the events they describe, and are based on the accounts of people who lived within that time. They can, therefore, be trusted as complete and factual. In light of them, the fanciful stories recounted in *Macmûat-al Tavârîh-al Mavlaviyya* by id-i Sahîh Ahmed Dede, who died in 1229 H. (1813 A.D.)–four and a half centuries later–appear to be unreliable and of little historical value. Apart from some events that took place in his own time, whatever this author has to say is woven from his own imagination. According to his book, one day, when Mevlânâ was around 65 years old, he was passing by the Karatay Madrasah with his friends and the call to prayer was recited. His friends went inside, and Mevlânâ followed and gave his *salām*. After the prayer, they recited from the Qur'ān and someone gave a sermon, read the *Mesnevî* and chanted the *Ism-i Celâl* (Allāh). Then they recited another *ashir* (a ten-verse section from the Qur'ān), recited a *gülbâng* and *naat*, and played the *ney*. Mevlânâ and his friends then stood up and walked around the *madrasah* three times. Then with three breaks, bowing their heads in greeting at each break, they held a *semâ'*. At the end they recited an *ashir* again during which everybody sat down and listened. Following this, they stood up in celebration and "saw" each other. They prayed for "the owner of the good deed" and the ceremony ended.[138] It is clear that these lines were written with the objective of connecting the *mukabele* as a whole to the time of Mevlânâ, but they are not based on any reliable record.

Within *Sefîne-i Nefîse-i Mevlevîyân*, Sâkıb Mustafâ Dede published the treatise *İşârat-al Başâra*, which he attributed to Jelâleddîn Argun Chelebi. We do not believe this treatise belongs to Jelâleddîn Argun Chelebi,[139] but believe that the treatise was written in the eighth century H. (fourteenth century A.D.) and that it refers to a version of the *mukabele* from that time. The author makes it known that Burhâneddin İlyas Chelebi (the son of Argun Chelebi who died 798 H., 1395–1396 A.D.) practiced *semâ'*.[140] When he mentions Chelebi Salâhaddîn (a *Mesnevîhân* in Konya and one of the grandsons of Shah Melek, son of Emîr Âbid Chelebi who had died in 739 H., 1338 A.D.), he describes *semâ'* gatherings in which the *chelebis* of the highest rank turned in the middle, the other *chelebis* turned around them in a circle, the *khalifs* turned in a second concentric circle, and finally dervishes turned in a third circle. Even in this later period he tells us that ecstasy was essential to *semâ'*.[141]

Among the facts transmitted by Sâkıb Dede, the most significant are some words passed on orally from generation to generation; words which are full of technical terms,[142] but which may be summarized as

---

[138] Konya, Mevlânâ Museum, Book No. 5446, p. 111.

[139] Concerning Jelâleddîn Argun Chelebi and this treatise, please see *Mevlevîhood After Mevlânâ*, Abdülbâki Gölpınarlı, pp. 122–24 and pp. 382–84.

[140] Egypt; Matbaa-i Vahbiyya; 1283; I, p. 369.

[141] Ibid., p.369: "*. . . duhul-i daire-i hareket-i devriyye, mevkuuf-i icâzet-i ruhaniyyet-i Pir kuddise sirruhul-munirdir; hod-be hod meshk ve idmanla mu'tad degildir*"

[142] Ibid., p. 134: "*Menkunlest ki zeyn-ul mahafil-i Mevleviyye ve sem'-ul macami-ul Mevleviyye olan ayin-i hikmet-agin ve erkan-i ibret-beyan ve ādāb-i latafet-maab, mama-i uzama-yi tevhid u marifet olup hush-der dem ve nazar-ber kadem ve sefer der vatan ve halvet der encumen ve yad kerd ve baz gesht ve nigah dasht-i uzama-yi Naksh-bendiyye ve semâ''u safa-yi vecd u hal ve tecerrud-i alayik u teferrud-i emsal ve cezbe-i Zul-celal-i Shamsiyye ve ishkiyye ile memzuc u muhammer adab-i kudema ve sufiyye ve rusum-i suluk-i muluk-i hakiykatle muanven ve mestur olup hala beyn-el ihvan mutedavel olan hurde-i tarikat invaniyle ma'hude harekat ve shekenat-i mustahsene-i isharat-i azim ki*

follows: The *mukabele* which is performed, and the etiquette and *ādāb* which are followed, were received as a spiritual "unveiling" (*kashf*) by Pir Âdil Chelebi, and they have been accepted. Pir Âdil Chelebi was the son of Emir Alim Chelebi, who was the son of Shamsuddin Emîr Âbid Chelebi, who was the son of Sultân Veled. Pir Âdil Chelebi took on the rank of *chelebi* in 825 H. (1421 A.D.), after the death of Arif Chelebi II, who was known as Arif Chelebi the Younger, who was the son of Emîr Âdil Chelebi, who was the son of Ulu Arif Chelebi. Pir Âdil Chelebi held the rank for thirty-nine years, until his death in 865 H. (1460 A.D.). There is no doubt that the reason he was called *Pir* is that he established the ceremony of *mukabele.*

Nevertheless, let us add this:

Abışka Noyan, who was known as the *Kösepeygamber* ("the prophet with little or no beard") came to Konya to visit Sultân Veled during the time of his leadership of the order. They organized a reading of the Qur'ān and "the mysteries" (*tilâvet-i esrar*: possibly referring to reading the *Mesnevî*), and Sultân Veled offered commentaries on spiritual meanings and realities. At this gathering some friends fell into ecstasy and began weeping and crying out loudly. Abıshka asked, "Why are they shouting and weeping?" Sultân Veled replied, "If good news comes to you from the greatest Khan, what will you do? The soldiers in the army of the faithful cry '*Allāhu Akbar!*' When they are fighting against the blasphemers, they cry out loudly to frighten them. Well, this is like that."[143]

As we mentioned previously, Ulu Arif Chelebi and his singers organized a welcome ceremony for the fountain sent back from Karaman. In the *semâ'* gathering in Tabriz, also mentioned earlier, the Qur'ān and *ghazals* are first recited before *semâ'* begins.[144] And again at the gathering of Chelebi, Qur'ān, *Mesnevî* and *ghazals* are

---

ledel-vakifin ilave-i hassa-i reftar-i salikan-i tarikatimizdir; bil-cumle nevbet-i vilāyāt-i Pir Adil'de berahin-i keshfiyye ile istihsan ve istihbabi numayan olmagila tergiyb-i iltizam ve tertib-i gayri-nizam ile tezyin-i cunbish u aram ve tahsin-i reftar u guftar-i ihvan u hullan buyrulup shive-i revish-i pak ve meyve-i menshe-i tabunakleri hasre-tul-urefa ve hayretuz-zurafa olmushtur."

[143] *Manâkıb-al Ârifîn,* II, pp. 818–19.

[144] Ibid., pp. 846–48.

recited first.[145] For the *Mesnevî*, there was a *rahle* ("folding table" on which to place an open book when one is seated on the floor) in the *türbe*,[146] and someone called Sa'adeddîn-i Mesnevîhân was the *Mesnevîhân-i Veledî*.[147] This person, who was one of the narrators, may have been appointed to serve as *Mesnevîhân* during the time of Sultân Veled, and he may have taken that particular title for that reason. It is also possible, however, that he read the *Mesnevî* of Sultân Veled, or oversaw its reading. Sırâceddin-i Mesnevîhân was a *Mesnevîhân* who was praised by Sultân Veled.[148] Sultân Veled gave him his khalifhood, signed his *hilâfet-nâme* ("diploma of khalifhood"), bestowed on him the *ferace*, and sent him to Amasya.[149] With *cherağ* ("guidance"; "light") and *ijâzet* ("permission") given to the khalif, he was authorized to perform *semâ'* rituals.[150] Ulu Arif Chelebi gave khalifhood to Tâjeddîn-i Mesnevîhân and *semâ'* began in Lâdik.[151]

As we can see from the references above, while ecstasy was still essential to *semâ'*, gatherings had begun to become more organized in simple ways. The format consisted of the recitation of the Qur'ān first, then of the *Mesnevî*, then of Mevlânâ's and perhaps also Sultân Veled's *ghazals*, and then commentaries on their meaning. The gatherings included the presence of those who served by offering recitation and singing. We believe that *semâ'* began after these recitations, and ended with another recitation of an *ashir* or perhaps with a *gülbâng*. These practices were all part of the first Mevlevî rituals.

Even after *semâ'* had become ritualized under the name *mukabele*, Dîvâne Mehmet Chelebi (who died near the close of the tenth century H., sixteenth century A.D.) still performed *semâ'* during journeys. The followers of Yûsuf-ı Sîne-Châk (died 953 H., 1546 A.D.) gathered together in Eyüp Sütlüce on the tenth day of Muharrem in 954 H. (1547 A.D.), cooked *ashura*, and then, to let their blood flow for the

[145] Ibid., pp. 878–79.
[146] Ibid., p. 923.
[147] Ibid., p. 979.
[148] İbtidâ-Nâme; *Mesnevî-i Veledî; with the corrections and introduction of Celâleddîn Humâyî;* Çaphâne-i İkbâl-Tehran; 1315.
[149] *Manâkıb-al Ârifîn,* II, p. 880.
[150] Ibid., p. 921.
[151] Ibid., p. 932.

sake of Imām Ḥusayn (grandson of the Prophet), had their heads, arms, and chests cut with shaving knives before performing *semâ'*.[152] Shûrî, a dervish of Yûsuf-ı Sîne-Châk, used to whirl in harmony with any musical instrument he heard playing, and would sometimes engage in *semâ'* even without music.[153] However, these types of *semâ'* were all done outside of the *tekke*. In Mevlevî *tekkes*, *semâ'* had turned into a ceremony, and, through the authority of the rank of *chelebihood*, the *mukabele* was being performed in a consistent style.

Have additions been made to the *mukabele* as time went on? It is impossible for us to make a statement of certainty on this subject. However, one cannot believe that Mevlevîs—who are extremely obedient to the rules of their tradition—would do such a thing casually. Concerning an earlier form of *mukabele*, we have a *mesnevî* of 50 couplets which we can call a treatise in prose, by Dîvâne Mehmet Chelebi. In this *mesnevî*, no mention is made of reciting a *naat*. Actually, the composition of the *naat* was the work of Itrî, who died in 1124 H. (1712 A.D.). According to oral tradition, when Itrî composed this masterful composition, it was so loved by the rank of *chelebihood*, they announced to everyone that it should be sung before the introductory improvization with the *ney* (*taksîm*). In our opinion, after the *mukabele* was established during the time of Pir Âdil Chelebi, the only thing added to the ceremony was the recitation of the *naat*.

---

152 *Mevlevîhood After Mevlânâ*, pp. 124–25.
153 Ibid., p. 211–12.

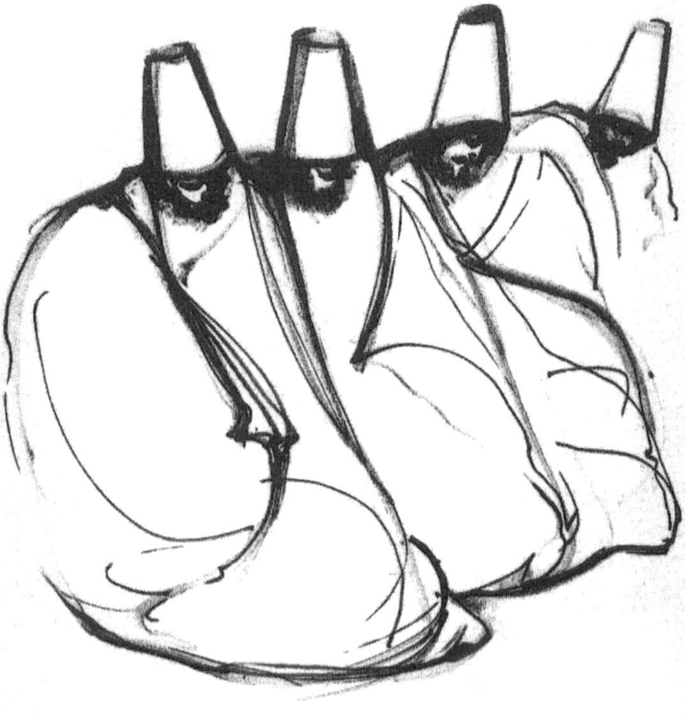

III

Mevlevî Mukabele

Semâ'hâne

S*emâ'hâne* is a compound noun made according to the rules of Persian grammar, which means "house of *semâ'*" or "the place where people perform *semâ'*." Sufi *ṭarīqahs* have a large circular room, which almost always has a niche; this room is called a *tevhidhâne* or *mukabelehâne*, and it is the place where they do *dhikr*. A part of this space was separated for those who would come, sit, and watch the *dhikr*. The place where the Mevlevîs engage in *semâ'* is always called the *semâ'hâne*.

The *semâ'hâne* is a large circular room with a floor made of walnut wood. The floorboards fit very tightly together and the wood gains a luster as though varnished because of years and years of *semâ'*. One goes into the *semâ'hâne*, which is a separate building within the *tekke*, through an outside door which is called *cümle kapısı*. In the area on the right just inside this door, there are shelves to place *pashmaks* (shoes). On the left side, above the separated space for the visitors, one climbs some stairs to enter a modest-sized space with a railing at the front. The front side of this space overlooks the *semâ'hâne*; the *neyzens*, *kudümzens*, *âyinhâns* (those who recite the *âyins*) and the *naathan* (the one who recites the *naat*) are positioned here. This area is called *mutribhâne*, or simply *mutrib*, which means "the place of the musicians." The area surrounding the *semâ'hâne* floor is also separated by a railing, creating a narrow seating area. This is the space for male visitors, called *züvvâr*, who come to watch and enter into ecstasy or a spiritual state, or who simply come out of curiousity or love of the Mevlevî path, or with a fondness for the ritual and music. The floor of this space is covered with rugs and carpets, and is entered by going through the *cümle kapısı* and then turning right. If the *züvvâr* are too numerous for this space, they might also sit in the space on the left side under the *mutrib*, or upstairs next to the *mutrib*. Above the space designated for male visitors, there is a space for female visitors, reached by going through an exterior door and then up some stairs. The front side of this space overlooking the *semâ'hâne* is covered with a thin lattice that rises to the ceiling.

At the front of the *semâ'hâne*, in the space for the *züvvâr*, is the prayer niche and on the right is the pulpit. On the left side, under the same roof but in a space separated from the *semâ'hâne* by a facade coming close to the ceiling, are the *türbe* of the first shaikh of the *dergâh* and the *türbes* of the shaikhs who followed him. The sarchophaguses of the *yatırs*, or saints, are also placed here, covered with large green cloths and embroidered drapes of the finest quality; their *sikkes* and *destârs*, some with and some without the *istiva*, lend a special grandeur and spirituality to the place. Across from the *türbe*, usually in the right corner of the *semâ'hâne* is the *Mesnevî kürsüsü* ("*Mesnevî* platform": an elevated place to read the *Mesnevî*).

One enters the *semâ'hâne* after one passes through the *cümle kapısı* and then through the door which is across from the niche, in front of the low balustrade (*parmaklık*) that separates the visitor area. Above the niche, like the prayer niches in mosques, there is a tablet on which is written a section of *āyāt* 3:37 from the Qur'ān, referring to *al-mihrâb*, or a section from 2:144 which indicates an orientation towards the Ka'bah.

Although the construction is supported by its side walls, the actual place where *semâ'* is performed is under the middle dome supported by columns. Aligned with the niche and at the front of the *semâ'hâne*, the *post* of the shaikh is spread. At a certain place above the *post*, there must always be an inscription that reads, *Ya Hazret-i Mevlânâ*. Beside this, tablets on which are written the names of *Chây Yâr*, the great ones of the religion and the elders of Mevlevîhood, are also hung on the wall in appropriate places. There is an imaginary line down the middle of the *semâ'hâne*, running from the edge of the shaikh's *post* to the middle of the *semâ'hâne* door; this is called the *Hatt-ı İstiva*, and one must never step on this line. The *post* of the shaikh is spread in a way that its center aligns with this line and its edge points towards the door.

Mukabele

This Arabic word means "to meet (face to face)." The Mevlevî ritual is known by this name because, as we shall see, Mevlevîs bow to each other during the *Devr-i Veledî* and look into each other's face, blessing the divine manifestation within each other's essence as they do so. The *ṭarīqahs*–called the *sofu ṭarīqahs* ("conservative orders") by Mevlevîs–follow the way of reaching God by chanting the Divine Names (*Asmāʾ*). Also, in their *dhikr* ceremonies a semicircle is formed in front of the shaikh, therefore their ceremonies are also called *mukabele*.

On the day or night of the *mukabele*, the *meydanjı* puts on his *tennûre* and drapes his *khirka* over his shoulders without putting his arms through the sleeves. At the door of the *semâ'hâne*, he seals his feet and bows his head, and then enters the *semâ'hâne* with his right foot. Without stepping on the *Hatt-ı Istivâ*, he walks towards the *post* of the shaikh. He kneels down in front of the *post*, which is spread upside down on the floor or folded over itself, and he "sees with" the *post* (*görüshmek*). He then puts it on his left shoulder and stands up, holding it with his right hand so that it does not slide down. He walks with small steps to the door of the *semâ'hâne*, turns around, bows his head, and exits. He goes to the chamber of the shaikh and with the *post* still slung on his back he seals his feet and bows his head to the shaikh. By saying, "*Eyvallah!*" the shaikh gives his permission for the *mukabele* to take place. Then the *meydanjı dede*, standing across from the cells and facing the *qiblah*, seals his feet, bows his head, and with a loud voice, stretching the last syllable as much as his breath will allow, shouts, "*Abdeste, tennûreye sala!*" ("Call to ablution and the *tennûre!*"). Then he goes to the *semâ'hâne* and enters there with a *niyâz*, approaches the shaikh's position and spreads out the *post*. Again he kneels down and "sees with" the *post*, and then exits the *semâ'hâne* with a *niyâz*. He approaches the *müezzin dede*, "sees with" him and asks him to recite the call to the prayer (*adhān*).

The *müezzin dede* recites the *adhān* in the garden of the *dergâh*. In the meantime, the *dedes* and the visitors who have come to join the *mukabele* do their ablutions, and the dedes put their *tennûres* over their shoulders and prepare for the *mukabele*. Then it is time for the *ṣalāh* ("ritual prayer").

To put on a *tennûre*—which is kept folded inside out—one holds the shoulders of it with both hands, kneels facing the *qiblah* and recites three *Sūrah al-Ikhlāṣ* (Qur'ān 112) and a *Fātiḥah* (Qur'ān 1) for the spirit of the Blessed Pir. One then "sees with" the *istivâ* on the collar of the *tennûre*, before passing one's head through it. In this way, the *tennûre* which was folded inside out is put on right side out. One then stands up, "sees with" the *elifî nemed*, ties it round one's waist, and checks that the folds of the cloth are distributed correctly. Finally, one drapes one's *khirka* over one's shoulders.

Next, beginning with the *dede* who has the highest rank and longest service, the *meydanjı dede* calls on each cell one by one. He opens the cell door slightly and with a slow, rather soft, low and harmonious voice (lengthening the *Ya* a little and the last syllable), he says, "*Buyrun yâ Hû!*" and without turning the door "into a secret" (*sırlamak*: i.e. "without closing it"), he moves on to the next cell. In this way, he stops by every cell. Those who hear this invitation stand up with a dignified calmness and head towards the *semâ'hâne*. When entering the *semâ'hâne*, there is no specific order based on rank; whoever comes first bows the head and enters right foot first. Once inside, however, one does not sit at the first place one finds empty; according to one's rank, one sits at the appropriate place. Those who will perform the *semâ'* stand with their feet sealed at the right side of the *post* (viewed from the front), below the *Mesnevî kürsüsü* ("platform") on a carpet with wooden skirting surrounding the *semâ'hâne*. The *ser-tabbâh* ("chief cook") stands at the top end of the *kursu*, then the *semâ'zenbashı* ("chief semâ'zen"), and then the *türbedâr dede* ("caretaker of the *türbe*"). At the lower end, the *dedes* in order of rank, and then the sympathizers, take their places. If there is not a large crowd, after the sympathizers, the kitchen souls stand, again in order of rank. If there is a large crowd and this row will not contain the brothers, then the kitchen souls stand on the left side, from the lower end of the *türbe* to the door. If the shaikh has young sons, they sit in line after the kitchen souls in order of age.[1]

[1] The son of a shaikh is called a *shaikh-zâde*. Some say that *shaikh-zâdes* were

After everyone takes their places, the *mutrib heyeti* ("musicians") also enter, but not into the *semâ'hâne* itself. They offer *niyâz* in front of the door that leads to the *semâ'hâne* and go up the stairs on the left. Within the *mutrib*, the *post* of the *neyzenbashı* is on the right, in front of the *türbe*. The post of the *kudümzenbashı* is in front of him, at the side of the *türbe*. Next to the *neyzenbashı*, according to rank, are the *neyzens*, and next to the *kudümzenbashı* is the second *kudümzen*. Amidst these are *halilezens* ("cymbal players") and *âyinhâns* ("singers of the *âyins*"). They all wait standing with their feet sealed. Finally, the shaikh enters wearing a *sikke* with *destâr* on it, his arms inside the sleeves of his *khirka* and clasping his hands together in front of him. The *meydanjı dede* walks a little way behind him, on his right. The shaikh enters through the door of the *semâ'hâne*, stepping with his right foot first, and the *meydanjı dede* follows him. Both of them seal their feet and bow their heads. This means, "*Salām,*" but it is a silent greeting. Those in the *semâ'hâne*, as well as the musicians, all bow their heads at the same time. The shaikh goes directly to his *post* but with slow steps, and stands for the supererogatory *ṣalāh* appropriate to the time. Those in the *semâ'hâne* put their arms through the sleeves of their *khirkas*, and form a standing row for *ṣalāh*.

Meanwhile, the *imām dede* has approached the prayer niche. Among the Mevlevîs, the shaikh does not perform the role of imām, and each *tekke* has its own imām to lead *ṣalāh*.[2] Then the *züvvâr* also make a row behind the imām, and *ṣalāh* begins. After they complete the supererogatory *rak'āt* as in the mosques, one of the musicians

---

positioned just after the *dedes* or even higher than them. But this would be according people status due to birth which is against the spirit of Mevlevîhood. After Mevlânâ, Sultân Veled received instruction from Chelebi Hüsameddin and then Shaikh Kerîmeddîn, recognizing them as guides and presenting them as such. Only after Shaikh Kerîmeddîn did Sultân Veled feel that he had the authority to represent his father and become leader of the lovers of Mevlânâ. The educator of Shaikh Hüseyin Fahreddîn Dede (1911) allocated him a place even lower than the most inexperienced kitchen soul; only after many years, recognizing his ability, did the educator make him sit on the *post* while he himself sat below.

[2] In order to understand why Mevlevî shaikhs do not take on the role of imām, please see *Mevlânâ Celâleddîn*, III Edition, p. 235.

recites three *Sūrah al-Ikhlāṣ* and a *Fātiḥah*. Again, the *müezzin dede* in the *mutrib* recites the *iqamah,* the call to the obligatory *ṣalāh*. The brothers in the first row move up to the shaikh's row, and the ones at the back fill in the next row, and they perform the obligatory *ṣalāh* together. There is nothing different about this *ṣalāh* compared to that performed in a mosque. However, if it is the afternoon *ṣalāh*, after the obligatory *ṣalāh*—or if it is at night and the night *ṣalāh* has been done, after the last supererogatory *ṣalāh* and after the *witr ṣalāh*—the *müezzin* or one of the musicians says, "*Allahumma antas Salām wa minkas salām, tabarakta ya Dhal-Jalāli wal-Ikrām*" ("O my God, You are Peace and from You comes peace, blessed are You, O Possessor of Majesty and Infinite Generosity").

Following this, one of the musicians with a beautiful voice, in a low, mellow tone rather than a melodious one, says "*Fa'lam 'annahū*" ("Know then"—Qur'ān 47:19) and then the *imâm dede*, the shaikh, and all the brothers join in reciting the *kalimāt at-tawḥīd* that is, *Lā ilāha illā Allāh*. Each syllable is stressed and the last is lengthened as long as the breath. The *kalimāt at-tawḥīd* is repeated three times, but in the last two instances *Fa'lam 'annahū* is not included. After the last *kalimāt at-tawḥīd*, the musicians say, "*Muhammedür Rasûlullâhi hakkan ve sıdkaa. Ve salli ve sellim ve bârik alâ es'adi ve eşrefi nûri cemî-il enbiyâi vel mürselîn, vel hamdû billahi rabbil âlemîn,*" and in this way the *dhikr* is completed. They then chant with prayer beads (*tesbih chekmek*) and pray. After the prayer, the shaikh slowly says "*Fātiḥah*" in a loud but mild voice. Immediately, everybody prostrates where they are, entreats, and stands up. The shaikh also "sees with" the place of prostration and stands up. Everyone except the shaikh takes their arms out of their *khirkas* and returns to the positions they were in before the *ṣalāh*. If they are not going to read the *Mesnevî* together, the brothers go back to the positions they took when they first entered the *semâ'hâne*. The shaikh sits on his *post* facing them, takes his place and makes *niyâz* to the *post*. Everyone else also sits and makes *niyâz*. The shaikh opens his arms with his hands turned towards his face, his fingers straight with the little finger and ring finger touching one another, and recites the *Post Duası* ("Sheepskin Prayer").

Reading the Mesnevî

If the *Mesnevî* is going to be read (which, unless there is a valid excuse, is absolutely necessary), as soon as the shaikh says, "*Fātiḥah*," the *meydanjı dede* makes *niyâz* and stands up together with the other souls. He spreads the *Mesnevî seccade* (the rug kept on the *Mesnevî kürsüsü*) on the floor just in front of the *kürsü* with the longer side aligned with it. When the shaikh "sees with" the floor and stands with the brothers, he approaches the *kürsü* without stepping on the *seccade*. The *meydanjı* picks up the *pîsh-tahta* (a small wooden desk used as *rahle*) which is kept leaning against the railing by the *kürsü*. He takes the left arm of the shaikh and helps him up onto the *kürsü*. During this time everyone is standing on their feet, conscious of not turning their backs to the *türbe*. Once on the *kürsü*, the shaikh sits down and "sees with" the *pîsh-tahta*. The brothers in the *semâ'hâne* also sit down and "see with" the floor, facing the *kürsü* and not turning their backs to the *türbe*. While the brothers are sitting down, a knowledgeable *dede* called the *qaari'-i Mesnevî*, which means "the one who reads the *Mesnevî*," who is appointed to this task, sits on the *Mesnevî seccade* facing the *qiblah*. Without turning his back to the *türbe* he makes *niyâz* and "sees with" the floor. Then after the *ʾAʿūzhu/Bismillāh*, he reads the lines from the *Mesnevî* which will be elucidated upon that day. Then after another *ʾAʿūzhu/Bismillāh*, the shaikh repeats the first line that the *qaari'* read and begins an exegesis. Before the commentary, if he wishes, he reads these lines which contain a prayer:

Iy Huda iy fazl-i tu hacet-reva
Batu yad-i hich kes nebved reva
In kader irshad tu bahshidei
Ta bedin bes ayb-i ma pushidei
Katre-i danish ki bahshidi zi pish
Muttasil gerdan be deryaha-yi hish
Katre-i ilmest ender can-i men
Va rehanesh ez heva vez hak-i ten[3]

---

[3] Written with red ink in I. *Tefsîr-i Mâşâallâhu kan*: "O God, the One whose favor permits the frailty of nature! It is not appropriate to associate anything

Sometimes these lines are read instead:

Iy Huda-yi pak-i bi enbaz u yar
Dest gir u curm-i mara derguzar
Yad dih mara suhanha-yi rakiyk
Ki tura rahm avered an iy refiyk
Hem dua eztu icabet hemzitu
Eymeni ez tu himāyāt hem zi tu
Her hata goftim islahesh tu kun
Muslihi tu iy tu sultan-i kuhun[4]

After these couplets, he reads the couplet he wishes to elucidate and begins the exegesis. He ends it with these two couplets:

Inchunin fermud Mevlânâ-yi ma
Kashif-i esrarha-yi kibriya
In ne necmest u ne remlest u ne hab
Vahy-i Hak Allahu a'lem bis sevab[5]

A short *ashir* recited by one of the musicians follows this. After the *ashir*, the *Fātiḥah* is not recited. The shaikh then reads the *Post Duası* ("Sheepskin Prayer").

---

with You. And it is You who have granted this guidance, too. Until now, You have veiled so many shameful deeds of ours. Make the drop of knowledge and understanding that You have granted previously join with its source, the Sea of Knowing. I have a small drop of knowledge in my soul; may You liberate it from the air, from the earth of the body."

[4] Written with red ink in II, *Fil-enreaty*: "O God, who has no equal; who is the Friend and the Beloved! Hold our hand and forgive our mistakes! Make us remember subtle and meaningful words that will make You compassionate towards us, O You who are our Comrade! Prayer comes from You, and the acceptance of prayer. Safety comes from You, and protection, also. If we say anything wrong, please correct our words, O You who are the Sultan of words! The One who corrects is also You!"

[5] "Our Mevlânâ, who explains the secrets of God Most Great, has said as follows: 'This is not knowledge of astrology, nor fortune-telling, nor a dream.' Well, Allah knows best; this is the revelation of theTruth."

Post Duasi ("Sheepskin Prayer")[6]

Bârekallâh ve berekât-ı Kelâmullâhrâ. Evvel azamet-i buzurgvârî-i Huda cetle celâluhû ve amme nevâluhû, kâffe-i enbiyâ-yı izam ve rüsül-i kiram salevâtullâhi ve selâmuhu aleyhim ecmain ervâh-ı tayyibeleriyçün. Hassaten sultân-ül enbiyâ, burhân-ül asfiyâ Hazreti Muhammedinil Mustafâ sallallâhu taâlâ aleyhi ve sellemin pâk, mutahhar, musaffa, azîz ü lâtif ruh-i mukaddes-i şerifleriyçün ve Çhâr yâr-ı güzîn-i bâ safa ve Fâtımatüz-Zehrâ ve Hadîcetül-Kubrâ ve Âyişetus-Sıddıyka ve Hazret-i İmâm Hasan-ı Alî ve Hazret-i İmâm Huseyn-i Veli ve şair Eimme-i sâdât, zurriyât-ı mukaddese-i Rasûlullâh ve Şühedâ-yi deşt-i Kerbelâ ve Âşere-i mübeşşere ve Ezvâc-i mutahhara ve bâkıy Ahsab u Ansâr-ı izam, Tabiin, Tebe'-i tabiîn ve Eimme-i müctehidin-i zevil-ihtiram ervâh-ı mukaddese-i şerîfeleriyçun, rıdvanullâhi taâlâ aleyhim ecmain. Ve mecmû'-ı evliyayı agâh ve ârifan-ı billâh ve alal husûs Hazret-i Sultânel-Ulema ve Hazret-i Seyyid Burhâneddîn-i Muhakkık-ı Tirmizi ve Kutb-ul âşıkıyn, gavs-ül vâsılîn, Sultân-ül kümmelîn Hazret-i Mevlânâ ve Mevlel-ârifîn mettaanallâhu bi envâri sırrıhil yakıyn ervâh-ı mukaddese-i şerifeleriyçun ve Hazret-i Şeyh Şemseddin-i Tebrîzî ve Hazret-i Çelebi Husâmeddîn ve Şeyh Salâhaddin-i Zerkûb-ı Konevi ve Şeyh Kerîmeddin, Sultân ibn-i Sultân Hazret-i Sultân Veled Efendi ve Vâlide-i Sultân ve Muhammed Alâeddin Efendi ve Hazret-i Ulu Arif Efendi ve Âbid Efendi ve Vâcid Efendi ve Bahâeddin Âlim Efendi ve Mazhareddin Âdil Efendi ve Muhammed Âlim Efendi ve Pir Âdil Efendi ve Cemâleddin Efendi ve Husrev Efendi ve Ferruh Efendi ve Sultân-ı Dîvanî Muhammed Efendi ve Bostân Efendi ve Ebû-Bekr Efendi ve Ârif Efendi ve Pir Huseyn Efendi ve Abdülhalim Efendi ve Hacı Bostân Efendi ve Muhammed Sadreddin Efendi ve Haci Muhammed Ârif Efendi ve Haci Ebû-Bekr Efendi ve el-Hâc Muhammed Efendi ve Muhammed Said Efendi ve Sadreddin Efendi ve Fahreddin Efendi ve Mustafâ Safvet Efendi ve Abdülvahid Efendi . . . ervâh-ı tayyibekeriyçün, nevverallâhu merâkıdehum ve caalel cennete mesvâhum ve cemi-i güzeştegân-ı çelebiyân-ı hulefâ ve meşâyih-i fukara, ahibbâ ervâh-ı tayyibbeleriyçün, bakiyler selâmetiyçun, izzetlu, faziketlu çelebi efendimizin selâmetiyçun, asâkir-i müslimîn ve huccâc-ı Beytullâhül-Haram selâmetiyçün ve güzeştegân-ı şair turuk-ı aliyye ervâhiyçün, şarkan ve garben kâffe-i mü'minin ü mü'minât ve erbâb-i hukuk

[6] For a complete translation see: https://www.dar-al-masnavi.org/golpinarli-2.html

ve aşâb-ı hayrat ervâhiyçun ve bu meclis-i şerifte hâzır olan ihvanin dünyevi ve uhrevi murâdât-ı hayriyyeleri hâsıl olmaklığıyçün, vakt-i şerif hayrı, hayırlar fethi, şerler defi, niyâzlar kabulü, murâdât husûlü, demler, safâlar izdiyâdı ve Hak taâlânın aziz rızâ-yı şerifiyçün celle ve alel Fatita. Rûh-ı pür fütûh-ı Hazret-i idüs-sakaleynrâ salevat: Allahümme salli alâ idina Muhammedin ve alâ âlihi ve sahbihi ve sellim. Azamet-i Hudârâ tekbâr: Allahu Ekber! Allahu Ekber! Lâ ilahe illallâhu vallâhu ekber Allahu ekber ve lillâhil hamd. Assalâtu vesselâmu aleyke yâ rasûlullâh, assalâtu vesselâmu aleyke yâ Habiballâh, assalâtu vesselâmu aleyke yâ nûre Arşillâh assalâtu vesselâmu aleyke yâ idel evveline vel âhırin ve şef'-al müznibîn ve selâmün alel mürselin velhamdü lillâhi Rabbil-âlemin.[7]

After the *Post Duası*, the shaikh "sees with" the *rahle* and steps down from the *kürsüsü*. While he "sees with" the *rahle*, everyone makes *niyâz* to the floor, stands up, and returns to their place to stand and wait. The *meydanjı* "sees with" the *Mesnevî sejjade*, and puts it back onto the *kürsü*. When the shaikh returns to his place, he sits down and makes *niyâz* to his *post*. The brothers (*ihvan*) sit in unison with the shaikh and make *niyâz* to the floor. If they have not read the *Mesnevî*, the shaikh sits on the *post* after the ritual prayer, makes *niyâz* to the floor together with the brothers, and reads the *Post Duası*.

When the *Post Duası* finishes, the *naathân* in the *mutrib* recites the *naat* composed by Itrî. The *naat* begins with "*Yâ Hazret-i Mevlânâ, Hak Dost!*" When the *ism-i Pir* ("name of the Pir") is mentioned, everyone bows their heads along with the shaikh, and when the word *Dost* is pronounced, they slowly raise their heads. The *naat* is listened to in respect and awe (*huzû' ve huşû'*). During its recital people usually close their eyes, due to the pleasure that arises within. To make a sound following the recital, to say "Ah!" or cry or sigh loudly, is absolutely forbidden; each soul has been warned previously by his *dede* not to make such a sound.

After the *naat*, the *kudümzenbashı* beats the *kudüm* with *lâ-re-lâ-re* notes. The *neyzenbashı*, or a *neyzen* chosen by the *kudümzenbashı*, begins the *taksîm* in the same *makam* as the *âyin* that will later be performed. He visits other *makams* that complement this *makam*, and at the end

---

[7] *Evrâd-i Mavlaviyya*, 1283 edition; *hashiye*: marginal note, pp. 31–32.

of the *taksîm*, which does not last very long, he returns to the *makam* of the *âyin* and another ney accompanies him with *dem* sounds. Immediately after the *taksîm* ends, the *peshrev* composed according to the rhythm of *Devr-i Kebîr* begins. The *peshrev* begins with the *kudümzen-bashı* beating the *kudüm* with drum sticks (*zahme*). At the first beat of the *zahme* , the shaikh and those in the *semâ'hâne* all say "Allāh" inwardly, forcefully strike their hands upon the floor, and stand up. This stroke is called the *Darb-ı Jelâli*: "Stroke for the sake of the *İsm-i Jelâl* (Allāh)," the 'Slap of Glory.'" The word *Jelâli* is also a reference to blessed Mevlânâ. Among the musicians, the *neyzens* also stand up at this point. Only the *kudümzens* and the *halîlezens* remain seated.

Devr-i Veledî ("Sultân Veled Cycle")

The shaikh comes to the front of the *post* and bows his head, and everyone bows with him. Then, without turning his back to the *semâ'hâne*, the shaikh turns right and leads a slow walk round the main part of the *semâ'hâne* in a halting, rhythmic gait. They walk following the rhythm of the *peshrev*: having stepped with the right foot, the left foot follows but pauses midway to allow the toes to rest briefly on the floor before moving fully forward. The next step sees the right toes do the same. When the shaikh has progressed three steps away from the *post*, the person behind him stops near the *post* and seals his feet, bows his head, and without stepping on the *Hatt-ı Istivâ* steps first with his right foot then his left to the other side of the *post*. Without turning his back to the *post*, he then turns to face the other way, seals his feet, and stops. The person behind him comes to the *post*, and the two souls look into each other's faces—especially between the eyes and the eyebrows—as they put their right hands on their hearts within their *khirkas,* and bow their heads with sealed feet. The one in front, without turning his back to the *semâ'hâne*, then turns around to follow the one who preceded him, walking in the same manner. In this way, each soul bows their head to another soul in front of the *post* and makes *niyâz jemâl-jemâle* ("beauty to beauty" or "face to face"), blessing the Divine Breath in the human being and the manifestation of the maturity of Absolute Being. The shaikh and those following him stop one step before the sarcophagus of the greatest shaikh in the *türbe*, and in honor of his memory and all those in the *türbe*, bow their heads. At the far side, one step before the door of the *semâ'hâne* which is directly opposite the *post*, they stop again and bow their heads. During this bow, they do not turn to face one another. The one who bows his head opposite the *post* steps forward with his right foot, and, avoiding stepping on the *Hatt-ı Istivâ*, continues to walk following the tempo. On the other side, one does not bow one's head when passing the *türbe*. When the shaikh comes to the right of the *post* according to his perspective (which is to the left according to the perspective of the *post*), he stops. The *nevniyâz* who has the lowest rank and is the newest member, is in front of him. In this way, the representative of the Path and the newest member, often a child or young enough to be called so, bow their heads to each other. This completes the first *devr*, or cycle, and the second *devr* is performed in the same way. During the third *devr*, the souls walk a little more quickly and the last one in the line moves away from the *post* without waiting for the shaikh. He bows his head, turns around and continues walking–because when this last *devr* is completed, the shaikh will be sitting on the *post*. At the same time, without letting others notice, the *semâ'zens* who are taking their places loosen the *tıyg-bend*, or wool string, that they tied to the *tennûre* a little below their waist (to pull the *tennûre* upwards so that it did not brush the floor). When they get to their places, again without letting others notice, they "see with" it (*görüshmek*) and place it on their breasts.

The walk in the *Devr-i Veledî* is a refined art requiring great skill; this is the real *mukabele*. One who knows the music and can express the elegance of a Mevlevî walks with graceful dignity in time with the tempo. Doubtless, the poet who composed the following couplet in Farsi was referring to this walk during the *Devr-i Veledî*:

Mestane eda naz u revish Mevleviyane
Bir mevhibedir dad-i Huda Mevleviyane

They look drunk, these Mevlevîs, yet so poised and beguiling (*naz*)!

It's a paradox gifted by God just for the Mevlevîs!

During the most recent era, we can say that there was no Mevlevî who could walk like the shaikh of Bahariye, Büyük Nazif Efendizâde Shaikh Huseyn Fahreddîn Dede (1329 H., 1911 A.D.). We have heard from our elders that Abdülvâhid Chelebi (1325 H., 1907 A.D.) said, "Ah! My shaikh! I wish my rank permitted me to walk behind you during the *Devr-i Veledî* so I could try to imitate your steps and your posture." During the *Devr-i Veledî*, the ability to pay attention so that the space in between the *semâ'zens* remains the same, to be conscious of the steps of the *semâ'zen* in front of one, taking the same step in the same style at the same time, and keeping the same posture during the entire walk, really depends on both familiarity with the music and having a feel for what it really means to be a Mevlevî. During the *Devr-i Veledî* the shaikh and the *sâliks* inwardly chant the *Ism-i Celâl* (Allāh).

In Mevlânâ's *türbe* in Konya, which is called the *Huzur* ("Presence") or *Huzûr-ı Pir* ("Presence of the Master"), the *semâ'hâne* is opposite the chamber where Mevlânâ lies, and one accesses it through the large archway on the left of the *türbe*. We feel we must mention that the Presence, the *Chelebi Makam* ("Station of the *Chelebi*"), the *Mesnevî kürsüsü*, and the *Sultân Veled Devri* all have an exceptional character when compared to other *dergâhs*. Inside the *semâ'hâne*, the *Mesnevî* and the *naathan* are positioned in a space to the right. Farther inside–on the right as one enters from the Presence– is a large space for visitors, with downstairs reserved for male *züvvâr* and the upstairs for women. The *post* of the *Chelebi* is spread out facing the Presence. Below this on the left, towards the space for the *züvvâr*, are respectively the places of the *tarikatchi*, *Mesnevîhân*, *ashchıbashı*, *türbedâr* of Mevlânâ, and the *türbedârs* of Shams and Âteshbâz. Behind them is the *mutribân* ("musician's area"). The *dedes*, the *matbâh janları* ("kitchen souls"), and the sympathizers stand in front of the *züvvâr*, but if it is very crowded, the *matbâh janları* sit on the left side of the *semâ'hâne* in front of the *masjid* wall. During the *Devr-i Veledî*, the *mukabele* is not oriented around the *post* of the shaikh, but rather around the Presence. One passes by the shaikh's *post* with a bow.

Semâ' and Selâms

During the third cycle of the *Devr-i Veledî*, when the shaikh arrives near the *post*, the *peshrev* ends and a ney *taksîm* ("improvisation") begins. This *taksîm* lasts until the shaikh is seated on his *post*. When the shaikh is seated the recitation of the *âyin* begins, and everybody bows their heads together at the same time as the shaikh. The *semâ'zens* hold the collars of their *khirkas* with the finger tips of their right hands and "see with" the *khirkas* (*görüshmek*). They lift the *khirkas* upwards a little, take them off, shake them lightly, and without turning their backs, turn to fold them in three so that the lower part is on the floor and they might be held by the collar when picking them up again. In such a way they are left on the rug where they sit. This movement is done suddenly and briskly. The *semâ'zens* are then left in their *destegüls* and *tennûres*, and with the right arm uppermost they cross their arms over their chests and place their hands on their shoulders, fingers straight but with a little space between them. In this way, the elbows come to chest level, and the hands and the fingers grasp the back of the shoulders; the feet are sealed. All the *semâ'zens* have now revealed their *tennûres*; only the *semâ'zenbashı* keeps his *khirka* on his shoulders.

The shaikh steps towards the front of his *post*, he bows his head and everyone bows with him. The *semâ'zenbashı* puts his arms through the sleeves of his *khirka* and approaches the shaikh. He stops before the *Hatt-ı Istivâ*, bows his head to the shaikh, whose hands are just a little outside of his *khirka*, and "sees with" the shaikh's right hand which is uppermost. Then the shaikh bends down and kisses the *semâ'zenbashı's sikke*. This means that the shaikh gives his permission for the *semâ'*. After "seeing with" the shaikh, on the left side of the *post* (as one faces it), and at a distance that will permit *semâ'zens* to pass to the outer circle, the *semâ'zenbashı* seals his feet, bows his head, and remains standing. The *semâ'zens* bow their heads along with him. Following this, the *semâ'zens* begin to walk one by one, stepping with their right foot first. As each one comes before the shaikh, he stops before the *Hatt-ı Istivâ*, bows his head and "sees with" the hand of the shaikh, who kisses his *sikke*. If the approaching *semâ'zen* is of the required ability, the *semâ'zenbashı* (who is standing with his face towards the

the shaikh and the *post*) pulls his right foot backwards, which means that the middle circle is open and he should take a place there. The *semâ'zen*, beginning with his right foot, takes three short steps towards the center and begins *semâ'*. If the *semâ'zen* is not as skilled, the *semâ'zenbashı* moves his right foot towards the center and forward, informing him that he deems it appropriate for him to perform *semâ'* in the outer circle. Then the *semâ'zen* takes three steps towards the outer edge and enters *semâ'* there. To point at a place with the head or hand, or to say something even in a whisper, is absolutely not allowed; such an act is disrespectful and breaches the rules of *ādāb*.

So that the space will be open for those who follow him, the first *semâ'zen* to enter the *semâ'* must move forward quickly while turning so that eventually he is nearby the *semâ'zen* who has yet to enter the *semâ'*, who is still approaching the presence of the shaikh. After the last *semâ'zen* enters the *semâ'* in the same fashion, the *semâ'zenbashı* bows to the shaikh and begins to direct the *semâ'* from within the *semâ'hâne*, following the path of the *semâ'zens*. If there is a *semâ'zen* who is not moving forward, the *semâ'zenbashı* approaches him. When the *semâ'zen* sees his shadow, he begins moving forward. If someone has moved too far and his *tennûre* is in danger of hitting the person in front, the *semâ'zenbashı* walks between them and directs the one at the back to go backwards and the one at the front to go forwards. The *semâ'zenbashı* always bows his head one step before the *Hatt-ı Istivâ* and passes over it without stepping on it. He should not direct the *semâ'* from outside the circle, and he must be especially careful that the arms of the *semâ'zens* do not hit his face or *sikke*.

As the *semâ'zen* turns counter-clockwise while doing the *chark* ("turn"), he drags his *direk* ("left leg") along the floor backwards and steps with the right. *Semâ'* possesses a quality that is impossible to describe exactly. It is impossible to do so because, although the truth of the ecstasy is the same for everyone, the pleasure that one feels and the state one acquires vary according to one's temperament. However, we can establish a few principles. First of all, *semâ'* is to offer oneself to the *âyin* that is being played and sung, giving oneself to its harmony and timing one's movements with it. But this happens spontaneously and it comes from the heart. Each time the *semâ'zen* begins the *chark*, he says, "Al-" and when he steps on the floor again he says, "-lāh," thereby completing the *Ism-i Jelâl*. In this way, he inwardly chants the *Ism-i Jelâl* in harmony with the ceremony. After the *semâ'zen* begins to turn he opens his arms. The forearms move down from the shoulders to the chest, extending both arms upward. The right hand is opened upwards as if in supplication, the fingers together, except for the thumb. The left hand is turned downwards, fingers a little bent. The *semâ'zen's* head tilts to the right; his face looks towards his left arm and fingers. The eyes are half closed, so everywhere is somewhat blurred. While repeating the *Ism-i Jelâl*, he gazes on contingent existence as if in a dream, knowing that the Truth beyond this dream is Absolute Existence. He is lost in ecstasy; he is in the realm of annihilation. But as the *dedes* say: "The feet of the *semâ'zen* can see." Without any trouble, he can sense the presence of the one in front of him and the one behind him, and he moves without brushing his *tennûre* or arms against another. In this sense, he is also in a state of sobriety. The one engaged in *semâ'* reaches annihilation from this state of sobriety and experiences multiplicity in unity and unity in multiplicity. It is quite common that he sheds tears quietly and obliviously; there is no end to their taste. His heart beats to the *Ism-i Jelâl*, his footsteps move with it. The voice he hears is His Voice; his journey is from himself to Himself. Free from vain posturing, his ecstacy and rapture belong to the Self. When the late Hakki Dede, one of the Bahariye *dedes*, did *semâ'*, he became so ecstatic that he did not even hear the *selâmbashı*. Tears dripping from his beard washed his *destegül*. The *semâ'zenbashı* approached him and tapped his foot (against the floor) to warn him of the *selâmbashı* ("beginning of the *selâm*"), but Hakki Dede didn't even hear it. Eventually, the *semâ'zenbashı* hugged Hakki Dede, allowing him to turn a few times; then sobbing deeply, Dede would come to himself and stop.

* * *

Reflections on the opening of the arms

Some *semâ'zens* do the *semâ'* for a while before opening their arms. They slowly lift their arms with their hands opposite each other and pointing downwards, touching their bodies until they reach their shoulders. Still pointing downwards and opposite each other, the hands rise to the head and only then are the arms fully opened. The late poet İbrahim Zuhuri Dede, who had a cell (*hüjre*) in the Bahariye, opened his arms like this and taught along these lines. There are also those who touch their hands (again pointing downwards and opposite each other) against their sikkes and do the *semâ'* for a while in this position before opening their arms. However, I suspect that these are styles borrowed from *Bektâshihood*, because the *niyâz* of one *Bektâshi* branch is as follows: elbows are opened out from the body and hands rest on the chest as fingers are uplifted. Again, some *dedes* wouldn't lift their arms until they reached the shoulders; they stayed in the *niyâz* position while their hands were lower than their shoulders with the fingers spread–as we mentioned before. This position is a form of *niyâz* from yet another Bektâshi branch. However, as these kinds of opening styles would ruin the uniformity of the ceremony, they should not be preferred or even tolerated. For example, the *semâ'zen* who has made *niyâz* in front of the shaikh might have already opened his arms while the arms of the *semâ'zen* in front of him are still at his chest, or the arms of the one before him are at the edge of his *sikke.* To those who tolerate these irregularities in the name of "joy" or "temperament," we must reply with these words of the *erens*: "Spill blood, but don't violate the law!"

* * *

When the ceremony reaches the point called the *selâmbashı* ("beginning of the *selâm*"), the *semâ'zens* must pause and the ritual slows its momentum. At that moment the *semâ'zens* stop where they are, in a position that faces the *post.* As they come to a halt, they bring their arms back to the first *niyâz* position. After glancing upwards, they seal their feet and close their eyes, and in this way are able to keep from getting dizzy. The *semâ'zens* who are next to each other shuffle closer and lean against each other's shoulders, and this helps them to avoid falling over. In this way, groups of two, three, or four *semâ'zens* leaning against each other are formed here and there around the *semâ'hâne.* If there is a *semâ'zen* who has fallen into ecstasy and has not heard the *selâmbashi*, the *semâ'zenbashı*, without lifting the heel of his foot, taps lightly on the floor with the tip of his toe to get his attention. At the moment when the *selâm* begins, in order not to end up in front of the *post*, each *semâ'zen* keeps on turning for a while if they are near to it. After the *semâ'zen* in front of him proceeds, the one closest to the *post* traces almost a semi-circle in front of it–that is, he turns very fast towards the center while passing by the *post*. This is another tradition within the *semâ'* ceremony.

In the first *devr* after the last *semâ'zen* enters the *semâ'*, the shaikh bows his head and goes behind the *post*, and then steps onto the *post*. At the *selâmbashi* ("beginning of each *selâm*" or "cycle of turning"), he walks out from behind the post, bows his head, and everyone bows with him at the same time.

After the *Devr-i Veledî*, while the shaikh proceeds from his post and makes *niyâz*, he silently says in Arabic words which translate as follows:

Turn in the circle of true existence.
Be in harmony with your capacity,
with your created nature.
Be in active submission.

كُونُوا دائِرَةً عَلىٰ وُجُودِكُم وَعَامِلَةً عَلي شَاكِلَتِكُمْ

When the first cycle (of turning) ends and the shaikh comes forth from the post, while he is bowing, again he silently recites in Arabic:

May Allāh's peace and wellbeing be upon you
O beloved ones who whirl in the circle of love,
May He make your listening and your intention sound.
May He bring you safely
to the center of true beginning.

سَلامُ اللهِ عَلَيْكُمْ اَيُّهَا الْدّائِرُونَ فِىْ دائِرَةِ الْمَحَبَّةِ سَلَّمَ اللهُ اسْماعِكُمْ وَنِيّاتِكُمْ وَأَوْصَلَكُمْ اِلَى
اَلْمَبْدَاءِ اَلْحَقيقْيِّ بِاَلْسَّلامَةِ

Then the shaikh returns to the *post*, and again he bows, and everyone bows together with him. Before the beginning of the *selâm*, from the right side of the post (as one is facing it), the *semâ'zenbashı* who has been at the head of the *semâ'zens* walks to the front of the *post* and bows to the shaikh, as he did at the beginning of the first cycle; however, he does not kiss the hand of the shaikh a second time. Together with the *semâ'zenbashı*, everyone bows again. After the *semâ'zenbashı* takes his place, the *semâ'zens* come one by one just as they did for the first cycle (but without kissing the shaikh's hand), bow, and enter the *semâ'*. As with the first *cycle*, the *semâ'zenbashı* indicates a place to each *semâ'zen*. After the last *semâ'zen* enters the *semâ'*, the *semâ'zenbashı* makes *niyâz* to the shaikh and begins his task of walking among the *semâ'zens*. This *selâm*, which is after the first cycle, is known as the first *selâm*.

After the second cycle, when the *selâm* begins, everyone stands in place as they did before. The shaikh comes forth from his post, bows his head, and recites these words silently within:

May Allāh grant you total soundness
O travelers on the Way of Love and Friendship.
May the Beloved remove the veils from your eyes
that you may see the secrets of turning and of the true center.

سَلامُ اللهِ عَلَيْكُمْ اَيُّهَا الْسَّائِرُونَ فى طَرِيقِ المَوَدَّةَ وَالخُلَّةِ وَكَشْفَ عَنْ بَصيرَتِكُمُ الغِشَاوَةَ
حَتّٰي تَرَوْنَ اَسْرارِ الدَّوْر وَالمَركَزِ الحَقيقيْ

This is known as the second *selâm*. The *semâ'zenbashı,* who is now at the head of the *semâ'zens*, leads them as they bow towards the shaikh who has returned to his post and who also bows towards them. He then walks toward the shaikh and bows to him again. The *semâ'zens* make *niyâz* together with the *semâ'zenbashı*. Again the *semâ'zenbashı* walks to his place and makes *niyâz*, and the *semâ'zens* enter the third cycle. When this cycle finishes, again the shaikh proceeds from his *post* and silently recites these words:

The peace of Allāh upon you
O lovers and truthful ones,
Your turning has become complete.
Your inmost souls have become ripened.
Allāh has made you ones who have attained
To the Truth of Certainty.

سَلامُ اللهِ عَلَيْكُمْ اَيُّهَا العَاشِقُونَ وَالصَّادِقُونَ تَمَّتْ اَدْواركم وَطَابَتْ اَسْرارَكُمْ وَجَعَلَكُمْ
الواصِلينَ اِلى حَقيقَةِ اليَقينْ

Everyone bows together with the shaikh for this third greeting (*selâm*). Then everyone enters the *semâ'* as they did before. This cycle is the fourth and final part, and it has a special feature compared to the other three. The *semâ'zenbashı* does not direct anybody to the center; instead everyone goes to the outer circle. When the first *semâ'zen* bows to the shaikh and begins *semâ'*, the *semâ'zen* moves quickly around towards the right side of the shaikh, and starts turning on the spot in the right corner of the *semâ'hâne*. If there are many *semâ'zens*, that first *semâ'zen* holds the *direk* just to the right side of the *post*, without coming too close to it, and does *semâ'* there. The *semâ'zens* who follow him hold the *direk* with enough space between each other so that their *tennûres* do not collide. After the last *semâ'zen* enters the *semâ'*, the *semâ'zenbashı* makes *niyâz* to the shaikh and returns to his initial position, where he stands with his feet sealed (*mühr-pây*). The reason the *semâ'zenbashı* does not walk or direct anyone to the middle is that the shaikh will also enter the *semâ'* during this cycle. After the *semâ'zenbashı* returns to his place, the shaikh bows and grasps the right side of his *khirka* with his left hand and brings it over to the left side; with his right hand, he holds the right collar of his *khirka* near the shoulder, his palm and thumb over the collar and his fingers wrapped round the inside. In this way, he begins the *semâ'* by slightly opening the *khirka* at chest level and, walking directly to the center under the chandelier, holds *direk* there. That is the middle of the *Hatt-ı Istivâ* and the center of the *semâ'hâne*. This place is also called the *kutup noktası* ("polar point"); it is the place of the *makam chelebisi*, the *chelebi* who represents Mevlânâ and his path. We can also say that it is the place of the pole (*qutb*) who is the inheritor and receiver (*mazhar*) of *Hakıykat-i Muhammediyye*, the Truth of Muḥammadhood. The shaikh whirls here as a deputy or representative for him. In the final part when the *âyin* ends, the *saz semâ'* (an instrumental form of Mevlevî music) begins, followed by the *taksîm* ("improvisation"). The *semâ'* of the shaikh is called the *post semâ'* and it is very slow. During this phase, the *taksîm* of the solo ney mixes with the creaking, padding sounds of the feet of the *semâ'zens* on the wooden floor and the rustling sounds of the *tennûres*; out of this, a harmony is formed which is so pleasing that one cannot finds words for it. While the shaikh slowly returns to his *post*, the ney *taksîm* also winds down. The arrival of the shaikh at his *post* and the ending of the *taksîm* is simultaneous, and immediately the *mutrib* begin the recitation of the *ashir*, starting with the *ʾAʿūzhu/Bismillāh*. The *semâʾzens* who hear the *ʾAʿūzhu/Bismillāh* stop where they are, prostrate on the floor, "see with" it, and then sit with their heads bowed. Their hands rest on their shoulders as they did when they first entered the *semâʾ*.

Within this last cycle, especially if there are many *semâʾzens*, some of the old *dedes* and the *nevniyâz* do not enter the *semâʾ*; instead they put their *khirkas* on their shoulders, seal their feet and stand in place during the *semâʾ*. The task of these souls, together with the *semâʾzen-bashı*, is to drape the *khirkas* of the kneeling *semâʾzens* over their backs. They take the *khirka* from the floor, "see with" it, and then put it on the back of the *semâʾzen*; the *semâʾzen* then "sees with" the collar of the *khirka* and puts it on. The ones who drape the *khirkas* do not turn their backs to the *semâʾhâne* as they quickly perform this service. Then they also go to their places to sit down, make *niyâz* to the floor, and begin listening to the *ashir*. Everyone takes a seat wherever they happen to be at the end of the cycle, not where they were in the beginning; so the *khirkas* that are placed on their shoulders may not be their own. After the *mukabele*, the souls take back their own *khirkas* from one another. This last cycle is sometimes inadvertently referred to as "the fourth *selâm*"; actually, because the *selâms* are made after the first, second, and third cycles, *semâʾ* has three *selâms* (the moments of greeting when upon the shifting of the music the shaikh steps forward in greeting and offers a prayer); the fourth cycle completes the *semâʾ*.

The *ashir* does not last long because the *semâʾzens* are perspiring from their exertion and may need to put on fresh clothes. Here, let's repeat: it is not appropriate to make a noise, show excitement, sigh, groan, or say, "Allāh" while the *ashir* is being recited. Everyone remains self-contained and silently listens to the *ashir* in an ecstatic state. While the one who recites the *ashir* from the mutrıb says, "*Subḥāne Rabbike Rabbil-ʿizzati ʿammā yasifūn. Wa salāmun ʿalal-Mursalīn. Walḥamdu lillāhi Rabbil-ʿālamin*,"[8] the *dua-gû dede* prostrates

[8] *Limitless in His glory is thy Sustainer, the Lord of almightiness, [exalted] above*

and then stands; he puts his arms through the sleeves of his *khirka* and bows his head, half facing the shaikh and close to the shaikh's right-hand side. Bringing his open hands together with fingers straight, he recites the prayer with *lahn-ı mahsusi.*

Dua-gû Duası

Bârekâllâh ve berekât-ı Kelâmullâhrâ. Semâ'râ, safârâ, vefârâ, vecdü hâlât-ı merdân-ı Hudârâ. Evvel azamet-i buzurgî-i Huda ve risâlât-ı rûh-ı pâk-i Hazret-i Muhammed Mustafârâ. Ve Çhâr Yâr-ı güzîn-i Habîbullâhrâ. Ve Hazret-i İmâm Hasan-ı Alî ve Hazreti İmâm Huseyn-i Velî ve Şühedâ-yı deşt-i Kerbelârâ. Ve evliyâ-yı agâh ve ârifân-ı billâh, alel husûs Hazret-i Sultânel-ûlemâ ve Hazret-i Seyyid Burhâneddîn-i Muhakkık-i Tirmizî, Kutbül-ârifîn, gavsül-vâsılîn Hazret-i Hudâvendgârrâ. Ve Hazret-i Şeyh Şemseddin-i Tebrîzî ve Çelebi Husâmeddîn ve Şeyh Salâhaddîn-i Zer-kûb-ı konevî ve Şeyh Kerîmüddîn, Vâlide-i Sultânrâ ve Sultân ibni Sultân Hazret-i Sultân Veled Efendi. Ve Hazret-i Ulu Arif Efendi ve Âbid Efendi ve Vâcid Efendi ve Bahâeddîn Alîm Efendi ve Mazhareddin Âdil Efendi ve Muhammed Âlim Efendi ve Arif Efendi ve Pîr Âdil Efendi ve Cemâleddîn Efendi ve Husrev Efendi ve Ferruh Efendi ve Sultân-ı Dîvânî Muhammed Efendi ve Bostân Efendi ve Ebûbekr Efendi ve Arif Efendi ve Pîr Huseyn Efendi ve Abdülhalîm Efendi ve Hacı Bostân Efendi ve Hacı Muhammed Arif Efendi ve Hacı Ebûbekr Efendi ve el-hâc Muhammed Efendi ve Muhammed Saîd Efendi ve Sadreddîn Efendi ve Fahreddîn Efendi ve Mustafâ Safvet Efendi ve Abdülvâhid Efendi . . . râ. Ve sair çelebiyân-ı hulefâ ve meşâyih-i fukarâ-yı mâzîrâ. Ve mezîd-i hayât-ı çelebiyân-ı hulefâ ve meşâyih-i fukarâ-yı bâkıyrâ. Ve alel husûs pîşevâ-yı erbâb-ı tarikat ve cedd-i buzurgvâr-ı hakıykat selâmet-i Hazret-i Çelebi Efendirâ. Ve mansûr u muzaffer şuden-î asâkir-i dîn-i İslam ve mahkûr u münhezim şuden-i a'dâ-yı dîn-i dûzah-encâmrâ. Ve selâmet- i huccâc-ı Beytullâhrâ. Ve rûh-ı revân-ı bânî-i in dergâh (Dergâhın kurucusuyla o zamânâ dek geçen şeyhlerin adları, "Dede Efendirâ" diye anılır). Ve Safâ-

---

anything that men may devise by way of definition! And peace be upon all His message-bearers! And all praise is due to God alone, the Sustainer of all the worlds! (Qur'ān 37:180–82, Muhammad Asad, *The Message of the Qur'ān*, The Book Foundation, 2003.)

yı vakt-i dervîşân, hâzırân, gaaibân, dûstân, muhibbân, ez şark-ı âlem tâ be gârb-ı âlem ervâh-ı güzeştegân-ı kâffe-i ehl-i îmânrâ. Ve rızâ-yı Hudârâ Fâtihatül Kitâb berhânîm azîzan.

After the *Fātiḥah* is recited, the *duajı dede* ("prayer" *dede*) recites the following:

> *Azamet-i Hudârâ tekbîr: Allahu ekber Allahu ekber, lâ ilahe illallâhu vallâhu ekber, Allahu ekber ve lillâhil hamd. Assalâtu vesselâmu aleyke yâ Rasulallâh, assalâtu vesselâmu aleyke yâ Habîballâh, assalâtu vesselâmu aleyke yâ nûre Arşillâh, assalâtu vesselâmu aleyke yâ idel evveline vel âhirin ve şefi'-al müznibîn ve selâmûn alel mürselîn vel hamdü lillâhi rabbil-âlemîn.*

After this, the shaikh says "*Fātiḥah*", makes *niyâz* on the *post*, and stands up; everyone does likewise, following the shaikh's lead by prostrating, making *niyâz* and standing up. If there is a tomb (*türbe*) in the *semâ'hâne*, the shaikh makes a half-turn towards it, bows his head (*bash kesmek*), raises his hands, and recites *Sūrah* 10:62 slowly in a solemn voice but without melody:

> *Eûzü billahi mineşşeytanir racîm; Bismillâhir rahmânir rahim. Elâ inne evliyâallâh, lâ havfun aleyhim ve lâ hum yahzenûn. Sadakallâhul azîm ve sadaka rasûlihil kerîm ve nahnü alâ zâlike mineşşâhidîn eşşâkirînel âmînin, veihamdü lillâhi rabbil-âleminel fatiha.*

After the *Fātiḥah* is recited, on his *post* he turns toward the *semâ'hâne*, and slowly says the following:

> *Ervâh-ı tayyibeleri şâd u hândan ve berekât-ı rûhâniyyet-i aliyyeleri ihsân oluna. Dem-i Hazret-i Mevlânâ, sırr-ı Şems-i Tebrîzî, kerem-i İmâm- I Alî, Hû diyelim.*

In this *gülbâng*, the last syllables of the words *håndan* and *ihsân* are extended. After the *gülbâng*, those in the *semâ'hâne* and *mutrib* bow their heads (*bash kesmek*) and say, "*Hū*" with all the power their voices can muster and as long as their breath can last. The shaikh then bows his head again and says, "*Esselâmu aleyküm*" with a solemn voice. This greeting (*selâm*) is for the souls (*jans*) in the *semâ'hâne*. Everyone bows their heads with the shaikh and the *semâ'zenbashı* responds to the greeting by saying, "*Ve aleykümüsselâm ve rahmetullâhi ve berekâtuhû.*" In this sentence, the last syllable of the word *selâm* is extended and *Hū* is said on a long exhalation of the breath. During the response to his greeting, the shaikh has left his post and is slowly walking towards the door. By the time the shaikh arrives at the place just under the chandelier and at the center of the *semâ'hâne*, the response to the greeting should be finished. The shaikh bows his head there again, and the others bow their heads with him. Under the chandelier, the shaikh seals his feet (*ayak mühürlemek*) and looks towards the *mutrib*; he bows his head and says, "*Esselâmu aleyküm*" in the same manner as before. This second greeting is for the *mutrib*. The *neyzenbashı* from the *mutribân* responds to the greeting in the same manner. By the end of the response to the greeting, the shaikh should have arrived at the door. At the door he turns towards the *semâ'hâne* without turning his back to the tomb (*türbe*). He bows his head to those in the *semâ'hâne,* in the direction of the *post*. Everyone bows their heads in response. He leaves through the door with his left foot (he had entered with his right foot; this is how one should enter and exit a *masjid*) and he goes to the *harem* to change his clothes.

Following this, those who are in the *semâ'hâne* walk out, turning to the *semâ'hâne* one by one at the door and making *niyâz* as they leave. The *türbedâr dede* and *meydanjı dede* remain as the last ones. If the *mukabele* is performed at night, the *türbedâr dede* puts the candles to rest (*sırlamak,* "into a secret") by blowing into a long pipe. Only the oil lamps of the *türbe* remain lit. The *meydanjı dede* bows and "sees with" (*görüshmek*) the *post*, folds it in half or puts it on his left shoulder. After this service, they leave the *semâ'hâne*; the ceremony has been completed.

Garipler Semâ'ı ("Semâ' of the Poor Ones")

Those among the *dedes* and *jans* (souls) whose thirst for the ecstacy of *semâ'* is not yet quenched stay in the *semâ'hâne* after everyone has left and the candles have been put to rest. Without taking off their *khirkas*, they hold them with their left hands, the right hand holding the collar and opening it a little at the chest, and they then make eighteen *charks* ("turns") in the style of the shaikh. Because this *semâ'* is done in dim light, with only the lamps of the *türbe* burning, it is called *Garipler Semâ'-ı* ("*Semâ'* of the Poor Ones"). After doing their eighteen additional turns, the souls leave the *semâ'hâne* in the same way as the others.

Niyâz Âyini ("Ritual of Entreaty")

It sometimes happens that the shaikh, or one of the souls or *muhips*, or someone attending the *mukabele* who knows of the *erkân* ("customs") of Mevlevîhood, falls into a state of ecstasy and wants the *mukabele* to go on. He offers a *niyâz* incorporating the number of *nezr-i Mevlânâ*: that is, he sends a *niyâz* to the *mutrib* to the amount of nine or eighteen, or some other multiple of nine. This is a *jemile* ("favor") and it belongs to everyone; it is spent by the *dergâh* or divided equally among the souls as a *berk-i sebz* ("souvenir"). The *niyâz* is sent to the *mutrib* before the fourth cycle ends, and it is left on the *kudüm* of the *kudümzenbaşı* after he "sees with" it.

If a *niyâz* is offered, the last *peshrev* in the fourth cycle is not played; the *neyzenbashı* plays a short *taksîm* in the *segâh makam* and begins the *niyâz mukabele*. The *Hüseynî Âyini* then begins, which contains the first couplet of one of Mevlânâ's *ghazals*:

> O Lovers! O Lovers! I turn the earth into jewels!
> O Musicians! O Musicians! I fill your tambourines with gold.[9]

Then the shaikh also sends a *berk-i sebz* to the *mutrib*, and it is placed on the *kudüm* of the *kudümzenbashı*. The *kudümzenbashı* takes what has been sent, "sees with" it, and places it on his right; the *niyâz mukabele* then begins.

During the *niyâz mukabele*, the *âyin* called the *Niyâz Âyini* ("Hymn of Entreaty") is sung and its lyrics consist of two parts. The first part is this:

---

[9] *Iy ashikan iy ashikan men hakra govher kunem*
Iy mutriban iy mutriban deff-i shuma pur zer kunem

I cast this body of mine whirling like a moth
around the candle of your soul.
The archives of this heart I cast into the rosy flames of fire.
When I was a drop, I threw myself into the ocean.
Alas! I lost my path in the valley of separation.
I can't describe this deep pain of my heart, such a sorrow I have.
If you love the Master, don't make me speak of it, this grief I have.
I lost my heart to the coquettish glance of that charmer.
My mind was lost in the lovelocks of that heart-breaker.
My reason was lost in the yearning to unite with the beloved.
My soul vanished in the pain of absence and separation.
My heart has burned in the fire of separation, such a sorrow I have.
If you love the Master, don't make me speak of it, this grief I have.[10]

[10] *Shem-i ruhuna cismimi pervane dushurdum*
Evrak-i dili atesh-i suzana dushurdum
Bir katre iken kendimi ummana dushurdum
Hayfa yolumu vadi-i hicrana dushurdum
Takrir edemem derd-i derunum elemim var
Mevlayi seversen beni soyletme gamim var
Gonlum benim ol gamze-i fettan ile gitti
Fikrim benim ol zulf-i perishan ile gitti
Aklim heves-i vuslat-i canan ile getti
Canim elem-i firkat u hicran ile gitti
Hecr ateshine yandi derunum elemim var
Mevlayi seversen beni soyletme gamim var

This poem which is in the *ayin ve naat* manuscript dating from the eighteenth to nineteeth century, and which is recorded as Persian writings no: 1606 in Ist. Uni. Library, has the headline *Nutk-ı pâk-i Sultân Veled.* But the second and the third stanzas are mixed with each other; there is a mistake in the rhyme in the third line of the second stanza; and the third line of the third stanza has a mistake in the *redif* (a word repeated at the end of every couplet of a poem) making the line defective. It is obvious that this language does not belong to Sultân Veled. In the second issue of *Istanbul Institute Magazine* (*Istanbul Enstitüsü Dergisi*), Halil Can informed us about an article of Rıfkı Melûl Meriç entitled "A biographical memorandum about the poets, calligraphers and musicians of the school of the Palace in 1131 H." (Ist. Istanbul Print., 1956, p. 138–168). In this article, Rıfkı Melûl

And the second piece is this:

Listen to my words, from a different place I will speak.
What the dervish needs is love for God the Guide.
Whatever the lover has is sacrificed for the Beloved's sake.
Semâ' is fidelity, joy for the soul, food for the spirit.

Come in love! Let's make a sound and echo it!
In our pain, let's make our "*Hū*" and "*Hayy*" reach heaven.
Let's beat the *kudum* and tambourine and play the *ney*!
Semâ' is fidelity, joy for the soul, food for the spirit.

Let's be bewildered in love for Mevlânâ and be his adorers.
Let's beat our breasts and rend our clothes!
This is our ritual and custom from our Sultan.
Semâ' is fidelity, joy for the soul, food for the spirit.[11]

Meriç refers to information about this poem from a *tezkire* ("biographical memorandum") of Kilârî Ahmed Refî', recorded as no. 1479 in the library of Istanbul Archeological Museum. Refî' writes that the poem belongs to someone named Ömer Chelebi and he gives the first stanza in the *tezkire* (p. 152). Ahmed Refî' also mentions Ömer Chelebi as being among the musicians and refers to him as "Dervish Ömer," commenting that he has a very beautiful voice and plays the tanbur (photographs from the *tezkire*, p. 9). In the manuscript in the museum of Ist. Uni. Library (property record 2. a) that the composer Abû-Bakr Çavuş/Sergeant from Eyup owned in 1142 H. (1729), the two stanzas of this poem are written (319. a.). Es'ad Efendi, in his *tezkire*, informs us that Dervish Ömer was a Mevlevî and that he lived during the period of Sultan Murad IV (Ist. Uni. Lib. Turkish Writings/Manuscripts, 2529, 32. B-33. b.).

[11] *Dinle sozumu sana direm ozge edadir*
Dervish olana lazim olan ishk-i hudadir
Ashikin nesi varisa ma'shuka fedadir
Semâ' vefa cana safa ruha gidadir

Ishkile gelin eyliyelim siyt u sadayi
Derd ile goke chikaralim huyile hayi
Chalalim kudum depredelim deff ile nayi
Semâ' vefa cana safa ruha gidadir

Ishile Mevlânâ'ya olup valih u hayran
Sineler dogup eyliyelim chak-i giriban
Sultanimizdan bize budur ayin u erkan

In the library of the Konya Museum, among the Abdülbâki Gölpınarlı writings and in a manuscript dating from the nineteenth century, the first stanza is as follows:

O Sufi! Our conversation fills the soul with joy.
To our pre-eternal bond with God it is fidelity.
Drink once of the dregs of our wine and see,
for difficulty it is a remedy.
Semâ' is joy, joy for the soul, food for the spirit.[12]

For the third stanza of this version, the first three lines from the first mentioned piece ("*Shem-i ruhuna*..." / "Candle of your soul...") are used, and the fourth line is the line repeated in all the stanzas. In this manuscript, the last stanza of the poem, which consists of five stanzas, is as follows:

Enter in love. Let's be seekers who are searching.
In fidelty, let's live joyfully, vibrating life!
Come to Blessed Mevlânâ, let's be his servant.
Semâ' is joy, fidelity for the soul, food for the spirit.[13]

It is possible that both the lyrics and the music of this second piece belong to Dervish Ömer.

During the *Niyâz Mukabele*, the stanzas below are added; the first of which is often attributed to Sultân Veled, but which actually belongs to Dîvane Mehmed Chelebi or Nev'î, having been translated

---

Semâ' vefa cana safa ruha gidadir

We have taken this from the eighteenth-century manuscript in the Library of Ibnülemin Mahmud Kemal (No: 3343, 55 b.).

[12] *Iy Sufi bizim sohbetimiz cana safadir*
Hakkile ezel ettigimiz ahde vefadir
Bir cur'amizi nush idegor derde devadir
Semâ' safa cana safa ruha gidadir
[Manuscript no: 82]

[13] *Ishkile gelun talib-i cuyende olalim*
Sidkila safalar surelim zinde olalim
Hazret-i Mevlânâ'ya gelin bende olalim.
Semâ' safa cana vefa ruha gidadir
[96. a]

from verses of Jamî'; and the second of which belongs to Eflâkî:

> I didn't use to know that, hidden or manifest, it was all You.
> Hidden from the flesh and the soul, it was all You.
> Within this universe, I used to ask for a sign from You.
> Then, at last, I knew that the universe was all You!
>
> Oh, the One who has created thousands of beings, such a Sultan is He
> that those who become His servants become the rulers of rulers.
> Whoever, today, is faithful to Veled and prostrates,
> if he is poor, he becomes a prince; if he is a prince, he becomes a sultan.[14]

The *Niyâz Âyini* ends with a *yürük semâ'î* (a musical piece in waltz rhythm) and a short *taksîm*; then the *ashir* begins and the *mukabele* ends in the manner described previously. If one accepts that the lyrics belong to the eighteenth century, the *Niyâz Âyini* and *mukabelesi* are late additions that have been generally admired and accepted.

Some Information Relating to Semâ'

Because underlying garments are seen when the skirts of their tennures open during the turning, *semâ'zens'* make sure that their under garments are as clean as their outer ones. Also, because they would perform *semâ'* barefoot, it is said that *semâ'zens* used to wear white gaiters that covered their ankles but left the soles of their feet bare.

---

[14] *Ben bilmezidim gizli iyan hep sen imishsin*
Tenlerde vu canlardan nihan hep sen imishsin
Senden bu cihan ichre nishan ister idim ben
Ahir bunu bildim ki cihan hep sen imishsin
Iy ki hezar-aferin bu nice sultan olur

Kulu olan kishiler husrev u hakan olur
Her ki bugun Veled'e inanuben yuz sure
Yoksul ise bay olur bay ise sultan olur

- If there is a visiting shaikh or *muhib* in the *dergâh* to whom an honorary *destâr* is given, they enter the *mukabele* together with the shaikh. From the perspective of the front, they are placed on the right of the shaikh, and from the perspective of the *post*, they are placed on the left. Ranked according to status, they sit very close to each other. During the fourth cycle, these honored guests enter the *semâ'* together with the shaikh. If there is only one guest with a *destâr*, he performs *semâ'* near the shaikh; if there are a number of them, they form a circle around the shaikh.The shaikh, the visiting shaikhs, and the *semâ'zenbashı* would wear *mests* ("leather socks") on their feet, while the feet of all the *semâ'zens* were bare.
- *Semâ'* wearing a *khirka* is done in the way we have descibed. However, on rare occasions, due to ecstasy or divine attraction (*jezbe*), sometimes the shaikh, or one of the visiting shaikhs, would hold the right or left collar of his *khirka* with his left hand and open out his other arm. In a picture by Kapûdân-ı Derya Hacı Vesim Pasha (d. 1910 A.D.) that depicts a *mukabele* held when Abdülvâhid Chelebi was visiting the *dergâh* of Kulekapısı, the right arms of both Huseyn Fahreddîn Dede, the Shaikh of Bahariye, and Abdülhalim Chelebi, the Shaikh of Manisa (1925), are open, and the one engaged in *semâ'* in the middle is in the *niyâz* position. During the shaikhhood of Ahmed Jelâleddîn Dede (1946), the last shaikh of Kulekapısı Mevlevîhâne, Orhan Selâhaddin Efendi used to join the *mukabele* with his *destâr* on, and in ecstasy would perform *semâ'* by opening his *khirka* and both of his arms in front of the *post*. He even used to join all of the four cycles. However, these occurances are the result of ecstasy or divine attraction (*jezbe*); essentially, one does not open one's arms when one is performing *semâ'* with a *khirka*.
- The *tennûre* of a *semâ'zen* when he is turning slowly opens in the shape of a triangle; when he turns fast, it opens in the shape of the domed lid of a copper serving dish. To allow the *tennûre* to open in this way, it has to be cut and sewn according to a certain pattern, and after one puts it on, the part gathered below the waist should be orderly, and the hem of the skirt should fall at

the same length on all sides.

- The color of the *destegül* and *tennûre* is generally white. But the *tennûres* of children and young *semâ'zens* may also be light yellow, orange, pink, green, and dark red. If the ones wearing the colorful *tennûres* are taken to the middle of the *semâ'hâne* and those in white *tennûres* make up the surrounding circle, a very beautiful harmony of colors is formed. Colored *tennûres* can be seen in the picture by Hajı Vesim Pasha.
- If some of the *semâ'zens* get tired after the first *selâm*, at the *selambashi* they may withdraw, put on their *khirkas*, and stand in their places with their feet sealed. In the picture by Hajı Vesim Pasha, five *dedes* on the right and five *dedes* on the left are standing with their *khirkas* on. There is no doubt that this picture depicts the fourth cycle of the *semâ'*, because the shaikhs enter the *semâ'* only during the fourth cycle. This is the practice because of the narrowness of the *semâ'hâne*, and so that the task of giving the *khirkas* back to the *semâ'zens* may take place. In the fourth cyle, there is no tradition that absolutely demands one join the *semâ'*.

Days of Mukabele, Nights of Grace

The *rivāyāt*, or oral tradition, which has been conveyed from mouth to ear, from ear to mouth, and from elder to youngster, tells us this: After the *mukabele* had taken its final form and was accepted by all Mevlevîs without objection, it was performed only when one fell into an ecstasy, when one received a divine attraction, or when a spirit of excitement, love, or enthusiasm appeared during a gathering for *sohbet*. There was no specific day or hour for *sohbet*. It went on in this way until the period of Sultan Selim III, who was a poet and musician and also a *muhib* of the Mevlevî Order. The Janissaries were aligned with the Bektâshîs; the sultan on the other hand, wishing to institute reforms, formed a spiritual alliance with the Mevlevîs, because theirs is a path open to accepting new ideas. Therefore, following his love and making inspiration his guide, he used to visit the Mevlevîhânes frequently, at unexpected times. Whenever the sultan came, the Mevelevis would hold a *mukabele*. One time, five times, ten times... the sultan's visits began to go on like this. The leaders of the Mevlevî Order started to get annoyed that instead of joy or divine attraction, the visit of the sultan had become the reason for the *mukabele*. Finally, the shaikhs got together and thought of a solution to this. They decided that in each Mevlevîhâne the *mukabele* would be performed one or two days a week. In the five Mevlevîhânes in Istanbul, these specific days were assigned as days for *mukabele*:

Friday: Kulekapısı (Galata)
Saturday: Üsküdar
Sunday: Kasımpaşa
Monday: Yenikapı (Mevlevîhâne kapısı)
Tuesday: Kulekapısı
Wednesday: Beshiktash (afterwards Bahariye in Eyüp)
Thursday: Yenikapı

This schedule was presented to the sultan with a letter reading, "At the exalted seat of your sovereignty, there is a Mevlevî *mukabele* everyday; whichever day you wish, you can honor that *dergâh* with your visit." From then on, the days assigned for *mukabele* were an established rule. Although this was the case, still, occasionally when the brothers came together for one reason or another, especially during the nights of Ramaḍān, a *mukabele* would be held. Besides these spontaneous *mukabeles*, the brothers also used to gather for *mukabele* on the twenty-seventh night of Ramaḍān (*Kadir Gecesi*, the "Night of Power"), the nights of the religious holidays, and the Candle Nights (such as the birth of the Prophet, the night of the ascension, etc.). These were referred to as *Ihya Gejeleri* ("Nights of Reanimation or Grace"), meaning that they should be passed in worship without sleeping.

In the cities outside Istanbul, excepting special circumstances, the *mukabele* was regularly held on Fridays after the midday prayer.

Shaikhs from Other Ṭarīqahs within the Mukabele

Mevlevîs regard themselves as the people of the truth. They call the other orders "*Sufi ṭarīqahs*", their shaikhs "Sufi shaikhs," and their dervishes "Sufi dervishes." The word *sufi* in this context, however, becomes *sofu*, meaning "conservative" in everyday speech, and is pronounced as such. Now and then, some of the shaikhs from other *ṭarīqahs*, who loved Mevlevî customs, would come to the *mevlevîhânes* in their own clothes. On certain occasions, many shaikhs would be invited to come as a group, such as during the month of Muharrem (when *ashura* is cooked), when the *tekke* held an opening ceremony after a repair or restoration, when a shaikh died, or when somebody was appointed to be his successor and there would be a gathering of the *post*. The shaikhs used to enter the *semâ'hâne* together with the Mevlevî shaikh, and they would join the *Devr-i Veledî* to the extent of their knowledge; then, like the *dedes* who did not join the *semâ'*, they would seal their feet and watch the ceremony. As the Mevlevîs bowed their heads, they also bowed; they sat down when the Mevlevîs sat down and stood up when they stood up; in other words, they would follow the lead of the Mevlevîs.

A Mevlevî in a Sufi Tekke

Mevlevî shaikhs, *dedes*, and *muhibs* also used to go to the *tekkes* of other *ṭarīqahs* as a kindness, upon invitation, or just because they wished to be there. In the Sufi *tekke*, even if the Mevlevî were not a shaikh himself, he would be placed next to the seat (*makam*) of the shaikh. While they were sitting and doing *dhikr*, the Mevlevî used to plunge into his own world, and when they stood up he also stood up, but would seal his feet where he stood and not join the *dhikr*. When the dervishes began *dhikr* with the name of Allāh, the Mevlevî would approach the center, bow toward the niche (*mihrab*), and begin the *post semâ'* with his *khirka*. Because *semâ'* gives a different taste, a different pleasure and spirituality to the *dhikr*, the Sufi shaikhs very much wanted Mevlevîs to come to their *tekkes*. However, the *dedes* used to discourage the *nevniyâzes*, saying that their *semâ'* would be spoiled, and did not often let them attend.

Within the most recent era, Mevlevîs wearing *khirkas* and *tennûres* attended the *dergâh* of Shaikh Murâd-ı Nakshbendî in Nishancı/Eyüp, and the *dergâh* of Ümmü Ken'an near Kıztashı, and they performed *semâ'* there. Although Seyyid Abdülkaadir-i Belhî (1341 H. 1923 A.D.), the shaikh of the Shaikh Murad Tekke, was a Nakshbendî shaikh, his father Seyyid Süleymân-ı Belhî (1270 H. 1853 A.D.) was a Mevlevî *khalif*; and he himself was also a Hamzavî (a Melâmî of Bayrami) regarded as the *qutb*, or spiritual pole, not only by Hamzavis, but by most *ṭarīqahs* including the Mevlevîs. The shaikh of Ümmü Ken'an, Ken'an Efendi, despite being a Rufâî, used to teach the *Mesnevî* and made his followers practice *Sultân Veled Devri*. In this way, it was as if he had brought the Rufâî and Mevlevî orders together.[15]

Ayn-ı Jem ("Unity Ritual")

This word which is originally *Ayn-ül Jem'* (please see **Ayn-ı Cem** in the glossary), has become the name of a ceremony. From one point of view, the *Ayn-ı Jem* is reminiscent of *semâ'* as it was during the period of Mevlânâ.

The *Ayn-ı Jem* is offered in remembrance of the family of someone who is funding through a foundation established for that purpose, or in gratitude for someone's wish having come true (in which case that person pays for the expenses), or because one of the lovers yearns for a special gathering of *semâ'* and *sohbet*. They are mostly performed at night, when, as a matter of fact, it gives great pleasure. There are also *Ayn-ı Jems* that are performed during the day, and they may even be arranged on a picnic site.

[15] For more information about the relationship of the Mevlevî order with other *ṭarīqahs*, and the positive and negative opinions of each concerning the other, please see our work *Mevlevîhood After Mevlânâ*, pp. 185–243 and especially the chapter "*Ṭarīqahs* Related to Mevlevîhood," Part IV of Section II, pp. 293–328.

When held at night, after everyone has eaten and performed the evening prayer, they enter a rectangular room called the *meydan-ı sherîf*, in just the same way as they enter a *semâ'hâne*; everyone takes their places, seals their feet and waits. The *post* of the shaikh has previously been spread out by the *meydanjı*. The shaikh is the last one to enter, and he bows and everyone bows with him. Then the shaikh turns towards those assembled in the *meydan*, sits down, prostrates on the floor and kisses his *post*. Everyone sits down together with the shaikh and makes *niyâz* to the floor. The *kahveci dede* ("coffee *dede*") or his assistant brings the coffee cups on a tray; beginning with the shaikh, according to rank, he serves coffee to the souls. When one has finished one's coffee one places the cup and saucer to one's right and a little behind one in such a way that it will not be seen. After the coffee is drunk, the coffee *dede* and, if necessary, his assistant, begin to collect the coffee cups. He goes in front of the person whose cup he will take, puts his left knee on the floor, raises his right knee, and bows his head. The soul relinquishing his cup and saucer takes them up, covers the rim of the cup with his left hand–fingers straight and closed–and gives them back with his right hand. This practice is based on the belief that a Mevlevî should not see a dirty nor shameful thing, nor does he show it; he covers it.

After the cups have been gathered, the *neyzenbashı* "sees with" the *ney* and begins a *taksîm*. Here we should give a brief discription of the *ādāb* of blowing the *ney*. After the *neyzen* "sees with" the *ney*, he says internally the *ʾAʿūzhu/Bismillāh* and then "*Allahū lā ilāha illā Allāhū*," and while he is saying the *Hū* he begins to blow into the *ney*. In this way, the sound of the *ney* becomes an extension of the *āyāt*. After the *taksîm*, the *âyinhâns* begin to recite the *âyin*. In front of the souls who are sitting, there are nine candlesticks on their right and nine candlesticks on their left. The *meydanjı* awakens these candles before anyone enters the room. While the *âyin* is being recited, those who wish to do so make *niyâz* where they are seated, stand up, bow their heads towards the shaikh, go into the open space, and begin *semâ'* with their arms in the sleeves of their *khirkas*. During the *Ayn-ı Jem* ceremony no one wears a *tennûre* or opens their arms. Also, during the *Ayn-ı Jem* no one stops at the beginning of the *selâm* unless they are exhausted, or have some other valid reason.

After the ritual is finished, the shaikh recites the *gülbâng* of *Ayn-ı Jem*:

> *İnâyet-i Yezdan, himmet-i merdân; mübarek vakitler hayrola; hayırlar fethola; sâhib-cem'iyyetîn muradı hâsıl ola; bil-cümle sâhib-i hayratın ervahı şâd ola; bu gitti, ganîsi gele; demler, safâlar müzdâdola. Dem-i Hazret-i Mevlânâ, sırr-ı Şems-i Tebrîzî, kerem-i Imâm-ı Alî, Hû diyelim.*

Altogether, everyone says "*Hū*" with a loud voice for as long as the length of their breath, and everyone prostrates on the floor and "sees with" it.

After the *gülbâng*, people sit crossed-legged. The *meydanjı* brings the fruit of the season. People eat and engage in *sohbet*, sherbets prepared previously are served, and the musicians sing *ilahis* from time to time. In this way, the conversation goes on until morning. While the call to morning prayer is being recited, the shaikh announces, "*Fātiḥah.*" After everyone has recited the *Fātiḥah* along with the shaikh, they "see with" the floor and stand up. The shaikh, followed by the souls, leaves the space after making *niyâz,* just as when leaving the *semâ'hâne*. They then proceed to the *masjid.*

Sheb-i Arûs ("Wedding Night")

The term *Sheb-i Urs* is also used. In Arabic, *arus* means "bride," and *urs* means "wedding," "festivity," or "wedding banquet." *Sheb-i Arûs* is a compound noun made with one Persian word and one Arabic word; it means "night of the wedding feast" or "nuptial night." *Ta'rîs* is a word which means "the journey of a traveler during the night and his lying down and sleeping for a little while around dawn." Bukhari reports the following *ḥadīth*:

> We were traveling together with the Prophet. We walked the whole night; at the end of the night we lost ourselves and fell asleep, and for the traveler there is nothing sweeter than this. When we woke up, we saw that the sun had risen; as a matter of fact the heat of the sun had woken us. First, such-and-such

a person woke up, and the fourth to wake up was Hattaboglu ʿUmar. Unless the Prophet himself stirred, we never used to wake him up, because we did not know what kind of a state he was in during his sleep. ʿUmar was a hard man; he recited the *tekbîr*, shouting "*Allāhu Akbar!*" in a loud voice, and did not stop reciting until the Prophet woke up. Once the Prophet was awake, they told him that the time for *ṣalāh* had passed. The Blessed Prophet replied, "Never mind," and we went on traveling a little further. Then we halted and made ablutions, someone recited the call to prayer, and we did the morning *ṣalāh* as a group. One person did not come to the *ṣalāh*. The Prophet asked him, "Why did you not come to the *ṣalāh*?" When the man said, "I had become *cünüb* ('religiously unclean') and there was no water," the Prophet told him, "You could have done the *teyemmüm* ('ablution using the soil of the earth when water is not available') and that would have been enough."[16]

Bukhari conveys another version of this tradition:

Bilâl told the Prophet, "I will wake you up," but he, too, fell asleep. After the sun had risen, the Prophet woke up and asked Bilâl, "What happened to your promise?" and when Bilâl apologized, the Prophet said, "Allāh takes away your spirits whenever He wishes and He gives them back to you again whenever He wishes." The Prophet ordered Bilâl to recite the call to prayer and everyone performed *ṣalāh* as a group.[17]

In volume I of the *Mesnevî*, Mevlânâ mentions this and says:

"O Bilâl, lift up your lilting voice
from the breath which I breathed into your heart,
that breath by which Adam was bewildered
and the hosts of Heaven made witless."

Mustafa lost himself in that beautiful voice,
prayer eluding him on the night of the *ta'rîs*.

---

[16] Al-Tacrid, Vol. I, p. 35.
[17] Ibid., p. 54.

He did not rise up from that blessed sleep
until the dawn prayer had advanced to noon.

So it was, on the night of the *ta'rîs*,
in the presence of the Bride,
his pure soul attained to the kissing of hands.[18]

The relationship between *Sheb-i Arûs* and this tradition concerning the *ta'rîs* is obvious. The birth of Mevlânâ into eternity was on the fifth day of the month *Jumādā al-ʾĀkhirah* in the year 672 (17 December 1273) while the sun was setting. Every year, Mevlevîs celebrate that day, which is in the sixth month of the lunar calendar, because, according to Mevlânâ, there is no death; the one who emigrates from this world is born into the world of meaning and lives within humanity.[19] In Konya, if the anniversary of this date fell in spring, summer, or autumn, rush mats (*hasır*: a rug made by sewing long straws or plant stems together) were spread, and upon them rugs (*kilims*), along the side of the pool facing the *türbe* in front of the *meydan odası,* and an *Ayn-ı Jem* was held in the open air. In winter, the *Ayn-ı Jem* was held in the *meydan.* In other *tekkes*, this night was always celebrated in the *meydan* room. When the ritual was over, the shaikh used to recite this *gülbâng* of *Sheb-i Arûs*:

Bishter a bishter a can-i men
Peyk-i der-i Hazret-i Sultan-i men

Vakt-i şerîf hayrola; hayırlar fethola; şerler def'ola; leyle-i arûs-ı rabbânî, vuslat-ı halvet-serây-i sübhânî, hakk-ı akdes-i Hudâvendgârîde ân-be ân vesîle-i i'tilâ-yı makaam ve fuyûzât-ı ruhâniyyet-i aliyyeleri cümle peyrevânı hakkında şamil ü âmmola, Dem-i Hazret-i Mevlânâ, sırr-ı Şems-i Tebrîzî, kerem-i İmâm-ı Alî, Hû diyelim. Hû…

[18] Couplets 1987–91.
[19] For more on Mevlânâ's thoughts concerning death, please refer to *Mevlânâ Celâleddîn*, third edition, pp. 124–26, 134–35.

Bayram Celebrations

During the first *mukabele* after the *bayrams*, on the Candle Nights (the four feasts when the minarets are illuminated: the Prophet's birthday, his conception, his night ascent, and the Night of Power), after the *dua-gû* prayer, then the ceremony of celebration occurs. Everyone places their arms through the sleeves of their *khirkas*. First the *semâ'zenbashı* walks forward, bows in front of the *post*, "sees with" the shaikh, seals his feet, and stands on the shaikh's right (this is on the left if one is facing the front, at the side of the *türbe*). The one after him then walks forward, "sees with" the shaikh and the *semâ'zenbashı*, and takes up the next position in the line. The next soul then "sees with" the shaikh, the *semâ'zenbashı*, and the soul who preceded him, and takes up the next spot. In this way, the last *semâ'zen* "sees with" the shaikh and all the souls before going to the very end and standing there. Before this "seeing with" begins, the *mutrib* have also come down so that the *neyzenbashı* and the *kudümzenbashı* take their places after the *semâ'zenbashı*, and the other members of the *mutrib* take their places according to rank.

After the ceremony of celebration, the shaikh invites everyone in the *türbe* to recite the *Fātiḥah*, and then recites the last *gülbâng*, and then everyone leaves the *semâ'hâne*.

Semâ' Meshki ("Practice")

After the *sikke* of one who has joined the Mevlevî Order (*intisab etmek*) has been blessed with the *tekbîr* by the shaikh, one of the *dedes* is assigned to teach him *semâ'*. This *dede* is both the *semâ' dede* of that soul, of that *muhib*, and he is his teacher. The *dede* takes his new *muhib* and leads him to the *matbâh* (kitchen); they bow and kiss the threshold before entering the *matbâh* and going to the room upstairs where the *post* is kept. Near the corner of this room, there are one or more nails hammered into the floor at equal distances from one another. They are made of brass, round and smooth so as not to cut the toes, and they are as big as the size of a toe. Around them the floor is slightly depressed. The *dede* first describes how to do *semâ'* and then demonstrates it himself. Then he has the *nevniyâz* adopt the *niyâz* position and they begin the *semâ' meshk* ("practice"). The feet of the *nevniyâz* are bare and he is in a state of ablution. First, he prostrates on the floor and "sees with" the nail. He puts his left hand with an open palm on his right knee and leans the elbow of his right arm on his left palm; he takes a pinch of salt out of the salt bowl near the nail and sprinkles it around the nail. The salt enables the foot to slide and it also keeps the foot from burning. Then he stands up and bows, crosses his arms on his chest with the right arm over the left, in such a way that the fingers will come to the back of the shoulders, with the hands grasping the shoulders. He positions the nail between his first and second toes. The left foot is like a column; it will never bend–the knee will not flex even a little. He angles his head a little to the right while turning his face to the left. In relation to the left foot, his right foot is perpendicular and a little removed from it. In this position, without the heel leaving the floor, the *semâ'zen* swivels his left foot to the right, and when the heel is turned to the right as much as possible, he takes his right foot off the floor, lifting it to the level of the left knee. Swiftly he steps once more on the floor perpendicular again to the left foot. During this movement, the left shoulder also swivels round to the back and so he finishes facing the same way as when he began the *chark* ("turn"). This series of movements is called a *tam chark* ("complete turn"). The *nevniyâz* is made to make nine *charks* on the first day. After that he "sees with" his *dede* and the *meshk* for that day ends. In the following days, according to the capability of the *nevniyâz*, the number of *charks* is increased to eighteen, twenty-seven, thirty-six, or another multiple of nine. After he has learned to do the *chark* well, he also learns to open his arms, then how to walk in the *semâ'hâne*, and how to do a half *chark* when necessary. The half *chark* is half of a complete *chark*. At last, after the *nevniyâz* has been "cooked" well in the *semâ'*, before dinner on a day of *mukabele*, a *müptedî mukabelesi* ("beginner's *mukabele*") is held.

Meshk is not only done in the *matbâh*; in the cells of the *dedes* there is a *semâ'* board on which one person can easily do the *chark*. After the first day, the *nevniyâz* does the *meshk* in the cell.

Because a Mevlevî begins *meshk* with a nail, and as it is also a spiritual path (*sülûk*) and service as much as it is a training, the expression, "the nail of the Mevlevî and the hoe of the Bektâshî" has been widely used by Mevlevîs. These words tell us that a Mevlevî begins his spiritual journey with *semâ' meshk* on a nail, while the Bektâshî does his service by digging the soil with a hoe.

The Mevlevî who has learned *semâ'*, according to his ability and talent, then studies the *Mesnevî*, learns how to blow the *ney*, practices the *âyins* and the *naat*, and, of course, learns about *usûl* ("rhythm"). During this time he also learns about *ādāb* and *erkân*. From this point of view, *Mevlevîhânes* are educational institutes or universities. When a *nevniyâz* who has practiced the *âyins* and the *naat* and learned how to blow the *ney* and beat the *kudum* becomes a master, he is included within the *mutrib*. The one who reads the *Mesnevî* increases his knowledge and, if he shows talent, is awarded an *ijâzet* to teach it. To teach the *Mesnevî* one must know *tafsīr* ("interpretations") of both the *Mesnevî* and the Qur'ān; know the *ḥadīth* ("traditions") of the Prophet; have *kalām* ("scriptural knowledge of the Qur'ān"); understand *taṣawwuf* ("Islamic mysticism"); understand *fiqh* ("Muslim jurisprudence"); have knowledge of history, including the history of different religions and sects; and have knowledge of poetry and the rules of literature and literary criticism.

Beginner's Mukabele

Although he belonged to the Nakshbendî order, İbrâhîm Halil also joined the Mevlevî order, and was known as Ashchı Dede, and was presented with a *destâr*. He writes in his memoirs that he completed his *semâ' meshk* in forty days.[20] This was the generally accepted

[20] *The Memoirs of Ashchi Dede*, Ist. Uni. Lib. Turkish scriptures. No: 78–80, vol. I, p. 205; vol. II, pp. 451–52. Ashchi Dede was only a nick name; his Mevlevî name was conferred as an honorary one, a blessing. His memoirs are important, because he conveys information about his era, the beliefs of the era, and the characteristics of those who lived in that period. İbrahim

number of days, but the training period could be longer or shorter depending on the student and the teacher. Completing the *semâ' meshk* is called *semâ' chıkarmak* ("to bring forth the *semâ*'").

When the *nevniyâz* has completed the *semâ' meshk*, his *dede* informs the shaikh and the *ashchı dede*. On a day of *mukabele*, before the meal, a *mübtedî mukabelesi* ("beginner's ceremony") is held. This *mukabele* is held in the *semâ'hâne* like other *mukabeles*, but the shaikh does not attend. The *ashchıbashı* stands below the *post*, and the *naat* is not recited. After a short *ney taksîm*, *Devr-i Veledî* is performed, and the *semâ'* begins. *Âyins* are not recited during any of the four cycles, and the *mukabele* is conducted with the *peshrev*. After the fourth cycle, the *ashir* is recited followed by the *gülbâng*, and, just like during the *bayram* celebration, one by one, everybody "sees with" those who have previously entered. Finally, the *nevniyâz* enters, "sees with" each person one at a time, and goes to the end of the line. While the *nevniyâz* "sees with" the souls, his *dede* walks behind him; he also "sees with" the souls and presents them with gifts from the *nevniyâz*. The *nevniyâz* and his *dede* also visit the cells of the *dedes* who have not joined the *mübtedî mukabele*; they "see with" them and present them gifts as well. The *nezir* (or more commonly, *niyâz*) is a gift like a tea cup and saucer, tea or coffee, or a piece of cloth.

Symbolic Significance of the Mukabele for Mevlevîs

As we have already mentioned, the earliest author to discuss the *mukabele* in its contemporary form was Divâne Mehmed Chelebi, the shaikh of Afyon Karahisar, who died in the second half of the sixteenth century. According to him, the Mevlevî has died in his being and self: the *külah* ("conical hat") on his head is his gravestone; his *khirka* is his grave; and, naturally, his *tennûre* is his shroud. The *ney* is the *sûr*, the horn that one of the archangels will blow to raise the dead. The right arc of the *semâ'hâne*, which has a circular form,

---

Halîl, a Nakshi dervish, was born in 1244 H., in Kandilli, Istanbul; and he served as a military secretary. He wrote his memoirs in 1317 H. The only copy is in the library of Istanbul University.

is the apparent world, relating to *shahadet* ("witnessing"), the *nasût âlemi* ("mortal realm"), and *halk* (the "people"). The left arc is the inner world; it is the unseen realm of meaning, symbolizing the *Gayb* (the "Unseen"), *melekût* ("heaven"), and the *emr âlemi* ("realm of commands," or God's kingdom). To rise and perform the *Devr-i Veledî* signifies coming back to life after death on hearing the sound of the trumpet. After having died before one dies (i.e. after having died as an ego: a selfish, imaginary, and relative being), it represents finding life in real Being through the breath and spiritual power of the *murshid.* The three cycles indicate the three stages of *yaqīn* ("certainty"): knowing, seeing, and becoming. They also refer to Absolute Being manifesting the inanimate world, the plant world, and the animal world . In the *semâ'hâne*, the point regarded as the starting point of the *Hatt-ı Istivâ*, which is where the shaikh is positioned, indicates the world of Absolute Being, and the point opposite it indicates the human being. Therefore, the right arc of the *semâ'hâne* shows the descent to the human being from Absolute Being, and the left arc shows the ascent back to Absolute Being from the human being. That is, the right arc shows the material descent, the maturity within matter; while the left arc shows the spiritual ascent, the journey towards spiritual maturity.

The first round of turning in the *semâ'* symbolizes the journey of the *Dhāt*–the "Self" containing all the Names and Attributes in an undifferentiated state–and the journey from a point. Through its journey, the Names and Attributes begin to manifest in the same way letters and words begin to manifest from a point. The shaikh is the one who has been favored with all the Names and Attributes, who has gathered and understood them, who represents the knowledge of God and the *Hakıykat-i Muhammediyye* ("Truth of Muḥammadhood"), and who is the translator of God. After the first round of the *semâ'*, God manifests Himself with His Name *Salām* ("Peace"), and the shaikh prays:

> You have become free of doubt and have known the oneness of God. You have reached the station of *'ilm al-yaqīn* ("certainty through knowledge"); health and joy be upon you!

During the second round, the lovers have turned the *vahdet* ("unity") into witnessing, and they have reached the station of *'ayn al-yaqīn* ("certainty through seeing"). At the end of this round, the shaikh says:

> You have taken your knowledge to the station of *shühûd* ("witnessing"); peace be upon you!

Within the third round the lovers' sight reaches the station of finding and becoming; their *seyr* ("journey") arrives at the station of *tahkıyk* ("investigation"). At the end of this round, the shaikh says to the lovers,

> Health and soundness be upon you! You have become completely annihilated; within Absolute Being you have lost yourself and your imaginary being.

The fourth round is the stage of residing within the Being of God and recognizing everything as real within its own station. Within this stage, they persevere in the station of *vahdet* and circle around their own centers.[21]

One sees that within the one word–*mukabele*–Mevlevîs signify the origin and resurrection (*mebde' ve maâd*), the unity of the Attributes and of the Self (*tawḥīd* of the *Ṣifāt* and the *Dhāt*), the stations of *yaqīn* ("certainty"), belief in the Unity of Being (*Vahdet-iI Vujud*), and its verification.[22]

Meanwhile, oral tradition informs us that Mevlevîs also perceive the following symbols within the *mukabele*:

- *Sharī'ah* ("law") is made of *ahkâm* ("judgements") and is based upon the *ẓāhir* ("apparent"); *ḥaqīqah* ("truth") is the *ahvâl*

---

[21] *Mevlevîhood after Mevlânâ*, pp. 473–76. The symbols within the *mukabele* are interpreted in almost the same way as we have described them here in the following: in *Minhâc-al Fukara*, by Rushûî-i Ankaravî; in Arabic *Al Tuhfat-al Bahiyya fi-t Tarikat-al Mavlaviyya*, by Kösec Ahmed Dede (died 1191 H., 1777 A.D.); in *Al Suhbat-al âfiyya*, by Shaikh Gaalip, which is a commentary on that; in *Işârât-al Ma'neviyya fi Âyin-al Mavlaviyya*, which is a short but valuable treatise by Mesnevîhân Feyzullâh Efendi, the shaikh of the Shaikh Murad Dergâh in Eyyup Nishanjı, and head of the *Reîs-al Kurrâ* ("Readers of the Qur'ān") in his period; and in various other treatises as well.

[22] *Minhâc-al Fukara*, pp. 68–76.

("circumstances") and is based upon the *bāṭin* ("hidden"). *Ṭarīqah* is the path that goes from the *ẓāhir* to the *bāṭin*; to travel on this path is known as the *sülûk* ("journey"). After coming from the apparent, the imaginary being of the one who reaches the Truth is annihilated. Such a person has reached the world of extinction, yet this is not the station of maturity. One has to pass through this station and see the manifestation of the actions and Attributes of the Truth, observing that the Truth becomes apparent on the mirror of the people. One has to know that the manifestations that become apparent through each receptor of favors are appropriate and real in relation to the receptor; one has to treat everything according to what it deserves. This is the station of *kemâl* ("maturity") known as *maʿrifah*. The *sâlik* ("spiritual traveler") who has traveled from *sharīʿah* to *ṭarīqah*, and from *ṭarīqah* to *ḥaqīqah*, within the first three of the four stages, stops at the center of *vahdet* ("unity") during the fourth stage and reaches the station of *maʿrifah*. The four stages of the *semâ'* point toward these stations.

- The *sâlik* who does *dhikr* with the *Ism-i Jelâl* (Allāh) is contemplating *āyāt* 2:115 of the Qurʾān: *And wherever you turn, there is the Face of God.*
- The right hand of the *sâlik* who opens his ams during *semâ'* is supplicating: it is open to the sky. The left hand is pointed downward. This means, "We take it from the Truth and give it to the people; we do not own anything ourselves; we do not exist; we are nothing but an image that serves a purpose but which only appears to exist." This posture also means, "We rise up to the sky and we rain upon the earth; we are *raḥmah* ("compassion") for the world. From the Attributes we arrive at the Self; from the Self we arrive at the world of Attributes, the world of appearance. We become annihilated within Blessed Muḥammad who was a *raḥmah* for the worlds."
- When the arms are opened, it looks like the letters *lām-aleph* of the Arabic alphabet, and it means *lā*. The body looks like the letter *aleph* drawn in the middle of this *lām-aleph*; in this way, *lā* becomes *illā*. *Lā* indicates negation while *illā* indicates affirmation; thus the *kalimāt at-tawḥīd–Lā ilāha illā Allāh* ("There is no

god but God")–is symbolized. By extension, the *sâlik* says, "My imaginary being does not exist; true being belongs to the Truth."

In this way, from beginning to end, the *mukabele* symbolizes *tawḥīd* ("oneness").

While the *mukabele* was being developed, were all of these considerations, as well as the ancient conception of how the heavens and the stars rotated, borne in mind? Although it is impossible for us to give a definite answer, we have to say that these symbols are not mere fancy; in fact, they are in accordance with the truth.

If one accepts that *semâ'* is essentially a means to take the *semâ'zen* to Real Being, a means of divine attraction that makes one lose oneself, or a state of joy that ensues from doing so, then it is clear that the Mevlevî *mukabele* is completely in accordance with the philosophy of Mevlânâ.

In conclusion, music and dance had magical or spiritual characteristics in primitive societies, but had an undisciplined format. *Semâ'* then developed a more measured, orderly form in the practices of the Alevîs and the Bektâshîs. In the Mevlevî *mukabele*, *semâ'* reached its highest ideal in a spiritually complete ceremony that is an expression of the Divine.

IV

Mevlevî Evrâdi

Mevlevî prayers, called *vird* (or *wird*, in Arabic) and *evrâd*, which is the plural, mean "words which are always read"; to read or recite them is regarded as a necessary task. In our Turkish language, metaphors such as *dilimin virdi*, "the *wird* of my tongue," or *Dilime vird edindim*, "I adopted it as a *wird* for my tongue," or words like *vird-i zebân etmek/edinmek,* "to make a *wird* of the tongue" in Ottoman have come from the meaning of the word. On the paths of *taṣawwuf*, each path has *evrâd* composed for reading at certain times, especially for reading after the morning *ṣalāh.*

Mevlânâ, in a *ghazal* of his in *Bahr-i Müctes* in *Divân-ı Kebîr* says:

> In order to reach the morning of your beautiful face,
> for a whole lifetime, this old earth reads *evrâd* every dawn.
>
> *Der arzu-yi sabah-i Cemâl-i tu omri*
> *Cihan-i pir hemihond her seher evrâd.*[1]

In one of his letters he says,

> The praying one (i.e. Mevlânâ himself) had been there for such a long time; and within this time, although I had watched and observed it from morning until evening for many days, they said that I had not been there. Why I stayed until the night *ṣalāh* and then went out was due to the suspicion created by two or three people who worship food and the jealousy within them. They don't even have an inkling about the "taste" of God. . . .

[1] Trans. V. III, poem CVII, p. 178, couplet 1696.

Everyday, five times, I do my *ṣalāh* together with the community; in addition to this, I also have twenty other *wirds*."[2]

In *Fihi ma-Fih*, Discourse 28, he says:

As for the *wird* of the attained ones (*erenler*): let me tell you as much about it as you can understand. This is their *wird*: in the morning, the celebrated souls, all pure angels, the ones that nobody can know but God—because God is very jealous and for this reason He hides even their names from people— yes, these come to visit and greet them.

And you see humankind entering the religion of Allāh in throngs.[3]
The angels enter unto them from every gate.[4]

You have sat down next to them, but you cannot see them, you cannot hear those words, those greetings and those smiles. This isn't surprising; a person who is ill and close to death sees imaginings. He or she is not even aware of the one who sits next to him or her; he or she doesn't even hear what that person says. Those realities are a thousand times subtler than these imaginings. One cannot even see these imaginings unless one becomes that ill; neither can one see those realities unless one dies; one cannot see them before death. The one who knows about the subtlety within the states of the attained ones, the visitor who understands their greatness, knows that many angels and many, many pure souls come into their presence with the dawn; and during such *evrâd*, that person waits and waits so as not to cause a difficulty for the shaikh. You know, there are servants at the door of the palace of the sultan. Each morning, they have *evrâd* to recite. Each of them has a certain station and a particular worship. Some of them worship at a distance, the sultan does not look at them; he pretends not to see them. But

[2] Letters; Ist. Inkilap ve Aka Books; 1963; Letter CXXXII, p. 198.
[3] The Holy Qur'ān, 110:2.
[4] The Holy Qur'ān, 13:23.

the servants both see the sultan and what he does. If a person becomes a sultan, from then on, this is his *wird*; let the servants come into his presence from all directions; because with him no servanthood remains. The injunction: "Acquire the nature of God!" has been actualized. This is a very great station and it would be a shame to speak about it, because its greatness cannot be comprehended by words... [5]

One sees that in his poetry, Mevlânâ uses *wird* as a metaphor of common usage. In his letter he alludes to the prayers and entreatings which are recited every day at certain times. And in *Fihi ma-Fih* he regards the sovereignty within the interior world of the one who has seen the greatness of God within himself, watching this power, doing this contemplation and this witnessing (*shühûd*) as a *wird.*

Did Mevlânâ recite a *wird*? What did he read or recite? We find information about this only in the oldest sources. There is no doubt that he followed the *sunnah* and that he recited the prayers read after *ṣalāh*, the Throne Verse (*Âyetül-Kürsî,* 2:255) and made *tasbīḥs* and prayed according to the prayers mentioned in the traditions of the Prophet. But, besides these what else did he recite?

Chun tu virdi terk kerdi der revish
Ber tu kabzi ayed ez renc u tebish

That is, what was or were the *wird* of Mevlânâ who said, "If you leave your *wird* during the spiritual journey, you will fall into trouble and stressful difficulty"?[6]

There is no record about this in the *Sipehsâlâr.* However, we see the following in the *Manâkıb-al Ârifîn*:

When he saw the advent of the month of *Muḥarrem*, Mevlânâ would recite this prayer:

My Allāh! You are the First and the Last! Your End has no end. And this year is the New Year. O Allāh! I wish from You, with

[5] Trans. Ist. Remzi Books 1959, p. 104.
[6] *Mesnevî*; vol. III; Trans. Ist. *Maarif* Pub. 1943, p. 32, couplet 349.

Your Compassion, that within this year I may be protected from the Devil whom one stones, that You might help me against the *nafs* which orders me to do so many wrongful deeds, that I might be occupied with things that bring me closer to You, and that I might avoid the things that will take me away from You. O Allāh, whose Grace (*Raḥmah*) is widespread, and who showers His Mercy especially on the faithful, and who possesses Greatness, Favor, and Grace, this is what I wish from You![7]

Again, Eflâkî conveys from Kadı Kemâleddin,[8] whom he refers to as "Malîk-al Hulefâ, Valîyy-Allāhu fil ard Shayh Mavla-ı Kâbî," that at the morning prayer, after performing the role of imām at the *madrasah* and when he sat down, Mevlânâ recited the following:

أعْدَدتُ لكُلِّ هَولٍ لا إلهَ إلّا ٱللّهُ وَلِكُلّ هَمٍّ وَغَمٍّ ما شاء ٱللّهُ
وَلِكُلّ نِعْمَةٍ الحَمدُ لِلّهِ وَلِكُلِّ رَخَاءٍ الشُّكْر لِلّهِ وَلِكُلّ أُعْجُوبَةٍ سُبحانَ اللهِ
وَلِكُلّ ذَنْبٍ اَسْتغْفِرُ اللهِ وَلِكُلِّ ضيقٍ حَسبِىَ اللهِ وَلِكُلِّ قَضاءٍ وَقَدَرٍ تَوَكَّلْتُ عَلَى اللهِ
وَلِكُلِّ مُصيبةٍ إنّا لِلّهِ وَإنّا إلَيْهِ راجعُونَ
وَلِكُلِّ طاعَةٍ وَمَعْصِيّةٍ لا حَولَ وَلا قُوّةَ إلّا بِاللهِ العَلِيّ العَظيمْ

The shelter within which I take refuge, the words I will say, and that which I think at each moment of fear, are the words and thoughts of "There is no god but God;" facing all griefs and troubles, I say, "Whatever Allāh wishes, occurs"; for each blessing that comes to me I say, "Praise be to Allāh"; for each comfort and abundance I say, "Thanks be to Allāh"; for each astonishing thing I see, I say, "Allāh is pure from incomplete attributes"; for each mistake, I say, "May Allāh hide that guilt and forgive me"; each time I find myself in difficulty, I say, "Allāh is enough for me"; against each accident of destiny, I say, "God is my support and in Him I trust"; each time a calamity occurs, I say, "Truly! We belong to Allāh and to Him

[7] V. I, p. 271–72. Eflâkî conveys this from *ashâb-ıhâbîr*.
[8] Kadı Kemâleddin-i was a famous scholar of the time who became a close disciple of Mevlânâ's.

we return";[9] each time I obey a command of His, and each time I make a mistake or each time I violate a command, all of my chanting and my ideas are formed by the thoughts, "There is no means or power except through Allāh, who is Most High and Most Great."[10]

Again Eflâkî says that Mevlânâ also used to recite these prayers after the morning *ṣalāh*:

اَللّٰهُمَ اجْعَلْ لِي نُوراً فِي قَلْبِى وَنُوراً فِي سَمْعِى وَنُوراً فِي بَصَرِي وَنُوراً
فِي شَعْرِى وَنُوراً فِي بشرى وَنُوراً فِي لَحمْيِ وَنُوراً فِي دَمِّى وَنُوراً مِنْ بَيْنَ يَدَىَّ
وَنُوراً مِن أمَامى وَنُوراً مِن خَلْفِى وَنُوراً مِن تَحْتِى وَنُوراً مِن فَوْقِى وَنُوراً عَن يَمينى
وَنُوراً عَنْ شِمَالِي   اَللّٰهُمَّ زِدْنِى نُوراً واعْطِنِي نُوراً واجْعلنِي نُوراً يا نُورَ النُورِ
بِرَحْمَتِكَ يا أَرْحَمَ الرَّاحِمِين

My Allāh! Illuminate my heart (*gönül*); illuminate my ear; illuminate my eye; illuminate my hair; illuminate my skin; illuminate my flesh; illuminate my blood; illuminate in front of me; illuminate behind me; illuminate under me; illuminate above me; illuminate my right; illuminate my left. My Allāh! Increase my light; give me light; turn me into divine light by Your Mercy , O Most Merciful of the ones who are merciful! O You who are the Source of Light (*Ya Nūr al Nūr*)![11]

The second one of these prayers is included in exactly this way within the *Mevlevî Evrâd,* today.[12] The third one, the Divine Light Prayer, is not within the text of the 1283 edition.[13] The words "as divine light" (*nūran*) have been taken into the commentary.[14]

---

[9] The Holy Qur'ān, 2:156.
[10] V. I, p. 287.
[11] V. I, p. 287.
[12] Ist. 1282, p. 36; 1328, p. 34–35; Bosnali Fâzil Pasha: *Sharh-al Evrad-al Musamma bi Hakayiki Azkar-i Mavlana*; Ist. 1283, pp. 166–67.
[13] In the 1283 edition, the main resources of the *ḥadīth* of the Prophet mentioned in the *Mevlevî Evrâd* have been indicated, and within the commentary the *ḥadīth* and Qur'ānic verses have been explained and interpreted.
[14] They are in the beginnings of the sentences and it has also been recorded

Eflâkî also conveys that when the sun is rising through the sky, or when he would see the moon, Mevlânâ would stop and recite this *āyāt:*

وَالشّمْسُ وَالْقمَرَ وَالنّجُومَ مُسَخَّراتٌ بِأمْرِهِ ألا لَهُ الخَلْقِ وَالأمْرُ تَبارَكَ اللهَ رَبُّ العَالَمِين

. . . and He has made the sun and the moon and the stars in service to His Command. Truly, all of creation and the command belong to Him. Blessed be Allāh, the Lord of the worlds![15]

Eflâkî also conveys:

In Mevlânâ Ihtiyâreddîn's[16] dream, God suggests to him to read the following prayer:

اللَّهُمَّ ارحَم وَتحَنَّن عَلىٰ سَيِّدِى وَسَنَدِى وَشَيْخِى وَمَكانِ الرُّوحِ
مِن جَسَدِى وَذَخِيرَة يَوْمِى وَغَدِى مَولَانَا مُحَمَّدٍ جَلَالِ الحَقِّ وَالدِينِ
وَعَلىٰ آبَائِهِ وأُمّهَاتِهِ وَأولَادِهِ وَخُلَفَائِهِ وَأتْبَاعِهِ اِلىٰ يَوْمِ القِيَامَةِ

"My Allāh, have mercy and tenderness upon my Master, the one whom I trust, my Elder, who is in the position of Spirit in my body, my nourisher of today and tomorrow, our Master Muhammad the Majesty of Truth and the Way (Mevlânâ Muḥammad Jalāl ul-Ḥaqq wad-Dīn), and upon his ancestors, his children, his khalifas, and his followers until the day of resurrection!"[17]

---

that they are contained within the *Evrâd-ı Halvati*; on p. 30 in the 1328 edition, ascribing them to Tirmizî and Bayhakıy, they have been included in a slightly different way; besides this, the version conveyed through Buhârî, Müslim, and Nasaî has also been included (pp. 50-51). In the commentary, it is in accordance with what Eflâkî conveys with the exception of the extra *Va nûran fî ızâmî* after *Va nûran fî demmî* (pp. 349–51).

[15] The Holy Qur'ān, 7:54.

[16] Imam İhtiyâreddîn was a close friend of Mevlânâ's. He was the one who performed the final washing of Mevlânâ's body and wrapped him in his shroud.

[17] This prayer is only in the footnote in the 1283 edition, and the last part differs only very slightly; on p. 38, 1328 edition, it is the last prayer, but the last part is quite different; pp. 51–52. It is in accordance with the commentary in 1283 edition; pp. 352–53.

Besides these, we see that Eflâkî has conveyed the following as well:

> When he was about to pass away, Mevlânâ called Sırâjeddîn Tatari to him and told him to recite the following prayer when in an expanded state of comfort as well as when contracted in distress:
>
> اللَّهُمَّ إنِى أتَنَفَّسَ لَكَ وَأمُدُّ نَفسِى إلَيْكَ اللَّهُمَّ إنِّي أشْتَاقُ إلىٰ مَولَانَا وَسِيلَةٌ إلَيكَ
> وَأشْتَاقُ إلىٰ عَافِيَةٍ وَسِيلَةٌ إلَيكَ حَتَّىٰ أسَبِّحَكَ كَثِيراً وَأذْكُرَكَ كَثِيرَاً
> اللَّهُمَّ لَا تَجْعَلْ لِى مَرَضاً يُنْسِينِي ذِكْرَكَ وَيُحَيِّطُ عَلَىَّ شَوْقَكَ وَيَقْطَعُ عَنِّي لَذَّةَ تَسْبِيحَكَ
> وَلَا تُعْطِينِي صِحَّةً يُطْغِيني وَيَزِيدُنِي بَطْراً وَشَرّاً بِرَحْمَتَكَ يَا أرْحَمَ الرَّاحِمِين
>
> "My Allāh! I inhale my breath only for You and with Your Power; I exhale my breath again only for You and with Your Power. My Allāh! I have a longing for Mevlânâ who has become a means for my reaching You; I also have a longing to be liberated and purified from difficulties, so that I may declare repeatedly that You are free from incomplete attributes, and so that I may remember You often. My Allāh! Don't give me a disease that may make me forget You, that might weaken the longing that I feel for You, that might take away the pleasure of declaring that You are free from incomplete attributes. But, with Your Compassion, neither give me health that may corrupt me, which might increase my egotism and wrong-doing, O Most Merciful One of the merciful ones."[18]

In addition to these prayers, in Eflâkî's work, there is also an "after the meal prayer" of Mevlânâ's, a will for his friends and those who follow him; and some Arabic words which are said to have been written by him as a remedy for malaria. Of these, we are conveying the table prayer and the will:

اللَّهُمَّ اَغْفِر لِصَاحِبِ هَذَا الطّعَامِ وَمَن سَعَىٰ فِي تَحْصِيلِهِ مِن الخُدَّامِ

[18] This prayer is absent in both of the editions; however, in the 1283 edition, it has been written as a marginal note before the previous prayer; p. 30. It is the same in the commentary; pp. 351–52. Please look at the "Explanations" of "The Letters" for Sırâjeddîn, p. 257.

بِحَقِّ مُحَمَّدٍ وآلِهِ الكِرَامِ يا ذَىَ الجَلالِ وَالإِكْرَام

O my Allāh! Forgive the mistakes of the owner of this meal and those who helped and served to prepare this! O You who are the Most Great and who possess the Greatest Grace and Benevolence! (Forgive them) For the sake of Muḥammad and his lineage![19]

أُوصِيكُم بِتَقْوىٰ اللهِ فِي السِّرِّ وَالعَلانِيَّةِ وَبِقِلَّةِ الطَّعَامِ وَقِلَّةِ
الكَلَامِ وَهِجْرَةِ المَعَاصِى وَالآثَامِ وَمُوَاظَبَةِ الصِّيَامِ وَدَوَامِ
القِيَامِ وَتَرْكِ الشَّهَوَاتِ عَلَىٰ الدَّوَامِ وإِحْتِمَالِ الجَفَاءِ مِن جَمِيعِ الأَنَامِ
وَتَرْكِ مُجَالَسَةِ السُّفَهَاءِ وَالعَوَامِ وَمُصَاحَبَةِ الصَّالِحِينَ وَالكِرَام
فَإِنَّ خَيْرَ النَّاسِ مَن يَنْفَعُ النَّاسِ وَخَيرُ الكَلَامِ مَا قَلَّ وَدَلَّ

I encourage you to always be conscious of God, to avoid mistakes in secret and in the open, while you are alone, or when you are with other people; to eat little and to speak little; to cease making mistakes and being rebellious; to continue fasting; to go on worshipping during the nights and always to turn away from the demands of the *nafs*; to take the troubles of all people as a burden upon yourself; to give up speaking with people who have small intellects and who are mean-spirited; and to be friends with and speak with pure and noble-spirited people; truly, "The best among human beings is the one who does good to human beings,"[20] and the best among words is the word that is succinct, whose intention is understandable.[21]

The first prayer is a prayer that is read once a year in the month of *Muḥarrem*, so it has no relation to the *wird*. The *āyāt* recited when

[19] This is in the first manuscript of *Manâkıb-al Ârifîn*, but it is not included in the later manuscripts; perhaps when Eflâkî was enlarging and revising it, he found this tradition weak. I, p. 1030.
[20] In "The Nefahât Translation" there is an extra saying: *Valhamdu lillâhi vahdeh*, that is "Praise be to Allah who is One" (Ist. 1289, p. 519). It is a *ḥadīth* ("tradition" of the Prophet); Câmi'-al Sagıyr, Egypt Pub. Hayriyya-1321, II, p. Veled Chelebi wrote a commentary about this will and had it published with the title *Hayr-al Kelâm*.
[21] II, p. 584.

the sun is rising and when the moon is seen is also a remembering of God. The table prayer and the testament will also have no relationship with the *wird.* And so, the prayer that Mevlânâ read after the morning *ṣalāh*, the Divine Light Prayer (*Nûr Duâsı*); the prayer based upon the dream of İhtiyâreddîn, and the prayer of which it is said that he told Sırâjeddîn-i Tatarî to recite it during the last phase of his life compose the nucleus of the *Mevlevî Evrâd.*[22]

---

[22] Besides the two editions of the *evrâd* mentioned above, there are also editions printed in 1280, 1282, and 1290 H. (1870, 1872, 1880 A.D. respectively). These prayers are included within these editions, too. In the *dergâh*, there are copies of the *evrâd* written in the years of 1290, 1317, 1322, and 1328 H. (1880, 1907, 1912, 1918 A.D.). We could not find an older manuscript. Abdülhalîm Chelebizâde Muhammed Bakır Chelebi's (1943) son Jelâleddîn Chelebi has the manuscript of an *evrâd.* This copy, written in a beautiful *naskhi* (a style of Arabic writing), is dated 1026 H. (1617 A.D.). On the first page is the record that shows to whom it belongs; e.g. this belongs to or this is the property of Abû-Bakr Chelebi. This Abû-Bakr Chelebi is the one who took the position of Chelebi in 1040 H. (1630 A.D.) and who was appointed to reside in Istanbul in 1048 H. (1638 A.D.), and who died on the seventh day after his arrival in Istanbul, on the twenty-seventh day of the month *Rabîulevvel* (Konya, Mevlânâ Museum, Abdülbâki Gölpınarlı Writings, No. 94, 143, b), and who was buried in the *türbe* in Yenikapı Mevlevîhânesi. In this copy of his, the prayer that begins with "*A'dadtu*..." after the *Asmā ʾ al-Ḥusnā* ("Beautiful Names"), the prayer of İhtiyâreddîn, and the prayer taught to Sırâjeddîn are absent.

In the *evrâd* given by Abdülvâhid Chelebi to the late Ali Haydar Bey, the father of Hüseyin Shükrü Ilıjak, the lawyer from Akshehir, we see a *salavat* ("greeting") to the Fourteen Innocent Ones (*Ondört Ma'sûm*: the Blessed Muḥammad, Blessed Fāṭimah and the Twelve Imāms) that begins with a *Bismillāh* after the *Asmā ʾ al-Ḥusnā* and then there is a *Nâdi Alî. Nâdi Alî* is the name of this quatrain in Arabic which means, "Call ʿAlī, he is the receiver (*mazhar*) of wondrous things [according to the way one reads, it may also mean: 'He is the one who does wondrous things']; in times of stress and trouble, you find him helping you. All my troubles and all my griefs will be dissolved thanks to your sainthood (*vilāyāt*), Ya ʿAlī, Ya ʿAlī!"

Nadi Aliyyen mazharil navaibi
Tacidhu avnan leke fin navaibi
Kullu hemmin va gammin sayancali
Bivilayatike ya Aliyyu ya Ali

It is said that during the Uḥud War, this was told by Gabriel to the Blessed Prophet and that the Blessed Prophet had called ʿAlī with these words

One sees that the *evrâd* also varies according to the joy and temperament of the one who gives it and of the one who receives

---

and that ʿAlī had then come and overcome the pagans; and it is recited with various addenda in Arabic or Persian, etc.; it is said that it has many properties (please refer to: Rıf'at Ahmed id; *Mirât-al makaasıd fi Daf'al mafâsid*; İst. Vezirhani, İbrahim Ef. Lithograph -1293, pp. 159–206). Acorrding to what has been said, *Nâdi Alî* is a quatrain of Di'bil-i Huzzâî (246 H., 860 A.D.). Alevîs and Bektâshîs give great importance to *Nâdi Alî*. There is even an anecdote that goes like this: In Iran, one of the people who call themselves *Ehl-i Hak* and who accept Alī as God was asked, "Why don't you do the *ṣalāh*?" He answered, "I am reciting *Nâdi ʿAlī* and that is the father of the *ṣalāh*!" (in Persian: "*Men Nadi Ali mihonem ki peder-i nemaze!*"). Please also refer to *Mevzûât-ı Kebîr* by Alîyy-al Kaarî; Ist. Matbaa-i Âmire, 1289, p. 93.

In *Nâdi Alî*, there are Persian compounds mixed with grammatically incorrect Arabic words and lines such as: *Yâ Aliyyu, yâ İlyâ, yâ Abû-I Hasan, yâ Abû-I Huseyn, yâ Abu't Turâb, Hall-i müşkil, server-i dîn, şâf'i-i yevmil-hisâb, Şâh-ı merdan, Şîr-i Yezdan, kudret-i Perverdgâr; Lâ fatâ illâ Ali lâ seyfe illâ Zül-fekaar. Her belâ ki pîş âyed def'kun Perverdgâr.*

After this comes *Sūrah al-Fātiḥah* with each *āyāt* commented on using words from the Twelve Imāms in grammatically broken Arabic; for example: *Sıratallezîne en'amte aleyhim, huva mutâbaat-al Askeriyy ellezî huva mutâbaat-al Hâdiyyi Sâhibu hâzel emr.* Even the last word of this sentence has been written with the *ain* as *al âmır*. At the end of this *evrâd*, we read this *ijazet*:

İn nâdi Aliyy-i Emîr-al Mu'minîn Haydar-i Kerrâr ve
Safger-i Girdgâr ve Şîr-i Perverdgâr ve Evrâd-ı Şerif-i
Hazret-i Mevlânâ kuddise sırruhul a'lâ bâ silsile-i tarîkat
ben in fakıyr resîdeest, men nîz Ali Haydar Bik
râ icâzet dâdem be in ki beher yevm in evrâd-ı
şerîf müdâvemet nümâyed ve bilâ özr-i şer'î
terk nekuned; Vallâh-al Muvaffik 3 Racab 306.

Post-nişîn-i Dergâh-ı
Hazreti Mevlânâ Kuddisa sırruhu
(seal)
İbni Mevlânâ Abdülvâhid bâ Meşîhat şud

The real form of this seal is *İbni Mevlânâ Muhammed bâ meşîhat şud Said* and Hemdem Said Chelebi had this well-proportioned seal engraved on his seal. After he died in 1275 H. (1858 A.D.), the Chelebis who took over the rank of Chelebi following him regarded this as a tradition and had their names engraved in the place of Said Muhammed Hemdem Chelebi and also included the other words.

it. In short, because we do not have an early copy in hand, it is impossible for us to say with certainy when the *evrâd* was composed. Because the oldest *evrâd* available to us was written at the beginning of eleventh century (seventeenth century A.D.), and because in the *Manâkıb-al Ârifîn* which was written in the seventh century (fourteenth century A.D.) there are no records about the existence of *evrâd* and the giving of permission to read *evrâd* to those who join the order (*intisab etmek*), we surmise that it was composed in the fifteenth or sixteenth centuries. Perhaps the *evrâd* was composed during the time when the kitchen services, the Mevlevî *mukabele*, and the other rules of behaviour and conduct (*ādāb ve erkan*) were also established.

By the Chelebi, the *khalīfah,* or the shaikh, the permission of the *evrâd* (*evrâd ijâzeti*) is given to the Mevlevî dervish whose *sikke* was conferred with the blessing of the *tekbir* (*Allāhu Akbar*). When the *evrâd ijâzeti* is being given, at the end of the *evrâd* which was printed or handwritten, it would be recorded and sealed that, "It is given with the condition that as it (the *evrâd*) has come to the person through the lineage (*silsile*), that person must read it in the morning after the *ṣalāh* and that he (or she) will never give up reading it unless there is a reason permitted by the religious law." We are including here examples of three *evrâd ijâzets* from the manual (p. 69) that belongs to *Mesnevîhân* Sıdkı Dede and which is archived as number 1176 in the Mevlânâ Museum, Konya:

> *Pîr-i dest-gîrimiz Hazret-i Mevlânâ Muhammed Celâleddîn Kaddese-nallâhu bi esrârihî efendimizin evrâd-ı şerifi icâzeti, silsile-i tarikat-i aliyyesiyle bu fakıyre vâsıl olup fakıyr de muhibbân-ı Mevlevîyyeden fülâna, mâni-i şer'-îsi olmadıkça günde bir defa kables-subh, ya ba'd ez namâz okumak üzere izin verdim. Vallâhul muvaffik vahuva yahdis-sebîl.*

> *Alhamdu lillâhi hakka hamdihî; vassalâtu vesselâmu alâ hayri halkıhî Muhammedin va alâ âlîhî ve sahbihî acma'în. Eceztu li kirâati hâzihil evrâdiş-şerîfetil-Mevlevîyyeti fi külli yavmin marratan alassabâhi lifülânin taleben limardâtillâhi tââlâ.*[23]

[23] "Praise be to God as He truly deserves to be praised; and peace and blessings upon the best of His creation, Muḥammad, and his folk, and all

İcâzet-i in evrâd-i şerif-i Hazret-i Mevlânâ Kaddesanallâhu bi sırrihil-a'lâ ba silsile-i tarikat-i aliyye-i on Hazret bemen resîdeest ve men nîz fulânrâ izn dâdem beon şart ki beher rûz kabl ez nâmaz-ı subh ya ba'd ez namaz müdâvemet nümayed ve begayr-i özr-i şer'i terkrâ reva nedâred ve becuz rızâ-yı Bâri taâlâ nehoned. Vallâhul muvaffiku va huva yahdis-sebîl.

In the 1283 edition, the main resources for the traditions of the Prophet mentioned in the *Mevlevî Evrâd* are indicated and within the commentary, the traditions and the *āyāts* are interpreted. Essentially, because at the end of this book, we will be giving the text as a document, we do not think that further explanation is necessary and so we are ending the chapter about the *evrâd* here.[24]

---

of his companions. Permission is granted to recite these noble Mevlevî prayers once every day at the break of day with the intention of seeking the acceptance and good-pleasure of God Most High."

[24] For the text of the *evrâd*, see *The Mevlevî Wird*, published by Threshold Society, 2000.

V

Ādāb & Erkan

İsm-i Jelâl

In the Holy Qur'ān there are many *āyāts* about remembering God. Verse 2:152 says, *Remember me and I shall remember you*; those who remember Allāh while standing, sitting, and lying down are praised in *āyāt* 3:191; and the frequent rememberance of God is enjoined in *āyāts* 3:41, 26:227, and 42:10. In *āyāt* 7:205, humankind is ordered to remember God quietly and in awe. *Āyāt* 8:2 speaks of those whose hearts tremble with awe when Allāh is mentioned, whose faith increases when His messages are conveyed to them. *Āyāt* 11:114 praises men and women who remember Allāh frequently, while *āyāt* 24:36 mentions houses of worship in which people are allowed to remember Allāh. In *āyāts* 33:10 and 33:41, as well as 37:3 and 87:5, remembrance of God is mentioned, and in 87:15 those who remember God are blessed.

The Prophet, too, praised *dhikr* circles as being gardens of Paradise,[1] and said, "Until the hypocrites say 'They are showing off!' remember Allāh."[2] He urged remembrance of God secretly[3] and said that the most elevated human beings are those who remember God.[4] Sufis attach great importance to the following two *ḥadīth*:[5]

> Listen and know: would you like me to inform you about the best of your deeds, the purest according to our Master (Allāh), the

[1] Cami, I, p. 29.
[2] Ibid., p. 30.
[3] Ibid., p. 30.
[4] Kunuz-al Hakaayik, I, p. 42.
[5] Risale-i Kushayriyya, p. 131.

> one that elevates your degree and which is better than feeding the poor using money and gold, or even better than confronting the enemy and chopping off their heads? To remember Allāh.[6]
>
> The apocalypse will not come as long as "Allāh, Allāh" is chanted upon the earth.[7]

Although experts in Islamic canonical law say that the *dhikr* mentioned in *ḥadīth* literature is not ceremonial, nor performed according to a specific ritual, Sufis who hold that *dhikr* using the Names of God is essential on the spiritual journey have from earliest times incorporated it within a ceremony. According to oral tradition (*rivāyāt*), the first Sufis saw *Lā ilāha illā Allāh*, *Allāh*, and *Hū* as the essentials of *dhikr*. Afterwards, they also added the Names *Ḥaqq*, *Ḥayy, Qayyūm*, and *Qahhār,* increasing the number of Names to seven, which corresponds to the seven levels of the *nafs*. The spiritual traveler might inform his shaikh about a significant dream he has experienced resulting in the *dhikr* being increased, or in the traveler moving onto the next Name; in this way, the seven levels of the *nafs* are ascended with seven Names. Later Sufis added other Names of God. Those who did the *dhikr* while they were sitting were called *Kuûdî,* while the ones who did the *dhikr* standing were called *Kıyâmî.* Besides this, *dhikr* has been classified into two catagories: silent or loud; the former known as *Zikr-i Khafî* and the later as *Zikr-i Jehrî.*[8]

In contrast to those Sufis who regarded recitation of the Names as essential for the spiritual journey, was a group whose adherents called themselves "the travelers of the path of Müsemmâ" (meaning "named; bearing a name") and *shuttâr/shakraks.* They did not distinguish themselves from common people through special clothing or ceremonies, nor did they frequent a *tekke* or special gathering place, and neither did they regard themselves as people of *taṣawwuf.* Because they cultivated the habit of seeing themselves as blame-

---

[6] Cami, I. p. 97.
[7] Ibid., II, p. 191.
[8] Harîrîzâde Kemaleddin Muhammed-al Harîri: *Tibyânu Vasâil-al Hakaayık fî Bayânı Salâsil-al Tarâık*; Ist. Fatih Lib. Vol. I, No. 430, 1. b-11. a, II, No. 431, 35 b-42. b.

worthy and less than everyone else, they took the name *Melâmet ehli* ("people of blame"), and they saw love and divine attraction (*jezbe*) as the essentials of the spiritual journey. Mevlânâ's father, his father's *khalif* and his own guide, Seyyid Burhâneddîn-i Muhakkık-ı Tirmizî, as well as Shams of Tabriz who had such an impact on Mevlânâ's life and came to be regarded as his *khalif*, belong to this second category.[9]

Judging by his father, his spiritiual guide, and his spiritual companion and *khalif*, Mevlânâ does not belong with those who considered *dhikr* (whether it be aloud or silent) to be essential to the spiritual journey. He is one of those like Abû-Bakr-al Vâsıtî (330 H. 932 A.D.) who said, "Those who chant His names are in greater unawareness than those who have forgotten to remember Him."[10] Mevlânâ indicates this with the following words:

We have said so much: reflect on the rest.
If your thought is frozen, practice remembrance of God.
Recollection of God brings thought into movement:
make remembrance the sun for this congealed thought.

Though divine attraction is, indeed, the essence of the matter,
brother, don't wait for it: exert yourself.
For to renounce exertion is like an act of disdain.
Can disdain be seemly for the devoted lover?[11]

And Mevlânâ deepens this understanding:

Our Sovereign has given the permission:
"Remember (*dhikr*) Allāh!"
He saw us in the fire and granted us light.

He said, "I so transcend your remembrance
that no image or description of yours can attain to Me.
One deceived by an image cannot find Our Self,
yet still, remember Me."

[9] Please refer to *Mevlânâ Celâleddîn,* III. Edition, pp. 49–66 and the second chapter, pp.140–52.
[10] Sulamî: *Tabakaat-al Sûfiyya*; p. 305.
[11] *Mesnevî* VI, 1475–78.

> The body's remembrance is imperfect imaginings,
> from which the Sovereign's Attributes remain remote.[12]

Seyyid Burhâneddîn-i Muhakkık-ı Tirmizî says that one should *dhikr* from the soul when doing *dhikr*[13] and adds, "There are two kinds of *dhikr*: the *dhikr* of the tongue and the *dhikr* of the heart. The *dhikr* of the tongue takes the servant to the *dhikr* of the heart. *Dhikr* means to escape the space of ignorance and enter the open space of sight."[14] From his *Maârif* we understand that Mevlânâ's father, Sultânel Ulemâ, also did *dhikr*.[15]

But all of these do not show that *dhikr* was of primary importance for Mevlânâ, or even for his father and his father's *khalif*, Seyyid Burhâneddîn. Even within his will, Mevlânâ does not mention *dhikr*. According to our perspective, his *dhikr*, and that of his father and *murshid*, suggest that rather than *dhikr* being essential to the spiritual journey, it is more of a courtesy.

In *İbtidâ-Nâme*, which is the primary source, and in subsequent sources (the two *Mesnevîs* of Sultân Veled, Sipehsâlâr, and *Manâkıb-al Ârifîn*), although *semâ'* is mentioned, there is no mention of a *dhikr* circle and no mention of Mevlânâ assigning someone a *dhikr*. Likewise, there is no record of Sultân Veled, Ulu Arif Chelebi, or Shemseddin Emîr Âbid Chelebi forming a *dhikr* circle or assigning *dhikr*. But the *Manâkıb* tells of how one day the Pervâne asked Mevlânâ, "Some of the old dervishes chant '*Lā ilāha illā Allāh,*' some chant '*illā Allāh*,' and the dervishes from Turkistan chant '*Hū, Hū*.' Some pious ones chant '*Lâ havle . . .*' some continue to chant "*Estagfirullâhil azîm ve bihamdihî*.' What is your *dhikr*?" Mevlânâ answered, "*Allāh, Allāh, Allāh*; we are the Allāhians. We come from Allāh and are returning to Allāh; my father also used to hear from Allāh, speak from Allāh, and chant, "Allāh." For Allāh has manifested Himself through all the Prophets with one of His Names; the manifestation

[12] *Mesnevî* II, 1715–18.
[13] *Maarif*; Badi'uz-zaman Firuzan-fer edition; Tehran Uni. Pub. 1339 Shemsi hicri; p. 62.
[14] Ibid., p. 66.
[15] Badi'uz-zaman Firuzan-fer edition; Tehran-1333 Shemsi hicri, Chapter V, p. 6; Chapter XVIII, p. 22.

of ours, as the Muḥammadans, is by the name Allāh that contains all the names," and he says that he chants the name Allāh.[16]

But let's repeat that because there is no record during the period of Mevlânâ, nor immediately after him, of someone assigning a chant of "Allāh" for a certain number of times, nor arranging a *dhikr* gathering, *dhikr* seems to be secondary compared to *semâ'*. For this reason, we accept the words, "*Dhikr* is not exuberance and overflowing; to reach the One whom one invokes is to be annihilated in Him. The invoker and the Invoked become one; one loses oneself, passing beyond one's existence into the Presence of the Truth,"[17] however we view these expressions as belonging to a much later period, especially the advice that the number of repetitions of the *dhikr* should be at least 3000.[18]

The *Ism-i Jelâl* (Allāh) used to be chanted as follows:

The shaikh sits on his post and the *dedes* and the *muhibs* form a complete circle to his right and left. The *meydanjı dede* takes in his arms a long *tasbīḥ* ("rosary") with large beads, kisses its *imâme* ("single, long bead"), presents it to the shaikh, and then spreads it around the circle (it is long enough to do so). Each person kisses the bead in front of him and holds the *tasbīḥ* with two hands, palms inside the circle. Slowly, and elongating the syllables as much as the breath will allow, the shaikh says, "*'A'ūzhu billāhi minash shayṭānir rajeem.*" In the same manner he then says, "*Bismillāh ar-Raḥmān ar-Raḥīm*" and begins the *dhikr*. To begin, "Allāh" is recited three times: first the syllable "Al" and then the syllable "lāh", the latter elongated for as long as the breath will allow, and with a brief pause between each repetition. After this, "Allāh" is recited without elongating the second syllable and with a brief pause between each repetition; as the *dhikr* progresses the second syllable is lengthened a little and the *dhikr* gets faster. Towards the end, the second syllable is no longer lengthened and the pause is diminished further, the syllables becoming faster and more forceful. While the first syllable is recited the head moves lightly upwards and during the second syllable it comes back again

[16] *Manâkıb-al Ârifîn*, I, pp. 250–51.
[17] *Minhac*, p. 89.
[18] Ibid., p. 92.

to its natural position. To turn the head to the right or left is not allowed. During the *dhikr*, the *tasbīḥ* is made to walk through the hands without tugging the beads; in this way, it moves towards the right within the circle. Towards the end of the *dhikr* the syllables become indistinct; two guttural sounds are heard. When he feels the *dhikr* had lasted long enough, the shaikh recites a long "Allāh" and everybody becomes silent. After this the shaikh recites the following *gülbâng*:

> *Allahu ekber a'zam kebîren vel hamdü lillâhi hamden kesîren ve sübhânallâhu bukreten ve asîlâ ve sallallâhu alâ eşrefi nûru cemi'il enbiyâi vel mürselîn; vel hamdü lillâhi rabbil âlemin.*
>
> *Vakt-i şerif hayrı, hayırlar fethi, şerler def'i, niyazlar kabûlü, murâdât husûlü, dîn-i İslâm nusratı ve kâffe-i ehl-i imân selâmetiyçün ve güzeştegân-ı mü'minin ve mü'minât ervâhiyçün* [silently]*: ve hassaten azîz, şerif, latîf cenâb-ı Vâcibül vûcudun rızâ-yı kerîmiyçün* [aloud]*: celle ve alel Fâtiha.*

In some manuscripts, as it was recited often, the *gülbâng* of the *İsm-i Jelâl* was as follows:

> *Vakt-i şerif hayrola; hayırlar fethola; şerler def'ola; Allahu azîmuş-şân, ism-i zâtının nûruyla kalblerimizi pür nûr eyliye; demler, safâlâr ziyâde ola. Dem-i Hazret-i Mevlânâ, sırr-ı Şems-i Tebrîzî, kerem-i İmâm-ı Alî, Hû diyelim.*[19]

Together with the shaikh, everybody says "*Hū*" for as long as the breath will allow and the ceremony ends.

When the *Ism-i Jelâl* is finished, the *meydanjı* gathers up the *tasbīḥ*, kisses its *imāme* and, carrying it in the same way as he had brought it, stands before the shaikh. The shaikh and the souls then make *niyâz* and stand up. The shaikh walks slowly to the centre, bows his head and gives a *salām*. As in the *semâ'hâne*, the *meydanjı* reciprocates the

[19] "May this moment be blessed. May goodness be opened and may evil be dispelled. May the Most Glorious God purify and fill our hearts with the pure Light of His Greatest Name. May all our moments, our journeying be resplendent. By the breath of our master Mevlânâ, by the secret of Shams of Tabriz, and by the generosity of Imām ʿAlī, let us say *Hū*, *Huuu*…"

salām. The ones opposite the shaikh move a little to the right and left, thereby opening a space in front of the door. Again, similar to the ritual in the *semâ'hâne*, bowing his head, the shaikh leaves the *masjid* (or room in which the *Ism-i Jelâl* is being chanted). Everybody bows their heads in response and leaves as if leaving a *semâ'hâne.*

The *Ism-i Jelâl* was chanted in the *masjid* of *dergâhs* after the morning *ṣalāh.* After it an *ashir* was recited. The *Fātiḥah* was then recited by the shaikh, after which the shaikh sat in contemplation before rising.

On *Ihya* nights, after the *ṣalāh* and before the *mukabele*, the *Ism-i Jelâl* was also chanted. If the *kudümzenbashı*, the *neyzenbashı* or the shaikh were sick and a substitute could not be found, the *mukabele* was not performed. Instead, under the direction of the *ashchı dede*, the *Ism-i Jelâl* was chanted in the *semâ'hâne* and this was deemed sufficient. Sometimes, during gatherings of the brothers when the conversation deepened and a state of ecstasy came over them, chanting also took place.

While the *Ism-i Jelâl* was being chanted, to show one's ecstasy outwardly (like in some Sufi *ṭarīqahs)*, to shout, to faint, to throw oneself onto the floor, to weep with a loud voice, or simulate ecstasy as if one had been caught by divine attraction was absolutely contrary to the Path; such a thing could not be done. If someone did it, the *meydanjı dede* or another *dede* immediately took that soul out of the circle. Essentially, because everyone had previously learned the proper conduct, no one did anything that would violate the *ādāb* and such a thing did not occur.

The authority to assign the *Ism-i Jelâl* belonged only to the *khalif*; for this reason, the shaikh who had not yet been endowed with khalifhood could not assign to others the *Ism-i Jelâl.* Just as it was assigned to *dedes*, it could also be assigned to outstanding *muhibs.*

The *meydanjı* took the one who was to be intiated into the *Ism-i Jelâl* to the *khalif.* Making him sit on his knees in front of him, the *khalif* spoke into his ear, "*Fa'lem ennehu La ilahe illAllah; Allah, Allah, Allah,*" and made him practice the manner of doing the *dhikr.* The number of repetitions begins with ten; but the number doesn't reach to thousands as Rasûhî says.

Meydân-ı Sherîf ("Sacred Space")

In Mevlevî *tekkes*, in a place close to the *matbâh* ("kitchen"), there is a rectangular room called the *meydan-i sherif.* At the entrance there is a place for making coffee, though sometimes coffee is made in a little room next to the *meydan*. In the *meydan* itself, there is a red *post* spread at the front, while to its right is a black *post* and its left a white *post*. The red *post* belongs to the shaikh, the black to the *kazanjı dede* ("cauldron" *dede*), and the white to the *meydanjı dede.*

After the morning *ṣalāh* is done and the *Ism-i Jelâl* has been recited, one by one, *dedes* enter the *meydan*. Lastly, the shaikh, usually accompanied in Konya by the *tarikatchi*, and in other *tekkes* by the *ashchıbashı,* bows his head and enters. All the *dedes* bow their heads together with him. As he sits down on his *post*, they sit down in unison and make *niyâz* to the floor.

The outer *meydanjı* then brings in morsels of bread on a tray and presents them to each person by kneeling in front of them. These morsels of bread are called *chörek*. The one who wishes to abstain communicates this by touching the tray with his index finger before bending forward a little and kissing his finger. The ones who wishes to partake kisses the morsel and holds it in their hands, waiting. Next, the *kahveji* ("coffee man") immediately brings the coffee and presents it to those who have a *chörek*. One who has taken the coffee, puts the *chörek* into his mouth and then drinks the coffee. The empty coffee cups are gathered in the manner we have previously mentioned. After this, everyone puts their hands on their thighs with fingers a little apart and the elbows touching the sides of the abdomen; they close their eyes and practice *murāqabah* ("meditation"). *Murāqabah* means to tie one's heart to the "owner of the time"—to the *qutb* ("spiritual pole") who is the inheritor of *Hakıykat-i Muhammediyye*—and to wait for *feyiz* ("enlightenment") from that soul. This state lasts for around five minutes; and then the person on the *post*, beginning with an *ʾAʿūzhu/Bismillāh*, recites aloud *Sūrah an-Naṣr* (110) from the Qurʾān. He then recites the *Fātiḥah* followed by this *gülbâng*:

> *Vakt-i şerif hayrola; hayırlar fethola; şerler def'ola; kulûb-ı âşıkan güşâd ola; demler; safâlar ziyâde ola; sâhibül-hayrâtın rûh-ı revanları şad ü*

handân ola. Dem-i Hazret-i Mevlânâ, sırr-ı Şems-i Tebrîzî, kerem-i İmâm-ı Alî, Hû diyelim.

Everybody says "*Hū*" for as long as their breath allows, kisses the floor, and stands up. The shaikh, *tarikatchı* or *ashchı dede* walks to the door, turns to the *meydan* and bows his head. Everyone bows with him and exits as they would from a *semâ'hâne. Muhibs* are not permitted to enter the *meydan.*

According to Mevlevîs, death is an illusory thing. Mevlânâ had become completely receptive of blessed Muḥammad's *feyiz*, and as there is someone in every period who is completely receptive of Mevlânâ, that person receives the *feyiz.* The one who knows who possessess this receptivity, makes *rabıta* ("spiritual contact") with that soul during *murāqabah*, tying their heart to them and visualizing them in front of their eyes. The one who does not know, connects to the *Hakıykat-i Muhammediyye.* Most Mevlevîs accepted Seyyid Abdülkaadir-i Belhî (1341 H., 1923 A.D.) as the *qutb* of that time. After he walked to the Truth ("passed away"), there were those who connected to his son Seyyid Ahmed Muhtâr (1352 H., 1933 A.D.), Ferruh Chelebi (1352 H., 1933 A.D.), Mesnevîhân Sıtkı Dede in Konya (1352 H., 1933 A.D.), and the Shaikh of Kulekapısı, Ahmed Jelâleddîn Dede (1366 H., 1946 A.D.).

Somat/Sımât ("Table")

Every moment, a Mevlevî is contemplating unity (*vahdet murakabesi*). *Hûş der dem* ("aware of every breath") he watches the manifestation of the moment he is in, his whole mind intent upon it, as it is evoked in the *āyāt*: . . . *those whom neither business nor striving after gain can turn from the remembrance of God* (24:37). He is not unaware of the Divine context of all his actions. From this point of view, eating is also a kind of worship, because it requires thankfulness.

A university professor, the late Ahmed Naim Bey (died 1353 H. 1934 A.D.) recounted how a shaikh invited him to dinner. Naim Bey said some thing like, "They have said that to be thankful for the *nîmet* ("blessing" or "food") is to see the One who has bestowed within that *nîmet.*" After the shaikh had thought silently for a while, he said, "We cannot say such words yet." A Mevlevî thinks about the power of the One who gives the *nîmet* and the wisdom of the one who eats it, and so sees the grace within it.

Among the Mevlevîs, the kitchen is a holy place; the raw get cooked there, the unripe mature. It is the station (*makam*) of Âteshbâz-ı Veli.[20] When the food is cooked, the *kazanjı dede* ("cauldron" *dede*) approaches, makes *niyâz* and opens the lid. The souls place the pot on the floor and the *kazanjı* recites this *gülbâng*:

> *Tabhı şîrîn ola; Hak berekâtın vere; yiyenlere nûr-ı imân ola. Dem-i Hazret-i Mevlânâ, sırr-ı Âteşbâz-ı Veli, kerem-i İmâm-ı Alî, Hû diyelim!*

> May the food be sweet, may the Truth give its abundance, and may it be divine light and faith for those who eat it. By the breath of our master Mevlânâ, the secret of Âteshbâz-ı Veli, and the generosity of Imām ʿAlī, let us say, "*Hū!*"

Altogether everybody says, "*Hū!*" When the time to eat comes, the *sofra* ("table") is set in the appropriate part of the kitchen. The table is a big, circular board. It is placed on a wooden stand made up from interlocking parts. The *posts* (sheepskins) are spread around the *sofra*. The spoons are placed along the edge of the table facing down, turned to the left with the handles on the right. Other Sufis place the spoon open, facing up, and say, "It is praying." The Mevlevîs place it facing down and say, "It is bowing in *niyâz*." The aim is not to display anything dirty and to hide what is shameful. At a meal everyone eats with a spoon, and each time one sips soup or some other food with the spoon, one replaces it facing the surface of the table. After the

[20] Âteshbâz-i Veli was said to be the cook in Mevlânâ's *madrasah* who came to Konya with Mevlânâ's father. His body lies under a *türbe* built in the Seljuk style on the side of the old way to Meram in Konya. His name was İzzeddin Yüsuf. Both from the inscription on the stone sachophagus under the *türbe* and that over the window of entreaty (*niyâz penjeresi*) on the upper part, we learn that he died on the fifteenth day of the month *Rajab* in the year 684 H. (16th September, 1285 A.D.). See *Mevlevîhood after Mevlânâ*, pp. 330–32.

spoons have been lined up, a pinch of salt is placed in front of everyone. A table cloth which is called a *dolaylı havlu* ("surrounding cloth") and which is long enough to reach around the circumference of the table is spread in such a way that half of its narrow side (about five inches) is placed on the table top and the other half falls freely upon the knees of those seated there. A table mat is placed in the middle of the table. The souls who serve water prepare the water jugs and glasses. The food is put into the serving bowls and they are lined up on the stone seat of the entrance hall of the kitchen used for eating. The dervish who is assigned to announce meal times, first before the chamber of the shaikh and then in the corridor where the cells are, seals his feet (*ayak mühürlemek*) and bows his head (*bash kesmek*) and with a loud voice calls, "*Hū . . . Somata sala.*" He lengthens the *Hū* a little and lengthens the *sala* as long as his breath allows.

Those in the cells arrive at the *matbâh*, bow their heads at the door, and enter inside by stepping right foot first. The shaikh also enters and altogether they sit down at the table and "see with" the *sofra*. The soup is placed in the middle. The soup is eaten from a single bowl and nobody talks during the meal. Everyone puts their index finger in the salt in front of them, tastes it and begins to eat. The spoon is always placed in the closed position and pointing to the left. While one is eating, one is not allowed to make sounds with the mouth, to look to the right or left, or to eat from in front of someone else. Everybody is kneeling. When the soup is finished, a dervish assigned to serve takes the pot away and another dervish brings more food. Depending upon the number of the people at the table, two or three souls, with their feet sealed, wait with a water jug in their left hand and a glass in their right hand; they wait on those who want water. The one who wants water breaks off a morsel of bread and holds it in the right hand level with the left shoulder. They glance at the water-bearer, who immediately "sees with" the lower part of the glass and presents it to the one who asks for it. Everyone stops eating and waits until the one who has taken the water drinks it. When the water has been drunk, the shaikh puts his hand on his heart and slightly bows his head as if to silently say, "*Ashk olsun!*" to the one who has drunk the water, who responds in the same way and "sees with" the lower part of the glass before presenting it back to the water-bearer. The water-bearer also "sees with" the lower part of the glass, returns to his place, refills the glass with water from the jug, seals his feet, and stands as he was before. When the *pilav* comes, everyone straightens up. The shaikh, or if the shaikh is not there the *ashchıbashı*, recites this gülbâng:

> *Ma sufiyan- rahim ma tabla-har-i shahim*
> *Payende dar yarab in kasera vu henra*[21]
>
> *Salli ve sellim ve bârik alâ es'adi ve eşrefi nûri cemî-il enbiyâi vel mürselin; vel hamdû lillâhi rabbil âlemînel Fâtiha.*[22]

After the *Fātiḥah*:

> *Nân-ı merdân, ni'met-i Yezdan berekât-ı Halîlür-Rahmân. Elhâmdü lillâh, eşşükrü lillâh, Hak berekâtın vere; yiyenlere nûr-ı îman ola; Erenlerin hân-ı keremleri, nân-u nimetleri müzdâd, sâhibül-hayrât-ı güzeştegânın ervâh-ı şerîfeleri şâd ü handân, bâkıyeleri selâmette ola; demler, safalâr ziyâde ola. Dem-i Hazret-i Mevlânâ, sırr-ı Âteş-bâz-ı Veli, kerem-i İmâm-ı Alî, Hû diyelim.*[23]

---

[21] This couplet (Trans. I, p. 226, couplet 2115) is the eleventh couplet of Mevlânâ's *ghazal* which begins with these lines:

Iy mir-i ab bigsha on cheshme-i revanra
Ta cheshmha gushayed zeshkufe bustanra

O chief waterman, open the flowing faucet!
Open, open, so the garden stirs and the flowers open their eyes.

The eleventh couplet translates as follows:

We are the Sufis of the road and we dine at the table of our King.
We are the ones nourished by His favour;
O our Sustainer, make this bowl, this table, and this favor eternal!

[22] "May peace and blessings and favors be upon all the most noble and illumined Prophets, and all praise belongs to God, Sustainer of all worlds. *Fātiḥah.*"

With the call of "*Fātiḥah,*" everyone would raise their hands and offer the *Fātiḥah* (Qur'ān 1). This is also a part of the Mevlevî *bayat* affirmation, declared when one enters the path of Mevlevîhood.

[23] "This is the sustenance of the noble ones, a gift from Yezdan (God), with the blessing of Abraham, Friend of the Merciful. Praise be to God, thanks be

Together with the shaikh, everybody says "*Hū*" in a loud voice for as long as the breath allows. Then everybody sits crosslegged, and one may even speak provided that not many people do so at the same time and it does not become too loud. If halva is being served, the *gülbâng* is recited when it arrives. When the food is finished, again everybody takes a pinch of salt, tastes it, "sees with" the table and stands up with the shaikh. The *somat gülbâng* used to be recited in a shorter form too:

> *Elhamdü lillâh, eşşükrü lillâh; Hak berekâtın vere; erenlerin nân ü nimetleri ziyâde ola; sâhibül-hayrâtın rûh-ı revanları şâd ü handan, bâkıyleri selâmette ola. Dem-i Hazret-i Mevlânâ, sırr-ı Âteş-bâz-ı Veli, Hû diyelim. Hû.*[24]

If someone has brought a sacrificed ram, the following words are added to both of the *gülbângs*: "*Niyâzi kabul, muradı hayr ile hâsıl ola*" ("May his entreaty be accepted and may his wish come true with goodness").[25]

Rüsûhî also records that the *somat gülbâng* that begins with "*Ma sufitan-i rahim*..." is recited as *ba'det-taam* at the edge of the table and that *ruz u sheb tezkar* is done.[26]

Besides these, there is also a *gülbâng* for the *bayram somat* ("holiday feast"), which we offer below:

> *Iy zeban kaasir zi add-i cud-i la tuhsa-yi tu*
> *Key zebanem shukr kerded der hor-i ala-yi tu*
> *Ozr-i taksirat-i ma chendan ki taksirat-i ma*
> *Shukr-i ni'metha-yi tu chendan ki ni'metha-yi tu*[27]

---

to Allah; may the Truth bestow its blessings; may the food we are about to eat be transformed into faith and light. May the generous feasts of the saints, their bread and blessings, ever increase; may the sacred souls of all generations who lived before, rejoice and be merry, and may those who remain be safe and in peace. By the Breath of Mevlânâ, by the secret of Âteshbâz-ı Velî, by the generosity of Imām ʿAlī, let us say *Hū. Huuuuu*..."

[24] Konya, Mevlânâ Museum Lib. No: 1665.

[25] Konya, Mevlânâ Museum Lib. No: 1665.

[26] *Minhâc*, p. 12.

[27] Konya Museum Lib. 1661.

O God, the tongue can never describe Your generosity!
Could I ever have a tongue thankful enough to appreciate Your favors?
Our excuses are as great as our mistakes.
We need to offer as many thanks to You as You grant favors.

After this stanza, the author of which we have not been able to trace, the *somat gülbâng* is recited; however, the following sentence is added: "*Hak erenler hayırlı emsâl-i kesîresiyle müşerref eyliye.*"

Among the Mevlevîs, there is also a leather *sofra* called the *elifî somat*. This *sofra*, which when spread is long and narrow like the Arabic letter *aleph* and which can be rolled up like a scroll, is sometimes spread out in the *matbâh*. The souls line up along it facing each other. This *sofra* is mainly for eating light snacks, such as a breakfast that can be placed in front of everybody, and it is used on group travels. From time to time, it is also spread out as a complement.

Fish and nothing that comes out of the sea can enter the Mevlevî *matbâh*. This is probably because of their smell and the phosphorous they contain, and because they stimulate lust.

Muharrem and Ashûre

First let us say that Mevlânâ is an *eren* who has never been on the side of a political party, who has never seen one side superior to the other nor attempted to make his Path an instrument for propaganda for this side or that. His belief in the Unity of Being (*Vahdet-i Vüjûd*) was not theoretical or a merely abstract system, rather he gave it a practical and humanistic aspect. In the sixth volume of the *Mesnevî*, while describing the mourning of the Shia at the Antioch Gate in Aleppo on the tenth day of the month Muharrem, he states that rather than weeping for the martyrs of Karbala, one should weep for one's own state, for the ruined heart that does not see anything but this wasted earth.[28]

When Mevlevîhood was turned into a formal system, the other *ṭarīqahs* invited Mevlevîs to recitations of *mersiyes* (a form of classical

[28] Trans. Ist. 1946, pp. 66–67.

poetry in praise of a person) and to the cooking of *ashûre* (known as *aş*), and so Mevlevîs also adopted this tradition.

Mevlevîs would also cook *ashûre* themselves and the shaikhs of other *ṭarīqahs* were invited. On these occasions *ashûre* was eaten at the *somat*. When the *ashûre* was served a *gülbâng* was recited, and within it the memory of the souls of Imām Ḥusayn and the martyrs of Karbala (*Shühedâ-yı Kerbelâ*) were honored; but there was nothing especially different in the *mukabele*, and *mersiyes* were not recited. However, in *tekkes* that had an Alevian tendency and in the *dergâh* in Konya during the time of Abdülvâhid Chelebi, the *Hadîkatüs Suadâ* of Fuzûlî (a famous, classical Ottoman poet) was recited for ten nights of Muharrem. On the eleventh night the last chapter was recited and it was complete.

To Offer the Fātiḥah

In the *ṭarīqahs*, in order to bless a new undertaking or close a gathering, it is customary that a shaikh or somebody else present be offered (invited to recite) the *Fātiḥah*. Mevlevîs do this too. At the end of a gathering, after the recitation of the *ashir*, this *terjeman* ("proclamation for a particular occasion") is recited:

Feth-i fukuh-i kainat; Feyz-i fiyuz-i mumkinat;
Masdar-u mevrid-i sifat; Ahmed u Alra salaat.[29]

After this greeting to the Prophet, the word "*Fātiḥah!*" is spoken and *Sūrah al-Fātiḥah* is recited.

Sefer ("Journey")

When they are setting out on a journey as a group, when the

[29] "Greetings to Ahmed—the victory of victories, the spiritual abundance of abundance in the universe of possibilities, and beneficiary and channel for the Attributes of God—and greetings to his descendants."

boundaries of a city are passed, or when they are boarding a vehicle, one of the elder Mevlevîs recites this *sefer gülbâng* ("journey" *gülbâng*):

Bidih mera tu Hudaya derin huceste sefer
Hezar nusrat u shadi hezar feth u zafer
Behurmet-i se Muhammad behakki char Ali
Bedu Hasen be Huseyn u be musiy u Cafer[30]

Salâvâtullâhi ve selâmuhû aleyhim ecmaîn. Vakt-i şerif hayrola; hayırlar fethola; şerler def'ola; demler, safâlar müzdâd, gönüller şâd, muradlar hâsıl, seferler bî hater ola. Dem-i Hazret-i Mevlânâ, Sırr-ı Şems-i Tebrîzî, kerem-i İmâm-ı Alî, Hû diyelim.[31]

Everybody would then bow their heads and say, "*Hū!*"

In the manuscript of the *Mesnevîhân* Sıdkı Dede (1352 H. 1933 A.D.) in Konya's Mevlânâ Museum[32], there is a *sefer gülbâng* as follows:

Rahra ber ma chu bustan kun latif
Menzil-i ma hod chi bashed iy uerif

---

[30] "O Allah! On this celebrated journey, for the sake of the three Muḥammads, for the sake of the four ʿAlī's, for the sake of the two Ḥasans, one Ḥusayn, Mūsā, and Jaʿfar, give us thousands of favours and joys, thousands of openings and victories."

The three Muḥammads are İmâm Muhammed-ül Bâkir (114 H., 783 A.D.), İmâm Muhammedüt-Takıyyül-Cevâd (220 H., 835 A.D.), and İmâm Muhammedül-Mahdî (328 H., 940 A.D.). The four ʿAlī's are İmâm Alîyy ibni Abû-Tâlîb (40 H., 661 A.D.), İmâm Alî Zaynul-Âbidîn (95 H., 719 A.D.), İmâm Alîyyür-Rızâ (203 H., 818 A.D.), and İmâm Alîyyün-Nakıy (254 H., 868 A.D.). The two Ḥasans are the elder son of Blessed Alî, İmâm Hasan (53 H., 670 A.D.) and İmâm Hasan'ul Askerî (260 H., 874 A.D.). Ḥusayn is the İmâm Huseyn (61 H., 680 A.D.) who is the son of Blessed Alî and the brother of İmâm Hasan. Mūsā is İmâm Mûsal-Kâzim (183 H., 799 A.D.). And Jaʿfar is İmâm Ca'ferus-Sâdik (148 H., 765 A.D.). The stanza, by an unknown poet, commemorates the Twelve Imāms.

[31] "All praise and blessing be upon them. May this moment be blessed; may goodness prevail; may all negativity be dispelled; may our moments and breaths increase in peace; may hearts be happy; may our yearnings be fulfilled; may our journeys be remembered. By the breath of Mevlânâ, the secret of Shams of Tabriz, and the nobility of Imām ʿAlī, let us say *Hū*..."

[32] Konya, Mevlânâ Museum Lib. No: 1176.

El hamdu leke vel mulku leke vesh shukru leke ya Musta'an.[33]

This couplet from Volume II of the *Mesnevî* is the third one of the chapter starting with: *Vasiyyet kerden-i Peygamber sallAllahu aleyhi ve sellem mer on bimarra ve dua amuziyesh.* However, its second line is: *Menzil-i ma hod tu bashi iy sheriff.*[34] It means:

Make our path as subtle as a rose garden:
You indeed, O Highest One, are our destination!

We have not heard a *sefer gülbâng* like this.

During World War I, on the banner presented by Ahmed Jelâleddin Dede, the shaikh of Kulekapısı, to the Mevlevî regiment, the first *gülbâng* mentioned above was embroidered.

Burial Ceremony

Among the Mevlevîs, it is customary to chant the *Ism-i Jelâl* over the dead. If the one who has died is a shaikh or khalif, he is washed in the *matbâh* ("kitchen") while the *mutrib* recite an *âyin*. The âyin contains the opening couplet of Mevlânâ's *mersiye*, which was written when Selahâddîn-i Zer-kûb died. It goes as follows:

Iy zi hicran-i firaket asman bigriste
Dil miyan-i hun nisheste akl u can bigriste

O friend, whose loss causes even the sky to weep!
The heart languishes in blood; reason and soul begin to weep.

The *âyin* also contains the two other couplets from the same *mersiye* which follow the one above. It is a *segâh âyin* composed by Itrî.

The coffins of shaikhs, khalifs and *dedes* are wrapped with their *khirkas*, and *sikkes* with a *destâr* are placed upon them. As the coffin is being taken to the cemetery, those who follow it chant the *Ism-i Jelâl* using the same intonation as the three opening intonations at

---

[33] See p. 2.

[34] Nicholson ed.; p. 388, couplet 2553.

the beginning of a *dhikr*. After the body is placed into the grave, his *sikke* is put on his head, his *khirka* is laid on his body and his *hilâfet-nâme* ("certificate of khalifhood") is placed on his right (the side of the *qiblah*). There is no *telkıyn* ("final rites") after the burial. Those attending the funeral form a circle around the grave, and following the lead of the shaikh or one of the elders they chant the *Ism-i Jelâl*. The one directing the *dhikr* then recites the following *gülbâng*:

> *Vakt-i şerif hayrola; hayırlar fethola; Derviş . . . merhum, garka-i garıyk-ı Yezdan, hâcesi hoşnûd ola; Dem-i Hazret-i Mevlânâ, sırr-ı Şems-i Tebrîzî, kerem-i İmâm-ı Alî, Hû diyelim.*[35]

Altogether, everybody says "*Hū!*" They bow their heads and leave the graveside. During the burial, it is customary to recite prayers as well as *āyāts* and *sūrahs* from the Holy Qur'ān; the chanting of the *Ism-i Jelâl* comes at the end. But as we have already mentioned, there is no *telkıyn* nor a *tezkiye* ("purification"). While alive–or rather after he was revitalized following his metaphorical death–the Mevlevî heard his *telkıyn* and adopted it.[36]

As we come to the end of this chapter, let us recall another story. People said to Mevlânâ, "It used to be that *qaaris* (those who memorise and recite the Qur'ān) and *muezzins* (those who recite the call to prayer) led funeral processions, but now in your time, *kavvâls* and *mutrib* (singers and musicians) are at the front of the procession. Scholars are critical of this. What is the wisdom and meaning of this?" Mevlânâ replied, "*Qaaris* and *muezzins* bear witness that this person was a believer and died as one. Our *kavvâls* and *mutrib* witness that this person was a believer, a Muslim, *and* also a lover. The spirit of the human being exists in the prison of this world, at nature's threshold, for so many years. When it is liberated by the grace of God and arrives at its origin, wouldn't this state cause a *semâ'* of joy and thankfulness?"[37]

---

[35] "May this moment be blessed; may goodness prevail; may all negativity be dispelled. For the late dervish–and the submerging of the one immersed in God–may his Master be pleased. By the breath of Mevlânâ, the secret of Shams of Tabriz, and the nobility of Imām 'Alī, let us say *Hū*..."

[36] For more concerning the funeral ceremony of Salahâddîn-i Zer-kûb please see *Mevlânâ Celâleddîn*, Third Edition, pp. 112–13.

[37] *Manâkıb-al Ârifîn*, Vol. I, p. 233.

Mevlevî Headstones

The headstones of Mevlevîs, who refer to the cemetery as the *hâmûshân* ("silent ones") or *hâmûshhâne* ("silent home"), like the headstones of the Melâmî-Hamzavîs, do not have special characteristics in terms of epitaphs and signs. However, the inscriptions, which may be poetry or prose, are related to *taṣawwuf*. They begin with words such as *Hû*, *Ya Hû*, or *Ya Hazret-i Mevlânâ*. On top of the headstone of a shaikh or khalif there is a *sikke* with a *destâr*. If the lower part of the *sikke* is not visible outside of the destâr, that indicates that the person buried there is one of the *Chelebis* (even if it is not mentioned in the inscription). On the headstones of *dedes* there are bare *sikkes*. On the headstones of male or female *muhibs*, there is a *sikke* in relief on the front side of the stone; even if the headstone has a *serpush* ("cap") indicating an officer, this is still the case.

Among the Mevlevî headstones in Istanbul, there are those with *kalıplı sikkes* (stiff and straight) and *kalıpsız sikkes* (softer and more curved); those with *Seyfî* sikkes and those with *Shemsî sikkes*; those with *istivâs* and those showing various styles of *destâr*. But, unfortunately, neglect is ruining not only the Mevlevî headstones with their *sikke* adornments, but the thoughts of the period, its sentiments, and the arts of stonemasonry and engraving, all of which are part of our literature and history and like local museums, due to the truths they reveal.

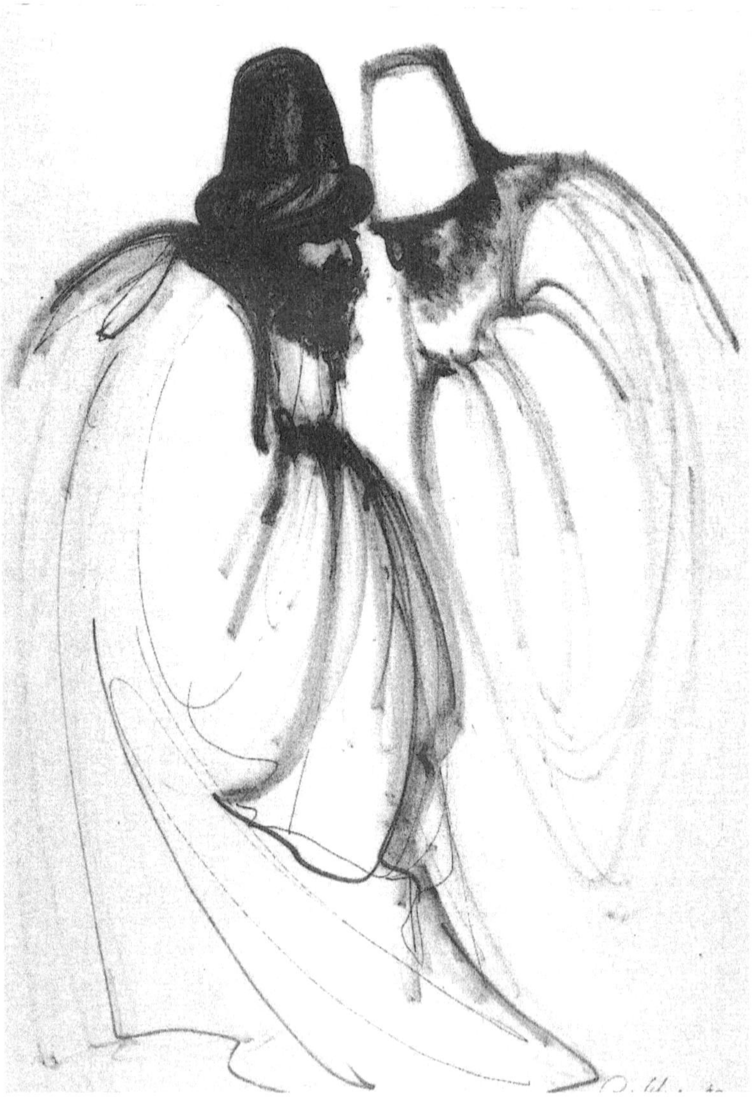

VI

Ranks of Mevlevîhood

Muhib

The word *muhib*, which means "one who loves," is a name given to those who have embraced Mevlevîhood but not yet accepted dervishhood. They make up the majority of Mevlevîs. Someone who wants to be a Mevlevî applies to a shaikh whom he loves and trusts. If the seeker is young, the shaikh makes sure that his parents agree with his decision.

A person whose application has been accepted brings a *sikke* to the shaikh. The shaikh himself, or the *ashchıbashı* ("head cook") who has his approval, initiates the person who wishes to be a *muhib*. The shaikh and the seeker make their ablutions, and the seeker kneels on the left of the shaikh, with no space between them, both facing the *qiblah*. The shaikh then invites the seeker to recite the following passages of repentance together with him:

> *Eûzü billâhis semî'il-âlîmi mineş-Şeytânir racîm. Bismillâhirrahmânir rahîm. Estağfirullâh, estağfirullâh estağfirullâhil âzîmüllezî lâ ilahe illâ huvel hayyül-kayyûmü ve etûbu ileyhi min külli zenbin eznebtuhû âmden ve hataen, sırran ve âlâniyeten feinnehû âllâmül guyûbi ve gaffârüz zünûbi ve settârül ûyûb. Eşhedü en lâ ilahe illallahu vahdehû, lâ şerike lehû ve eşhedü enne Muhammeden abduhû ve rasûluhû ve eşhedü ennel mevte hakkun vel cennete hakkun ven nâre hakkun ve ennallâhe yeb'asü men fil kubûri ve ileyhin müşûr.*[1]

[1] "From the accursed Satan, I take refuge in God who hears and knows all. In the name of God, the Infinitely Compassionate and Most Merciful, I ask forgiveness from God; I ask forgiveness from God; I ask forgiveness from God, who is the Most Magnificent of all, there being none worthy of worship

This is a wish to be forgiven by God, a repentance for guilt, and a renewal of faith. It can also be recited in a shorter or longer form. It has been reported that some shaikhs primed the seeker to have an *istihare* ("special dream"), while others prepared difficulties for the one wishing to be a Mevlevî, testing him through various words and deeds.

After this, the shaikh holds the *sikke* of the one who is going to be a *muhib* with his two hands and recites *Sūrah al-Ikhlāṣ* (112) once. He breathes onto the front of the *sikke* and recites it again, then breathes to its right side and recites it again, and finally breathes onto its left side. There are also those who recite the *Ism-i Jelâl* eighteen times and breathe into the *sikke*. Then, with his face directed to the *qiblah* and his legs bent beneath him, he has the seeker lay his head upon his left knee, holds the *sikke* towards the *qiblah* and recites these words:

> *Bi resmi Kutbül-ârifîn, gavsil-vâselîn, sultânül-kümmelîn, burhânül-mukarrabîn, kurratu uyünil-muvahhidîn, Mevlânâ ve Mevlel-ârifîn Muhammed Celâlül-Hakkı vel-milleti ved-din; kaddesenallâhu bî esrârihî ve mettaanâ bi fuyûzatihî; niyâbeten min sâhibil-emri.*[2]

He holds the *sikke* with both hands and kisses first its right and then its left side; then he has the seeker kiss it in the same way. He

---

but He. He is such that He is Ever-Living and Self-Subsisting, and I repent for all the sins that I have committed, consciously or unconsciously, secretly or openly; truly, it is He who knows completely what is hidden, who forgives sins completely, and who hides what is shameful. I bear witness that there is none worthy of worship but God, who is One and has no partner, and I bear witness that Muḥammad is His servant and messenger. I bear witness to the truth of death, the truth of the Garden, and the truth of the Fire; and that God resurrects those in the grave to be gathered again in His Presence."

[2] "According to the customs of our master and the master of the gnostics, who is the pole of gnostics, who comes to the aid of the attained ones, who is the sultan of the mature and who is the proof of those in proximity to God and who is the apple of the eye of those who recognize God as one; the Power and Majesty of the Truth, law and religion, Jelâl-i Muhammed (Mevlânâ)! May Allah bless us with His secrets and make us benefit from His spiritual abundance by representing the owner of the work and the command."

places the *sikke* on the seeker's head, and then, still holding it with both hands, he recites this *tekbir*: "*Allahu ekber Allahu ekber, lâ ilahe illallâhu vallâhu ekber, Allahu ekber ve lillâhil hamd*..."[3]

The shaikh rubs the seeker's back three times with his right hand, then has him raise his head from his knee and takes his right hand in both of his own hands, with the seeker also holding the shaikh's hand in the same way. Then they "see with" each other as they kiss each other's hands. The shaikh sends the new *muhib* to his *dede*, the person who is going to be his educator (*mürebbî*). The *muhib* whose *sikke* has been *tekbired* in this way, when instructed by his *dede*, seals his feet and bows his head to the shaikh. Without turning his back, he leaves the room. He is now a *nevniyâz*, and his *dede* takes him to his own cell and makes him begin the *semâ' meshk*.

The cell of the *dede* is a school for education (*terbiye*) and the spiritual journey (*sülûk*). The *nevniyâz* who completes the *semâ'*, according to his talent, practices *naats* or *âyins*; he joins the *mukabeles*; and he learns about courteous service (*ādāb*). He joins the *sohbets* and adopts the principles of *taṣawwuf*. He reads the *Mesnevî*, studies commentaries upon it, and absorbs its lessons. If he has a talent for poetry, the poems he reads and writes are analyzed and critiqued. If he is inclined to play music, he studies the *ney* or the *kudüm*. If he becomes proficient at it he may join the *mutrib*. If he develops a capacity, he is given the title of *Mesnevîhân*. Day by day, in every smallest detail, he is taught by his *dede* how to walk, how to lie down, how to get up, and how to speak to people and communicate with mindful signs, words, and actions. Over time at this school, he becomes a representative of Mevlevî *ādāb* and *erkan*; he becomes an example of Mevlevî grace and a *mürebbî* ("educator") in his own right.

The authority to *tekbir* the *sikke* belongs to the *khalif*, but as an honorary gesture the authority to *tekbir* the *sikke* may be given to those who have practiced (*meshk*) the *semâ'*.

---

[3] "God is Greatest; God is Greatest. There is no deity but God. God is Greatest; God is Greatest. All praise belongs to God..."

Dervish (Dede)

If a person who has accepted dervishhood sits on the *saka post* ("water-bearer's sheepskin") for three days and perseveres, then he puts on the *arâkıyye* and service *tennûre.* For one thousand and one days, he performs various services and completes his ordeal; and after "turning into a secret" in his cell for three days, he completes his *chile* ("seclusion") of eighteen days. He then becomes a *hûjrenishîn* and is called *dede* and *dervish.*

We will not repeat here the details of *chile ādāb* and *erkan* which are described in *Mevlevîhood After Mevlânâ,*[4] but we will repeat the *gülbângs* that are recited on various occasions.

When the *chile* has ended and the dervish is standing in position in the middle of the *meydan* after the meal (*somat*), the *tarikatchı* or *ashchıbashı* recites the following *gülbâng*:

> *Vakt-i şerif hayrola; hayırlar fethola; şerler def'ola; derviş kardeşimizin niyâzı kabul ola; âşıyân-ı Mevlevîyyede râhatı müzdâd ola; demler, safâlar ziyâde ola. Dem-i Hazret-i Mevlânâ, sırr-ı Şems-i Tebrîzî, kerem-i İmâm-ı Alî, Hû diyelim: Hû.*[5]

The following *gülbâng* is recited by the *ashchıbashı* to the dervish after giving advice to him following the *chile*:

> *Vakt-i şerif hayrola; hayırlar fethola; şerler def'ola; derviş kardeşimizin hizmetleri mübarek ola. Dem-i Hazret-i Mevlânâ, sırr-ı Şems-i Tebrîzî, kerem-i İmâm-ı Alî, Hû diyelim: Hû.*

This *gülbâng* is recited by the *meydanjı* at the door of a cell when he is taken there:

---

[4] Please see pp. 359–62.

[5] "May this moment be blessed; may goodness prevail; may all negativity be dispelled; may the entreaty of our dervish brother be accepted; may the one in love with the Mevlevi way continue in ease; may our every moment, every breath and every pleasure be filled with Light. By the breath of Hazrati Mevlânâ, the secret of Hazrati Shams of Tabriz, and the nobility of Imām ʿAlī, let us say *Hū*…"

Vakt-i şerif hayrola; hayırlar fethola; şerler def'ola; derviş kardeşimizin rahatı müzdâd ola. Dem-i Hazret-i Mevlânâ, sırr-ı Şems-i Tebrîzî, kerem-i İmâm-ı Alî, Hû diyelim: Hû.

The *meydanjı* then recites this *gülbâng* when he enters the cell:

Tebrîk-i mekîn ü mekân ve safâ-yı zemîn ü zaman; çerâğ-ı rûşen, fahr-i dervîşân; zuhûr-ı îmân; kaanûn-ı merdân. Dem-i Hazret-i Mevlânâ, sırr-ı Şems-i Tebrîzî, kerem-i İmâm-ı Alî, Hû diyelim: Hû.[6]

After reciting the cell *gülbâng*, the *meydanjı* takes the dervish to the Chelebi if they are in Konya or to the shaikh if they are somewhere else. The shaikh holds the right hand of the dervish who is kneeling down in front of him. His thumbs are straight and his palms are touching each other; his fingers hold the dervish's hand. He recites *āyāt* 48:10:

ʾInnal-ladhīna yubāyiʿūnaka ʾinnamā yubāyiʿūnal-lāha yadul-lāhi fawqa ʾaydīhim. Faman-nakath faʾinnamā yankuthu ʿalā nafsih. Wa manʾawfā bimā ʿāhada ʿalayhul-lāha fasayuʾtīhi ʾajran ʿaẓīmā.

Truly those who pledge their loyalty to you [Muḥammad] do no less than pledge their loyalty to God. The hand of God is over their hands. Then anyone who violates their oath does so to the harm of their own soul and anyone who remains true to what he/she has pledged to God, God will grant them a supreme recompense.

He then uses scissors to cut off a few hairs from the middle of the dervish's eyebrows and moustache and, with a *tekbir,* places the ceremonial *khirka* over the dervish's back.

Shaikh

The shaikh is the person who has the authority to manage a *tekke*

[6] Salutations to place and space, and the purity of earth and time; the lamp of the dawn, the dervish's honor; the manifestation of faith; the code of mercy, by the breath of Hazrati Mevlânâ, the secret of Hazrati Shams of Tabriz, and the nobility of Imām ʿAlī, let us say *Hū*..."

and educate *muhibs* and dervishes. This authority is conferred by the Chelebi, and it is confirmed with a written and sealed document called an *ijâzetnâme*. The *Shems dede* or the *Âteshbâz dede* is usually the one who brings the *ijâzetnâme*. On the first day of the *mukabele*, the one who has brought the *ijâzetnâme* sits on the *post*, and the person who is going to become a shaikh sits one rank below him. Before the *naat* is recited, the *meydanjı dede* brings the *sikke* with a *destâr*, holding it in his two hands. He stands a little to the right of the *Hatt-ı Istivâ* (viewed from the front). The *ijâzetnâme* is presented either to the *semâ'zenbashı* or the *dua-gû dede*, who reads it aloud and presents it to the person on the *post*. The person on the *post* "sees together with" the person who is to become a shaikh and presents the *ijâzetnâme* to him. The new shaikh "sees with" him as he receives it. Then after "seeing with" it, the *sikke* with the *destâr* is given to the person on the *post*. He takes off the *sikke* of the new shaikh sitting next to him, presents it to the *meydanjı*, and "sees with" the *sikke* with the *destâr*. He puts it on the new shaikh's head, and, holding his right hand, has the new shaikh sit on the *post* while he himself sits one rank below him. One always "sees with" the *sikkes* as they are being exchanged.

After this exchange the *mukabele* takes place. When the *mukabele* is over, as in the *bayram* celebration, the new shaikh "sees with" everyone in the *semâ'hâne* and then takes his seat on his *post* and recites the last *gülbâng*. Other Sufi shaikhs are invited to visit the *semâ'hâne* for this ceremony, which is called *ijlas* ("ceremony of sitting on the *post*"). Because the shaikh of Yenikapi Mevlevîhânesi in Istanbul was the representative of the Chelebi, *ijâzetnâme* was recited during the first *mukabele* there as well. The shaikh in whose *tekke* the *ijlâs* ceremony occured used to join this *mukabele*, and the celebration was performed again there.

If the shaikh had not gone through a *chile* to become a *dede*, after having sat on the *post* he used to go to Konya for eighteen days, where he would perform the eighteen services with a naked *sikke* (one without a *destâr*). Following this, his *sikke* with a *destâr* was *tekbired* once more by the Chelebi, and he would return to the place where he had become a shaikh.

Let us also mention this:

The great ones of Mevlevîhood have found that, according to the calculations of *abjad* (Arabic numerology), 1001 is the numerical value of the word *riza* ("acceptance" or "good pleasure"); and when they added the sum of 3 and 18 (making 21) to this number, they arrived at 1022, which is the numerical value of *riza-yi Hû* (God's acceptance or good pleasure). They perceived meaningful relationships within this equality.

Rather than being a spiritual task, shaikhhood was an administrative one. We do not see *ijâzetnâmes* of shaikhhood in the early periods; khalifhood and shaikhhood were the same. Actually, the one who becomes a shaikh must become a khalif too, if he is not one already. After all, if one notes that Burhâneddin Chelebi (son of Emîr Âdil Chelebi, who was the son of Ulu Arif Chelebi) sent Hajı İbrahim (son of Ahî Ahmed, who was the son of Anî Mahmud) as a shaikh from Edirne to Niğde on the tenth day of the month *Rajab* in 796 H. (1394 A.D.), one understands that the appointment of shaikhs by the Chelebi was adopted in later years in order to maintain cohesion and prevent confusion.[7]

Khalif

If the shaikh is a *sayyid* ("descendant" of the family of Blessed Muḥammad) he wears a green *destâr*; if not, a white one. If he is a *khalif*, his *destâr* is *duhânî* (dark, smokey violet–almost black). Chelebis wrap their *destâr* so that it covers the lower part of the *sikke* (i.e. so that the part of the *sikke* that touches the head is not seen at all). The *sikkes* of those who are not *chelebis* have one inch showing below the *destâr*. However, because the *chelebi* of the time sent his own *destâr* to the first shaikh of Yenikapı, Shaikh Kemâl Ahmed Dede (1010 H., 1601 A.D.), the shaikhs of Yenikapi wrap their *destârs* like *chelebis*. If the khalif is a *sayyid*, he can wear a green or white *destâr*, and if he is not a *sayyid*, he can wear the white *destâr* whenever he wishes.

[7] *Mevlevîhood after Mevlânâ*, pp. 398–400.

Conferring Khalifhood

An established khalif and the person receiving khalifhood sit together on a prayer rug facing the *qiblah*. The recipient is on the left of the khalif; the *sikke* with the *destâr* is on the khalif's right. The khalif recites āyāt 48:27 from the Holy Qur'ān:

Laqad ṣadaqallāhu Rasūlahur-ru'yā bil-ḥaqq. Latadkhulunnal-Masjidal-Ḥarāma 'in-shāa'al-lāhu 'āminīna muḥalliqīna ru'ūsakum wa muqaṣṣirīna lā takhāfūn. Fa'alima mā lam ta'lamū faja'ala min-dūni dhālika fatḥan-qarībā.

Indeed, God has shown the truth in His Apostle's true vision: most certainly shall you enter the Inviolable House of Worship, if God so wills, in full security, with your heads shaved or your hair cut short, without any fear: for He has [always] known that which you yourselves could not know. And He has ordained [for you], besides this, a victory soon to come.

After reciting this *āyāt*, a few hairs from between the recipient's eyebrows, or from his eyebrows and moustache, are cut off with scissors. The khalif "sees with" the *khirka*, and the recipient does the same before it is placed upon him with a *tekbir*. Then, as if he is pronouncing it over the *sikke* of a *muhib*, the khalif pronounces the *tekbir* over the *sikke* with a *destâr*. Next, they hold each other's right hand, thumbs straight and touching each other, while their fingers grasp the dorsal area of the hand. The khalif recites āyāts 48:10 and 48:18–19:

'Innal-ladhīna yubāyi'ūnaka 'innamā yubāyi'ūnal-lāha yadul-lāhi fawqa 'aydīhim. Faman-nakath fa'innamā yankuthu 'alā nafsih. Wa man'awfā bimā 'āhada 'alayhul-lāha fasayu'tīhi 'ajran 'aẓīmā. Laqad raḍiyal-lāhu 'anil-mu'minīna 'idh yubāyi'ūnaka taḥtash-shajarati fa'alima mā fi qulūbihim fa'anzalas-sakīnata 'alayhim wa athābahum fatḥan-qarībā. Wa maghānima kathīratany-ya'khudhūnahā. Wa kānal-lāhu 'Azīzan Ḥakīmā.

Truly those who pledge their loyalty to you [Muḥammad] do no less than pledge their loyalty to God. The hand of God is over their hands. Then anyone who violates their oath does so to the harm of their own soul and anyone who remains true to what he/she has pledged to God, God will grant them a supreme recompense. Indeed, well-pleased was God with the faithful when they pledged their allegiance unto thee [O Muḥammad] under that tree, for He knew what was in their hearts; and so He bestowed inner peace upon them from on high, and rewarded them with [the glad tiding of] an opening soon to come and [of] many boons of the struggle which they would achieve: for God is indeed almighty, wise.

He interprets these *āyāts* and then he recites the beginning of 47:19 into the recipient's right ear: *Fa'lam 'annahū lāa 'ilāha 'illal-lāhu* ... (*Know then, that there is no deity save God*...).

He says "Allāh" three times and directs him to chant the *kalimat at-tawḥīd* ("*Lā ilāha illā Allāh* . . .") three times after the morning prayer and after saying the *'A'ūzhu/Bismillāh* and "*Fa'lam*..." He also advises him to say, "*Muhammedur rasûlullâhı hakkan ve sıdkaa; ve salli* ..." and to recite the *Fātiḥah* just like during *ṣalāh*. They "see with" each other, and he expresses, as he congratulates him, the hope that his khalifhood will be good for everyone.

Because it was customary to bury the *hilâfetnâme* ("certificate of khalifhood") and the *meshîhatnâme* ("certificate of shaikhhood") together with the khalif or the shaikh when they died, only a few of them are left in our hands. Some of these were not put into the grave for some reason or other, while some are copies. In *Mevlevîhood after Mevlânâ*, we published translations from the Persian of a copy of the *hilâfetnâme* given to Seyyid Süleymân-i Belhîye (1294 H., 1877 A.D.), shaikh of the Shaikh Murad Dergâh in Eyup Nishanca, Istanbul, by Shems Dede Ahmed Dede; as well as a translation of the *hilâfetnâme* in Arabic given to Seyyid Ali, the shaikh of Medine, by Huseyin Fahreddîn Dede.[8]

Recorded as no. 92 in the archive of the Mevlânâ Museum in Konya, there is a *hilâfetnâme* of 209 lines. Its dimensions are 8.5x0.28, it has been written in the very beautiful *sülüs* style of calligraphy typical of that period, and it is in the form of a scroll. This valuable document, photographs of which we have previously published, is the *hilâfetnâme* given to Dervish Yûsuf ibni Ilyâs ibni Mûsa-l Kunavî

[8] See pp. 402–06; the photographs of the second translation are on p. 32 in the photographs at the end.

by Alîyy ibni Muhammed ibni Ârifül-Jelâliyyüs-Sıddıkıy, around the middle of the month *Rabī' al-'Ākhir* in 931 H. (1925 A.D.). On the same *hilâfetnâme*, it is recorded that Dervish Yûsuf ibni Ilyasül-Kunavî gave a *hilâfetnâme* to Chelebi Hızırshâh ibni Muhammed Chelebiyyül-Jelâliyyüs-Sıddıykıy (this part of the *hilâfetnâme* is comprised of five lines written in gold). This is the oldest document that we have today showing the Mevlevî lineage.

According to this *hilâfetnâme*, the lineage of khalifhood from Mevlânâ to Hızırshâh Chelebi, is as follows:

Mevlânâ–Sultân Veled–Jelâleddin Emîr Arif (Ulu Arif Chelebi)–Shemseddin Emîr Âbid Chelebi–Husâmeddîn Emîr Vacîd–Muzaffereddîn Emîr Âdil–Chelebi Muhammed–Chelebi Arif–Chelebi Burhâneddin–Chelebi Âbid–Chelebi Jemâleddin –his son Chelebi Âbid–Chelebi Aliyy ibni Muhammed ibni Arif– Dervish Yûsuf ibni Ilyâs ibni Mûsa-l Kunavî–Hızırshah Chelebi bin Muhammed Chelebi.

In this *silsile* ("lineage"), Mehmet Chelebi after Emîr Âdil must be Emîr Âlim Chelebi (794 H. 1395 A.D.), the son of Shemseddin Emîr Âbid Chelebi. Arif Chelebi who is after him, is Emîr Arif Chelebi, who was the son of Ulu Arif Chelebi's son Emîr Âdil Chelebi (770 H. 1368 A.D.). Emîr Arif Chelebi was the *makam chelebi* from 798 H., (the year of the death of Âlim Chelebi) until 825 H. (1421 A.D.). Chelebi Burhâneddin and Chelebi Âbid following him are not mentioned in later *hilâfetnâmes*. Chelebi Jemâleddin, whose name is mentioned after these two, is the Jemâleddin Chelebi who died in 915 H. (1509 A.D.) and who was the son and successor of Pîr Adil Chelebi, who died in 865 H. (1460 A.D.). Again, in the later *hilâfetnâmes*, Jemâleddin Chelebi gave khalifhood to Abdükadir Chelebi from Aksaray; he to Ahmed Efendi; he to Dîvâne Muhammed Chelebi; he to Fedâyî Mustafâ; and he to Hızırshah Chelebi.

Hızırshâh Çelebi is praised with these words in the *hilâfetnâme*:

> May Allāh lengthen his shadow and continuously increase his abundance and divine light; may He cause his life, his secret, his happiness and his joy to endure. He is the greatest secret of Allāh, the might of Allāh, the greatest divine light, the most everlasting and powerful evidence of Allāh, the Ka'bah of the people of wisdom, the *qiblah* of the lovers, the essence of the darlings,

the support of the beloveds, the one whom spiritual travelers obey, and the khalif of the Teacher of universes. He is Hızırshâh Chelebi, the son of Muhammed Chelebi, from the family of Mevlânâ and the descendants of Abū Bakr.

His name is Hızırshâh; his father's name is Muhammed; he is one of the *chelebis*; and the date is also correct. We think that such a perfect coincidence is implausible, and we therefore wish to conclude that this Hızırşah is the same Hızırşâh who was the son of Dîvâne Mehmed Chelebi. But there is an issue that makes us pause to reflect: in 931 H. Dîvâne Mehmet Chelebi was alive, so should the passage of praise not be written in the plural? We put aside this doubt because Mehmet Chelebi is never referred to as "the late," and he is never remembered with words which are traditionally used for someone who has passed away. Hızırshâh is the only one who could be praised to such a degree.

In the archives of the Prime Ministry Office, there is an item dated one month before the *hilâfetnâme* was conferred (20 *Rabīʿ al-ʾAwwal*, 931 H.), which says that Ali, Hasan, and Hûseyn (the sons of Hamza in Söke) should be exempt from paying taxes because their uncle is *Halife-i evliyaullâh Hızırşâh dâmet selâmetuhu*, one of the (grand)sons of Mevlânâ.[9] According to us, this Hızırshâh is the same Hızırshâh who was the son of Mehmed Chelebi.

Who is Yûsuf ibni Ilyâs ibni Mûsa from Konya?

In the library of the Mevlânâ Museum in Konya, there is a documented work[10] titled *Mürşidut-Tâlibîn*: this work was written by Mahmud Dede, the *Mesnevîhân*.

Upon the order of Sultan Murad III (died 1004 H., 1595 A.D.), in the month of *Dhu ʾl-Qaʿdah*, 998 H., Mahmud Dede translated *Savâkıb-al Manâqib*, which is a summary and translation of *Manâkıb-al Ârifîn* by Abdül-Vahhâb ibni Jelâleddîn Muhammed-i Hemedânî (who died in Madīnah in 954 H., 1547 A.D.). He completed it between 998 and 1004 H. and presented it to the Sultan. In the translation of *Savâkıb*, Mahmud Dede (who died in 1006 H.,1597–98 A.D.) says that

[9] *Tahrir defteri* (written survey of a province) from the year 935 H., No. 148, V. 209. *Mevlevîhood after Mevlânâ*, p. 114.

[10] No. 4005.

he served Abdüllatîf, the son of Sheik Sinan Dede, and was educated by him for fifteen years before taking the hand of his brother, Abdülkerîm the *Mesnevîhân,* and receiving khalifhood from him.[11]

In *Mürşidut-Tâlibîn*, Mahmud Dede writes that Sinan Dede was known as Black Yûsuf when he was a child. It is understood that the name of Sinan Dede was Yûsuf Sinan. In the *Menkabe*, the father of Sinan Dede is Ilyas Sufi from Karahöyük in Konya. In Edirne, Sinan Dede received khalifhood from Ali Chelebi, who is *fevkal-had sahib-kemal* and *ilm-i inshada bi nazir* and who is the son of Shehid Mehmed Pasha from the generation of Mevlânâ and the lineage of Abū Bakr.[12] Now, there is no doubt that Ali Chelebi, the son of Arif's son Muhammed, whose name is mentioned in this *hilâfetnâme*, is the same person.

Besides these, this *hilâfetnâme* contains the signatures of twenty-one witnesses. The first one of these signatures belongs to Jemâl Chelebi bin Mustafâ Mollazâde maddallûhu zilluhü. We do not know who this is. The second signature belongs to Dervish Mahmud ibni Üveys-al Mavlavî. As the second signatory, we can assume that he must have been a highly respected person. In Konya, without turning to the *dergâh*, if one turns to the right at the corner of the way across the cemetry known as *Üchler* ("Threes"), there is a ruined *türbe*. Here, two people are buried beside each other. One is Inil, or Inil Dede, who died in 960 H. (1552–53 A.D.). The epitaph on the other headstone reads: *Sultânül-ârifîn-burhânül vâsîlin-Mahmud Dede ibni Üveys Dede-Senetü hamse ve sittine ve tis'amie.*

It is possible that this person, who died in 965 H. (1557–58 A.D.), which is forty-one years before Mahmud Dede who was a *Mesnevîhân* and the translator of *Savâkıb*, was a *Mesnevîhân* too. The second signature belongs to this person.

In his own time, Mevlânâ was recognized as a very great shaikh and as an imām of the Hanafī school.[13] He was acknowledged as "the

---

[11] Ist. Uni. Lib. Turkish writings. 280; 4. b-10 b.

[12] 15. b-16. A.

[13] According to written evidence in a copy of the *Mesnevî* written in 677 H. (1278 A.D.), five years after Mevlânâ had passed into Infinity, which was donated to a foundation one year later as part of the deeds of trust. Konya, Mevlânâ Museum Lib. No: 51.

inheritor of the messengers and the prophets, the last among the expounders of Islamic law and the scholars who actually followed what they knew,"[14] and both he and his book have been praised. Epithets such as "Imām, the son of Imām, the pillar of Islam" have been attributed to him,[15] and he has been hailed as the "Expounder of Islamic laws." This view is not incorrect, because, although he is a Hanafī, he follows the traditionalists in not accepting analogy.[16] He accepts both free will and predestination as being reconciled within *taṣawwuf*, but he also analyzes and criticizes each of them from the view point of education, taming the ego, and ethics.[17] He regards those who get intoxicated with wine and cannabis as children, entitled neither to the rights of divorce nor barter.[18] He regards the *tekbîr* (the proclamation of God's greatness) at the beginning of prayer and the final *salām* as belonging to the pillars of *ṣalāh*.[19] Although one can give many more examples, because this is another focus of examination apart from our topic, we will not dwell on it further.

However, let us immediately say that Mevlânâ was not the founder of a *ṭarīqah*, and although he was exalted in *taṣawwuf* he never introduced a special garment, special forms of worship, or an extra practice of *dhikr*. The *ferecî* that he wore was the garment that scholars of his time used to wear. The *sikke* on his head was the Balkh *külah* (conical hat); it was the *külah* worn by scholars. His was a *kalansüver* like that which the Prophet used to wear, which he used to cover himself with when necessary.[20] The traditional *sarık* ("winding cloth") which he wrapped around his *külah* was the *sarık* of the prominent scholars. During the time of Mevlânâ, there was neither *tennûre* nor *destegül*, neither *elifî nemed* nor *habbe*. His home was at the *madrasah*; he earned his living by teaching lessons and writing *fatwās*. He strongly criticized those who bragged about their

[14] The same library, no: 53. *Mesnevî* written in 783 H. (1382 -83 A.D.).
[15] *Mevlevîhood after Mevlânâ*, p. 353; the translation of the text is in *Mevlânâ Celâleddîn*; III. Edition, p. 133.
[16] *Mevlânâ Celâleddîn*; III. Edition, pp. 169–71.
[17]. Ibid., pp. 182-87.
[18] *Mesnevî*, vol. III, Ist. 1943, p. 61, couplet 671–72.
[19] *Fihi Ma-fih* trans. Ist. 1959; Remzi Books; Chapter 3; pp. 9–10.
[20] Cami', p. 100.

title or *khirka,* as well as those who made themselves seem more than they really were. Shams expressed the same opinion.[21] In one of his letters, Mevlânâ says that he was appointed to direct a *tekke*, and, in describing those who stood against him, he makes a point of saying that he is not like other shaikhs.[22] His letters about the appointment to the *tekke* of a certain Hamîdüddîn and a certain Nusratüddîn,[23] as well as the handing over of a *tekke* vacated by a shaikh named Sadreddîn to Chelebi Hüsameddîn,[24] suggest that the *tekke* was a feature of Mevlânâ's life. Perhaps these places were *Ahî zâviyes* (small lodges for craftsmen belonging to guilds) where brothers gathered, studied their lessons, and made conversation. However, there is not even the slightest sign that a special ritual took place in these *tekkes*, nor that they belonged to a *ṭarīqah.* Via his state and words, Mevlânâ conveyed to those who gathered around him the path of his father and khalif, the *sayyid* Burhâneddîn, and especially the path of Shams. This path did not stray from piety and the law even as far as the width of a hair. He says:

Men bende-i Kur'anem eger can darem
Men hak-i reh-i Muhammad-i Muhtarem
Heskes ki cuz in suhan zimen nakl huned
Bizarem ezu vu zon suhan bizarem[25]

Yet this path is one that is based upon love and *jezbe* ("divine attraction"); it is not founded upon being but upon Non-Being. It accepts the practice of educating oneself and giving oneself to humanity, not of losing oneself. Mevlânâ says:

---

[21] *Mevlânâ Celâleddîn*, 3rd Ed., pp. 171–72.

[22] Letter CXXXII, pp. 198–99.

[23] Letter LXVIII, pp. 102–03.

[24] Letter LXXVI, pp. 116–17. He explains that besides the Ziyaeddin Vezir Tekye, Chelebi Husameddin is also shaikh of another *tekye* (LXXV, pp. 115–16).

[25] As long as I have life, I am the slave of the Quran.
I am dust at the door of Muhammad the Chosen.
If anyone makes anything else of my words,
I am appalled by him and whatever he says.
[Quatrains: 1331]

Ishest tariyk u rah-i Peygamber-i ma
Ma zade-i ishkiyim u ishk mader-i ma
Iy mader-i ma muhufte der chader-i ma
Pinhan shode der tabiat-i kafer-i ma[26]

This path is not the path of the Divine Names (*Asmā`*) and dreams (ruyâ); it is the path of being named or reflecting the meaning of the Divine Names (*müsemmâ*) and the highest point of observing and witnessing them (*rü'yet*). From this point of view, Mevlânâ's character was not preoccupied with forms. All these *semâ'* disciplines–to *chark*, to maintain the *direk*, to grant permission to chant the *Ism-i Jelâl*, to pass through a *chile*, to appoint someone to serve for eighteen days, and the *meydan* ceremony–were all established later; they were adopted from the traditions of the Fütüvvet and Kalenderîs–that is, the Melâmetîs. However, we must also assert that while these ceremonial customs were established, no divergence from essential principles occurred, and these traditions cohered around the thoughts and joy of Mevlânâ.

Sipehsâlâr writes of Mejdeddin wanting to pass through a *chile*: forty days worshipping and fasting in seclusion. When he insisted, Mevlânâ agreed and placed him into a *chile*, but, having begun with his friend, three days later he became hungry and went to the house of another friend to eat. He came back into the room and returned to the *chile* again–Mevlânâ was aware of this. Sipehsâlâr also conveys that Mejdeddin said of Mevlânâ, "When we have such a mercy from God as Mevlânâ, to hide in seclusion means to be deprived of blessing," and that he had left the *chile*.[27] *Manâkıb-al Ârifîn* also relates that Mevlana said, "This used to be within the religion of the Prophets Moses and Jesus, but it is not for the Muḥammadans; it is *bid'ah* (innovation)." Yet Sultân Veled still wanted to enter a *chile*, and upon his own insistence he remained within the *chile* for forty days.[28]

[26] Love is the path and direction of our Prophet.
We are born from Love. Love is our Mother–
O our Mother, hidden within our *chadur*,
concealed by our own *kafir* nature.

[27] Ahmet Avni Konuk trans., pp. 98–99.

[28] II, pp. 793–94.

According to the oldest stories, this is what is said about the *chile*.

As for the shaikhhood and khalifhood:

There is an oral tradition of how a shaikh was requested for a certain place. Mevlânâ said to Chelebi Husâmeddîn, "Thanks be to God that they wanted a shaikh; if they had wanted a dervish, either this poor one or you, my glance, would have had to go." This legend, which is attributed to others, too (e.g. Hajı Bektash), does not have a particular value other than that of legendary anecdotes and stories of its kind.[29]

Neither in Sipehsâlâr nor in *Manâkıb-al Ârifîn* is there a record or oral tradition relating to shaikhhood. In these two oldest resources, khalifhood has the meaning of shaikhhood. Sipehsâlâr lists Chelebi Jelâleddîn Ferîdun, Sırâjeddîn-i Bayburdî, Bahâeddîn, Fahreddîn-i Sivâsî, Evlâd-i Müderris, Kerîmeddîn Bektemüroğlu, Salahâddîn-i Fakıyh, Nizâmeddîn-i Hattat, Izzeddîn-i Erzinjânî, Mejdeddîn-i Marâgıy, Alaeddîn-i Amâsî and Husâmeddin Huseynül-Mevlevî among the khalifs. Some of these, such as Bektemüroğlu Kerîmeddîn, were Mevlânâ's khalifs. Sırâjeddîn-i Bayburdî is possibly Sırâjeddîn-i Mesnevîhân, who was a Mesnevîhân during the time of Sultân Veled and teacher of Eflâkî.[30]

Alâeddîn-i Amâsî, whom Sipehsâlâr mentions is the khalif of Chelebi Hûsâmeddîn, is the teaching partner of Sırâjeddîn-i Mesnevîhân. Chelebi Hûsâmeddîn wrote a *hilâfetnâme* for this person, bestowed a *ferecî* on him, and sent him to Amasya.[31] Bahâeddin is possibly Kâtibül-esrâr Bahâeddin-i Bahrî.[32] Selahâddîn-i Fakıyh's name is also mentioned in the letters.[33] Nizâmeddîn-i Hattat was the son-in-law of Salâhaddân-i Zerkûb.[34] Hûsâmeddîn Huseynül-Mevlevî was Sultân Veled's khalif in Erzincan. Ârife-i Hosh-likaa is a khalif in Tokat.[35] Ulu Arif Chelebi conferred

[29] Vilāyāt-name, *Manaqib-i Haci Bektash-i Veli*; Abdülbâki Gölpınarlı edition; Ist. Inkilap Books, 1958, p. 93.
[30] *Manâkıb-al Ârifîn*, I, p. 272.
[31] Ibid., II, p. 880.
[32] Letters; Explanation, p. 225.
[33] Ibid., p. 256.
[34] Ibid., pp. 254–55.
[35] *Manâkıb-al Ârifîn*, II, p. 928.

khalifhood on Melikûl-hulefâ Kemâleddîn, Muhyiddîn, and Tâjeddîn-i Mesnevîhân in Lâdik; a *zaviye* was established and *semâ'* began.[36] Let's record here that the *zaviye* mentioned here is not the literal *zaviye* but a *dergâh.*[37]

Reading *Manâkıb-al Ârifîn*, we understand that those who joined the path had some hair cut off with scissors, and a *cherağ* ("candle" or "light") and *ijâzet* ("certificate") were given to those who attained khalifhood and could set up a *semâ'* gathering.[38] Again, we learn from the same book that a khalif would wear a *fereci.*[39]

It is certain that this cutting of hair came from the *chhâr darb* shaving among the Kalenderiyye. But this is not confined to Mevlevîs; the Bektâshîs have it, too.[40] We know that shaving was a mark of being in a *ṭarīqah*—as in those who followed the path of Shihâbeddîn-i Sühreverdî (632 H. 1234 A.D.), author of *Âvârif-al Maârif*, in the seventh to eighth centuries *hijrah*—and to wear *shalvar* ("baggy trousers") was a sign of the people of *fütüvvet.*[41] However, for the Kalenderîs shaving meant to be *chhâr darb*: to have the hair, eyebrows, moustache and beard shaved off with a razor. The Rum Abdals of Anatolia and Thrace, the Haydarîs, and the Jâmîs did the same, but some of them didn't shave their moustaches. The first Bektâshîs practiced *chhâr darb.*[42] In the sixteenth century, some Mevlevîs also made a custom of it, but later this group disappeared.[43]

In his *Minhac-al Fukara*, Rüsûhî mentions this tradition which was spoken of only in books in his period. He says that *chhâr darb*

[36] Ibid., p. 935.
[37] For the other khalifs of Sultân Veled and Ulu Arif Chelebi, please refer to *Mevlevîhood after Mevlânâ* (pp. 44–45, 86).
[38] *Manâkıb-al Ârifîn*, II, p. 921.
[39] Ibid., p. 800.
[40] *Vilāyāt-Name*; see the chapter "Terms in *Vilāyāt-Name*"; p. 141. 3. b. Shaving.
[41] Abdülbâki Gölpınarlı: *The Futuvvet Organization and its Resources in Islamic and Turkish Lands*; Ist. Uni. Faculty of Economics Magazine, Vol. XI–separate printing than issue 1-4; Ist. Ismail Akgun Print., 1952, p. 18.
[42] Vahidi: *Manaqib-i Hacce-i Cihan ve Netice-i Can*; Ist. Uni. Lib. Turkish Writings No: 9504; 18: a-72; b. See especially the Sufis whom he refers to as "Shemsians" and whom he distinguishes from "Mevlevians": p. 65. b-72. B.
[43] *Mevlevîhood after Mevlânâ*; pp. 101–27, 207.

shaving belongs to the people of Melâmet in Mevlevîhood, and it is contingent upon the permission of the shaikh. If one does not have a shaikh, it depends upon one being aware of the state of one's *nafs*. In addition, he also refers to some fictitous stories attributed to blessed Mevlânâ and Jenâb-i Shems, attributing to Mevlânâ a little *mesnevî* named *tıraşhnâme*, which explains the symbolism of *chhâr darb* shaving. However, this *mesnevî* belongs to Shâhidî (958 H. 1550 A.D.).[44]

Although there is a Melâmet influence in *kıl kesmek* ("cutting a hair") transmitted from the Kalenderîs, it is also certain that it is a symbol for being cut off from everything except the spiritual path, and it is generally understood in this way.

Nev-rûz

This is a Persian compound name which means "the new day"; it refers to the first day of spring. This day was a holiday in Zoroastrianism. Later, this day coincided with a series of events during the Farewell Pilgrimage of Prophet Muḥammad. The day before *Bayram* (*Arefe*) was on 8th March, with *Bayram* being on 9th March. On the journey back between Makkah and Madīnah, at a place called Gadîru Humm, the Blessed Prophet said of ʿAlī, "To whomever I am a friend and protector, ʿAlī is also his friend and protector," and this occurred on the nineteenth day of the same lunar month, which was 21st March and *Nev-rûz*. This caused the followers of ʿAlī and *Ehl-i Beyt*, as well as the Sufis, to attribute an Islamic significance to 21st March, i.e. *Nev-rûz*. Alevîs and Bektâshîs regard this day as the birthday of ʿAlī. Those who regard the sun's entrance into Aries as a sacred event also influenced this belief.

The human being, feeling deeply that spring is an entrance into a new phase of life, love, growth, and liberation from winter's shroud-like white and murky black, adopts the celebration of this

[44] *Minhac*; Chapter One; pp. 11–20, especially p. 16. See also p. 272 of *Mevlânâ Celâleddîn* and p. 140 of *Mevlevîhood after Mevlânâ*.

day as an expression of our humanity. In this way, the tradition spread to those outside of the *ṭarīqahs* and was fortified (especially among the "elite" class) by *Bahariyes* and *Nev-rûziyes* imported from Iranian literature into Turkish *divân* literature. *Nev-rûz* was also celebrated in the royal palace, where the head astrologer used to present the horoscope for the new year to the sultan. This illustrates that *Nev-rûz* was accepted as the beginning of the new year—the result of accepting the Shemsî Hijrî Calendar (with *Nev-rûz* at the beginning) in 471 H. (1078 A.D.), during the reign of Melikshah of the Persian Seljuks (died 485 H. 1092 A.D.). Even the political rivalry between the Ottomans and Persians, which has lasted for centuries, was not able to cast a shadow on the importance of Nev-rûz.

Among Mevlevîs with an Alevî tendency, *Nev-rûz* is celebrated by drinking milk, just as it is among the Bektâshîs. Seven *āyāts* called the *Heft Selâm* (which begin with the word *selâm*) are written on a piece of paper, or inside a bowl that can be written on, with either Turkish ink or soil pressed and dried in the form of a seal or in a rectangular form taken from the area surrounding the resting place of Imām Huseyn (known as *Turbet* and *Ceher*). The writing in the bowl is done by dipping these seals into water. Then these writings are dissolved in milk. Some red coloring is also added to the milk to turn it pink (known as "sherbet for the new mother"). On *Nev-rûz*, instead of coffee, milk is served. During the first sip, the following prayer is recited: *Ya mubeddirel-leyli ven nehar, ya mukallibel-kulubi vel absar, ya muhavvilel havli vel ahval, havvil halena ila ahsenil-hal* ("O You who measure night and day, who turn hearts and eyes, who transform states and years, turn our states into the most beautiful state!")

The *Heft Selâm* ("Seven Greetings") are composed of the following *āyāts*:

> *Salāmun ʿalaykum-bimā ṣabartum fani ʾma ʿuqbad-dār.*
> *"Peace be upon you because you have persevered!" How excellent, then, this fulfillment in the hereafter!*
>
> [13:24]

Salāmun-qawlan-mir-Rabbir-Raḥim.
Peace and fulfillment through the word of a Sustainer who dispenses all grace.

[36:58]

Salāmun ʿalā Nūḥin-fil ʿālamīn.
Peace be upon Noah throughout all the worlds!
[37:79]

Salāmun ʿalāa ʾIbrāhīm.
Peace be upon Abraham!
[37:109]

Salāmun ʿalā Mūsā wa Hārūn.
Peace be upon Moses and Aaron!
[37:120]

Salāmun ʿalāa ʾIlyāsīn.
Peace be upon Elijah and his followers!
[37:130]

Salāmun hiya ḥattā maṭlaʿil-fajr.
Peace!... This until the rise of dawn!
[97:4]

Mevlânâ wrote many paeans to spring; he loved it very much. However, there is not even the slightest sign that *Nev-rûz* was celebrated in his time or in the resources close to his period. Without doubt, we can say that the celebration of *Nev-rûz* and the *Heft Selâm* was adopted at a later period by some Mevlevîs bound to *Ehli Beyt* (the family of Prophet Muḥammad). It was not a general practice either. It was celebrated in Bahariye Mevlevîhâne, and in Konya during the time of Abdulvahid Chelebi. Some *dedes* would serve milk to visitors. In Shaikh Murad Dergâh,[45] they definitely followed the custom of the *Heft Selâm.*

[45] As we have mentioned previously, although this *dergâh* was officially Nakshi, their shaikh was a Hamzavi and received Mevlevî khalifhood. His sikke had the *tekbir* conferred upon it for the *shaikh-zades* ("sons of the shaikh").

Heft Sin

The following, known as *Heft-Sin,* the first letters of which are *sin* (Arabic س) would be in small plates on the *Nev-rûz* table:

1. *Sirke* (vinegar)
2. *Senced* (silverberry)
3. *Sîr* (garlic)
4. *Sümâk* (sumac)
5. *Sebze* (green-leafed vegetable)
6. *Sünbül* (hyacinth, both its bulbs and leaves)
7. *Semnû* (halva with semolina or flour)

Also, on the table, would be a mirror as a sign of light and the Qur'ān to proclaim the correspondence to *sharī'ah.*

After the time of *tahvil* (the opening of the New Year), someone who is present at the table recites loudly "*Yâ Muhavillel havli vel ahvâl havil halenâ ilâ ahsenil hâl*" and this is repeated 365 times. The 366th time is the time of *tahvil* and "*Yâ müdebbirel leyli ven . . .*" is recited. The milk that is placed in front of everyone is drunk at the moment of *tahvil.* The *salawat* ("greetings" to Prophet Muḥammad) is recited, everyone "sees with" (*görüshmek*) each other during the ceremony for days and nights of grace (*ihya gejeleri*) and then they take a seat around the table again. If the time is convenient, food is eaten.

* * *

Let us finish by explaining (1) a custom that we forgot to mention in the section on *sefer* ("journey"); (2) the saying *cherağ dinlendirmek* ("to put the light to rest"); (3) the marriage *gülbâng*; (4) the belief in "April water"; (5) and the term *chelik* ("steel").

1. One who is not journeying takes in his right hand the hand of the person who is making a journey, just like during an initiation ceremony. Then, first into his right ear and then into his left, he breathes the following from *āyāt* 28:85: *'Innalladhī faraḍa 'alaykal-Qur'āna larāadduka 'ilā ma'ād* (*He who has*

laid down this Qur'ān in clear terms, making it binding upon you, will assuredly bring you back [from death] to a life renewed.) Then the *sefer gülbâng* is recited.

2. The *türbedâr dede*, before he puts to rest the lights in the *semâ'hâne* following the *mukabele*, recites:

   Çerâğ-i bâtın îken nûr-i Ahmed
   İyân oldu doğup şems-i Muhammed

   While the light of Ahmad was the hidden light,
   The sun of Muḥammad rose and became apparent.

   Breathing upon them through a pipe, he puts the lights to rest with the *terjeman* ("prayer") above. In the morning, he also puts the oil lamps and the candles of the *türbe* to rest with it. If the candle or oil lamp is within reach, instead of putting it to rest with a breath, he licks his thumb and index finger and holds the wick between them. The reason is clear: if it is put to rest with the breath, it fumes and smells.

3. The following is the marriage *gülbâng*, which is recited immediately after the marriage is announced, or when the groom is entering the bridal chamber:

   Bâda mübarek ber cihan sûr u arûsihâ-yi mâ
   Sur u arûsirâ Huda bubrid ber balâ-yi mâ

   Vakt-i şerif hayrola; hayırlar fethola, şerler def'ola; demler safâlar müzdâd ola; Hak erenler mübarek ve müteyemmin eyliye; hayrul-halefler ihsan eyliye. Dem-i...[46]

[46] May our banquets and marriages be a blessing to the world.
Banquets and marriage celebrations
are what God has apportioned to our earthly forms.

May this moment be blessed; may goodness prevail; may all negativity be dispelled;
May your breaths and joys increase in peace;
may God bless the saints and make them a source of good fortune;
and may He grant beautiful character to the carriers of the tradition.

4. "April water" is rainwater collected in the second of the Rumi Calendar months. It extends from 21st April to 21st May according to today's Western calendar. It is a very old belief that the rain that falls during this period is very enlightening, full of spiritual power and blessings, especially during the first week. The rain is collected and *sūrahs* 1, 2 (*āyāts* 255–57, "The Throne Verse," only), 112, 113, 114, and 109 are recited over it seventy times. Some people also recite *sūrah* 97 and recite *Allāhu Akbar* and *Lā ilāha illā Allāh* seventy times. Finally, the *salawat* is chanted over the water seventy times. These *sūrahs*, *dhikrs,* and *salawats* are breathed onto the water. Within this month, every morning and every night one drinks a little of the water. It is stored, and as it runs out more is added to it. People may offer some to the sick. Not only in *Mevlevîhânes* but in other *tekkes* too, there were beautifully decorated "April bowls" for the collection of this special rain water. The Mevlânâ Museum displays an April bowl presented by Abû-Saîd Bahâdır Hân (1305–25).[47]

5. **Çelik:** "Steel" (pronounced and sometimes spelled *chelik*). A *çelik* is a stick as long as an arm and as thick as an index finger. It is kept in the *meydan*, and *dedes* also have one in their cells. If a dervish does something contrary to the Path, violating the rules of the *tekke*, he is made to stand in the *niyâz* position and the shaikh or the *ashchı dede* hits him a few times below the knees with the *çelik*. This is not a beating, but a lesson in *ādāb* among the brothers. When necessary, especially during the *semâ' meshk*, *dedes* strike the *nevniyâzes* with the *çelik*.

[47] Mehmed Onder: *Konya, The Mevlânâ City*; Konya-Yeni Books, 1962, pp. 327–28.

VII

Mesnevîhânhood

Let us finish our book with more discussion of the *Mesnevî*, which is a great and unique work. We have mentioned it previously and quoted from it throughout this book.

Although Mevlevî shaikhs, especially a *mesnevîhân*, were all appointed to lecture about the *Mesnevî*, in some *dergâhs*, especially in Konya, there was a long, illustrious tradition of *mesnevîhânhood.* Unless he had an excuse, each Mevlevî shaikh was expected to recite the *Mesnevî* before the *mukabele.*

Since the time it was composed, the *Mesnevî* has spread throughout the entire Islamic world and has been deeply respected and loved by all thoughtful readers, who have appreciated its beauty and its knowledge of theology and *taṣawwuf.* It has been regarded by many as the third resource for Muslims after the Holy Qur'ān and the traditions of the Prophet.

In the land of the Ottomans, especially during the periods of reformation in the seventeenth and eighteenth centuries when experimental innovations were being made, places called *Dârül-Mesnevî* were opened to teach the *Mesnevî.* In the *madrasahs* and mosques, they also began to teach the *Mesnevî.*[1]

The *Chelebi*, or a *mesnevîhân,* would give a *mesnevîhân ijâzet* to a person who had the capacity for it and who had completed the necessary courses.[2] The *Chelebi* used to grant the *mesnevîhâns* the

[1] With regard to *Dârül-Mesnevî*, please refer to *Maârif Tarihi*, "The History of Education," by Osman Ergin; vol. I, Ist-1939, pp. 133–35.

[2] In *Mevlevîhood After Mevlânâ* we have given two examples of *ijâzetnâmes* conferring *Mesnevîhânhood.*

authority to wear the *destâr* too.

We have written about the method of teaching the *Mesnevî* in the chapter "Semâ' & Mukabele." Let's summarize here: One used to begin to read the Mesnevî with an *ʾAʿūzhu/Bismillāh* and end it with the couplets "*İnchünin . . .*" Then an *ashir* was recited, a prayer was made, and the lesson was finished.

Mesnevî suret buved cânesh tuyî
Hem cihet hem nur u erkanesh tuyî
Mesnevî-i ma dukkân-i vahdetest
Gayr-i vahid herchi bini u butest
Der dil-i men in suhan zon meymenest
Zon ki ez dil canib-î dil rovzenest

The *Mesnevî* is the face, its *Jaan* is You.
You are its direction, its light, and its support.
Our *Mesnevî* is the shop of Unity;
Whatever you see other than the One is just an idol.
The speech in my heart comes from That auspicious direction,
for, surely, there is a window from heart to heart.

15 *Jumādā al-ʾĀkhirah* 1383
2 November 1963

www.ingramcontent.com/pod-product-compliance
Lightning Source LLC
Chambersburg PA
CBHW031415290426
44110CB00011B/383
9780939660612